GCE AS Level

AS Level for AQA

Applied **ICT**

Series Editor:
K. Mary Reid

www.heinemann.co.uk
✓ Free online support
✓ Useful weblinks
✓ 24 hour online ordering

01865 888058

Inspiring generations

Heinemann Educational Publishers
Halley Court, Jordan Hill, Oxford OX2 8EJ
Part of Harcourt Education

Heinemann is a registered trademark of
Harcourt Education Limited

First published 2005

10 09 08 07 06 05
10 9 8 7 6 5 4 3 2 1

British Library Cataloguing in Publication Data is available
from the British Library on request.

10-digit ISBN: 0 435449 94 X
13-digit ISBN: 978 0 435449 94 0

Edited by Rebecca Harman
Designed by Lorraine Inglis
Typeset by Thomson Digital, India

Original illustrations © Harcourt Education Limited, 2005

Illustrated by Tek-Art/Thomson Digital, India

Cover design by Wooden Ark Studios

Printed by Printer Trento s.r.l.

Cover photo: © Zefa Images

Websites
There are links to relevant websites in this book. In order to ensure that the links are up to date, that
the links work, and that the sites are not inadvertently linked to sites that could be considered
offensive, we have made the links available on the Heinemann website at
www.heinemann.co.uk/hotlinks. When you access the site the express code is 994XP.
Please note that examples of websites suggested in this book were up to date at the time of writing.
It is essential for tutors to preview each site before using it to ensure that the URL is still accurate and
the content is appropriate. We suggest that tutors bookmark useful sites and consider enabling
students to access them through the school or college intranet.

Contents

Acknowledgements

Sharon Yull would like to thank Guido Gybels, Director of New Technologies, RNID, for his assistance with material relating to deaf people.

The authors and publisher would like to thank all those who have granted permission to reproduce copyright material.

Microsoft product screen shots reprinted with permission of Microsoft Corporation.
MSN Messenger screengrab Copyright © 2004 Microsoft Corporation
Yahoo! Messenger screengrab reproduced with permission of Yahoo! Inc. © Yahoo! Inc.
YAHOO! And the YAHOO! logo are trademarks of Yahoo! Inc.
PIPEX
Sky.com
RNID
Papercourt Sailing Club
Mr-Office.com
OwensDirect.com
Crown copyright material is reproduced with the permission of the Controller of HMSO
redhouse furniture design
Sage (UK) Limited
snowdrop.co.uk
Lottery tickets reproduced with the kind permission of Camelot Group plc, Operator of the National Lottery. The 'Crossed Fingers' logo is a registered trade mark owned by The National Lottery Commission.
Hewlett Packard
Hunter's Yard
Barclaycard
writersdock.co.uk
BBC
Winzip is a registered trademark of Winzip International LLC. All rights reserved.
ZipCentral
Adobe product screenshots reprinted with permission from Adobe Systems Incorporated.
Google home page and hit list screengrab © 2005 Google
AQA
Lycos, Inc
Macromedia

The authors and publisher would like to thank the following for permission to reproduce photographs:

Alamy Images/page 3
redhouse studios/page 31

Every effort has been made to contact copyright holders of material published in this book.
Any omissions or errors will be rectified in subsequent printings if notice is given to the publishers.

Introduction

This is one in a series of four volumes that covers the AQA qualifications in Applied Information and Communication Technology for GCE.
The books are organised like this:

* AS (Single Award), which covers units 1 to 3

* AS (Double Award), which covers units 1 to 7

* A2 (Single Award), which covers units 8, 10, 12 and 14

* A2 (Double Award), which covers units 8 to 15

The two AS Level (Single and Double Award) qualifications are covered by one book each.
The two A Level (Single and Double Award) qualifications are covered by two books each, one at AS and one at A2 level.

This book covers the seven units that are offered in the AS (Double Award):

* Unit 1: ICT and Society

* Unit 2: ICT and Organisations

* Unit 3: Data Handling

* Unit 4: ICT Solutions

* Unit 5: Fundamentals of Programming

* Unit 6: Computer Artwork

* Unit 7: Creating a Website

To complete the AS (Double Award) you should study Units 1 to 4, plus any two units chosen from Units 5 to 7. To complete the AS (Single Award) you should study Units 1 to 3 only.

Assessment

Your achievements on this qualification will be assessed through portfolios of evidence and a controlled assignment. The assignment will be assessed externally and the portfolios will be assessed internally.

Unit 1 will be assessed externally, and you will complete an assignment, set by the examination board. You will be given be given a scenario in advance and will be expected to do research and to prepare materials. The assessed work itself will be completed over a period of 15 hours under controlled conditions.

The remaining AS units will all be assessed internally. You will be expected to construct a portfolio for each unit. Further guidance on this is given in each unit.

Further information

You can find further information about this qualification at www.aqa.org.uk. Remember to search for GCE Applied ICT. You can download the complete specification, which gives full details of all the units, both AS and A2, and how they are assessed. This document is nearly 200 pages long.

Standard ways of working

In addition, 'Standard Ways of Working' runs as a common theme through all the units, and is covered in the preliminary pages. Students are advised to read this before starting on the units.

A Tutor Resource File will provide additional material for these units.

We hope you enjoy your studies and wish you every success.

K Mary Reid
April 2005

Standard ways of working

Introduction

As an experienced ICT user, you already know a great deal about how to get the best out of your ICT equipment. But you can probably learn some new tricks.

In this chapter you will be comparing the way that you work with the way that ICT professionals work. This should help you to act responsibly and legally, to watch out for your own safety, and to save time. Mastering these ways of working will definitely impress a future employer.

Evidence

These standard ways of working also apply to your work across all the units you are taking for this qualification. You should provide as much evidence as you can in each unit, to show that you understand and practice them. Hints about evidence are provided in each section.

Working safely

Avoiding hazards

You probably expect to be using a computer regularly over many years both for your studies and for work. You need to protect yourself from the risks of accidents or long term health problems. You will learn about Health and Safety regulations in Unit 1, but most of this is commonsense.

Wherever you use a computer, check for these hazards in the room around you:

* wobbly tables or desks
* not enough room to spread your papers or use the mouse
* sharp corners that someone could hurt themselves on
* lack of fire extinguishers, or extinguishers of the wrong type
* unsuitable furniture, of the wrong height and size
* too much heat or too little ventilation.

Avoiding bad posture

If you use a chair that is not comfortable and that does not support your back properly you will probably develop painful problems with your back. Employers are required to provide their employees with adjustable chairs, which can be adjusted in a number of different ways. If you are using an adjustable chair, find out how it can be changed to suit your physique.

You may not have an office chair at home, but you should try out different chairs and cushions to give the right level of support. If your back aches after using a computer then you do need to pay more attention to the seating.

Avoiding physical stress

Physical stress occurs if you sit in the same position for too long. This can be avoided by taking regular breaks. When you are sitting in front of a computer, ask yourself whether you feel relaxed, or whether any of your muscles are tensed. Try to reduce the tension by changing how you sit.

Preventing eyestrain

Employers are required to install suitable lighting in rooms where computers are used. The lights should be strong enough and not flicker. You should also avoid glare on the screens by positioning them so that they do not catch glare from bright sunlight or badly placed desk lights. Check the lighting at your place of study and in the room where you use a PC at home. You can also adjust the brightness and contrast on your screen so that it is comfortable to use. Your eyesight is precious, so do not risk damaging it by using a computer in poor light.

Managing cables

All cables used in a computer system should be:

* properly installed
* insulated to prevent electrical shock
* fastened out of reach so you cannot pull on them or catch your feet accidentally
* run around the edge of a room and not across the floor where they can cause trips.

Check the cables that are around the PCs that you use regularly. Also check the power sockets, so that you are not running too many multi-points off one circuit.

Managing the furniture

Here are some questions to ask about all the PCs you use regularly, whether at your place of study, at home, at work or at a library.

* Is the desk the correct height? If the desk is too high is there a footrest?
* Can the seat be adjusted – and has that been done? You should be looking slightly down to the screen.
* Is the screen placed so that it can be read comfortably?
* Is the keyboard placed in a comfortable position? You may find a wrist rest will help.
* Is there a pleasant view in the distance? This may seem an odd question, but you will find that re-focusing your eyes on things in the distance from time to time will relax them and prevent eye strain.

 Signpost for portfolio evidence

Describe your working environment. You should include the layout and suitability of the furniture, equipment, cables and lighting.

Managing your working time

Most computer users are tempted to miss breaks and carry on working for several hours, especially when they are absorbed in an activity. You should aim to take a brief break every hour or so. For five minutes or so get up, walk around, have a drink, or do another task. Your work on the computer will actually be more productive as a result. Your eyes will suffer if you look at a screen for long periods of time. Although you are unlikely to cause permanent damage to your eyes, they can become sore and tired. Employers have to provide eye checks for employees who spend a significant amount of their time working on a computer.

 Signpost for portfolio evidence

Keep a plan or log of your working time, showing that you are taking sensible breaks.

Keeping information secure
Protecting information from theft, loss and fire

Information is valuable. If you lose your own work then you may have to spend many hours re-doing it, and you may not be able to remember everything you wrote the first time. You may even fail a course because of lost work. Similarly, much of the information within an organisation is absolutely vital, and its loss could mean the serious loss of business.

Here are some sensible precautions that you, or an employer, should take:

* Keep all removable media (CDs, USB pens etc.) with you, or in a safe place. Important media can be locked away.

* Lock rooms that have PCs in them when there is no-one working on them.

* Store backups in a fireproof safe.

* Do not tell anyone your passwords, and do not write them down.

Protecting information from viruses

Virus protection is not an optional extra these days. You should refuse to work on any PC that is not adequately protected. Not only should the right kind of software be installed, but the virus definitions files should be updated regularly. In many systems, virus definitions are updated every few hours. This is because new viruses can be transmitted via email to many thousands of computers within minutes.

Networks normally have high levels of virus protection. You might like to check what level of protection that has been installed on the network that you use. On a home computer, you should download virus protection software if it is not already installed. You will have to pay a modest annual subscription to keep your virus definition files up-to-date, but this should not be neglected.

 Signpost for portfolio evidence

Provide evidence that you use virus protection software.

Protecting confidentiality

It is good practice not to use the names of living people in anything you write, unless you have their permission. For example, if you are asked, as a student, to write a report on the IT systems within an organization, you should explain to the member of staff what you are writing and ask permission to refer to them. You may like to send them a copy before you submit it.

If you have data about the customers or clients of a organisation, and you need to refer to them, then it is usual to 'anonymise' their names, addresses and any other identifying information. You can do this either by removing the data altogether, for example, by Tippexing out any handwritten information. Or you can use pseudonyms instead of the real names, in which case you should mention that you have done so.

If you are working for an employer, and your report is for internal use only, then it is acceptable to use real names in many instances.

When information is confidential then you should do all you can to keep it secure. Information may be confidential because it is about named people, or it may be confidential because it is important to the organization. You should not, under any circumstances pass this information on to anyone who has no right to know it. You should also take responsibility for making sure that no-one gets to see the information accidentally; that means that you should not leave confidential information on your screen and walk away, and you should not leave printouts lying around.

You will learn more about the laws that govern information about people in Unit 1.

If you want to protect your work from other people you can create a password for it. You may have to read the Help files for your application to find out how to do this. One word of warning – beware of creating a password if you do want to share a document with a teacher, assessor or work colleague.

 Signpost for portfolio evidence

You could show that you have password protected an important file.

Respecting copyright

You will learn about the laws on copyright in Unit 1. If someone writes anything, develops software, designs an image or creates an art object, they have the copyright for that item. That means that only they have the right to copy the material, unless they have given permission to someone else to do so. Copyright lasts throughout the author's lifetime, and for 70 years afterwards (when it is handled by the person's executors). Wholesale copying of material, especially when it is then sold by the copier, is illegal. This is often known as piracy, especially in relation to software.

One way to avoid infringing copyright is to acknowledge your sources. If you use or refer to work that someone else had done, then it is only fair to mention them. In certain circumstances you could be breaking the laws on copyright if you do not do so. There are several ways in which you can acknowledge a source:

✳ Use a direct quote, in quotation marks

"Be nice to nerds. Chances are you'll end up working for one." Bill Gates: Business @ *The Speed of Thought*

✳ Refer to it in the text

Bill Gates once wrote in his book Business @ *The Speed of Thought* that you should be nice to nerds. He said that the chances are you'll end up working for one.

✳ Use a footnote or end note

It has been said that you should be nice to nerds, because the chances are you'll end up working for one.[14]

At the bottom of the page, or end of the document, you will see this:

---

[14] Bill Gates: *Business @ The Speed of Thought*

What you should not do is to write something like this, without acknowledging that Bill Gates originally wrote it:

I think you should be nice to nerds. After all, the chances are you'll end up working for one.

You can also include the title, author and publisher of the book in a bibliography. Plagiarism occurs when someone passes off someone else's work as their own. It can happen in novels, in songwriting and in academic work.

The most serious form of plagiarism is when students submit coursework as their own, when it has been written by someone else. Examination Boards and Universities disqualify students who

are found to do this. In some cases the student copies coursework that has been previously submitted successfully; in other cases the student asks someone to write the coursework for them. This is not acceptable and may be illegal, even if permission has been given by the copyright holder.

You should, of course, not submit work under false pretences. You should also protect your own good work to make sure that no-one tries to pass it off as their own. One difficulty that some students have is in deciding how much help they should ask for with their work. The best advice is to discuss this with the teacher, who will know exactly how much support they and other people can give you.

 ## Signpost for portfolio evidence

You can show that you understand and respect copyright law by acknowledging your sources of information.

Keeping copies

You probably learnt to keep copies the first time your computer crashed and you had not saved your work! To avoid it happening again:

✳ save the file as soon as you start it, giving it version number 1 e.g. Customer Report v1.doc

✳ if you can, configure the software to autosave your work at regular intervals

✳ at regular intervals, save the file with a new version number, or even with a new name.

 ## Signpost for portfolio evidence

You can show that you keep copies by listing the contents of folders showing the names of the files you have saved.

Keeping backups

It is very reassuring to know that your files are backed up. If the system does malfunction then you will be able to retrieve the work that you have spent so much time over.

On a network, the complete system will be backed up at least once a day. This will happen automatically. You might like to ask the network administrator at your centre about the backup procedures that are followed.

Backup copies should normally be stored in a different building from the originals. On your home computer you are responsible for making sure that backups are created. You can do this in several ways:

* You can set up some software applications to make a backup of each file as you create it. Whenever you save the file the previously saved version is renamed as the backup copy. Look out for Options or Preferences in the main menus.

* Copy important files to an external medium such as a CD or external hard disk. You should do this on a regular basis. Important files could include your email address book, and key documents that you are working on for assessment. Make sure that you keep the backup copies somewhere safe.

* Use the Backup utility that is provided with some versions of operating system software.

Managing your work

Planning your work

When you begin a piece of work you should always decide when you are going to finish it. You may be set a deadline by your employer or teacher, but you would be wise to aim to finish it before the deadline. If it is a substantial project that will take many days or weeks, you can work backwards from the deadline to decide what you need to achieve at key dates. Draw this up as a plan at the beginning.

You may need to provide several different types of documents and files. Again, list what you need to do and fit them into the plan. If you do all this at the beginning you will not be in danger of getting to the end and finding that key components are missing.

 Signpost for portfolio evidence

Keep a work diary, plan or log of your activities.

Identifying your work

On any document you should always include this information in the header or footer:

* your name

* any other essential details about you e.g. your department at work or your centre number

* the date on which you completed this version of the document.

This identifies you as the author of the document.

For assessment purposes you will have to produce further evidence to authenticate the work. This can be in the form of a monitoring checklist kept by a teacher, or witness statements. You will also be required to sign a statement that you have competed the work yourself.

 Signpost for portfolio evidence

The header or footer on documents should identify you as the author.

Using appropriate filenames

Which of these is a sensible file name?

* myfile.doc

* janejones.jpg

* Doom.pdf

* Unit 3 Project v1.doc

Of course, what counts as 'sensible' depends on what you are going to do with the file. At work, you would probably have to pass a file to someone else to use or to read and comment on. The filename should clearly identify:

* what the file contains

* the version number (where appropriate).

 Signpost for portfolio evidence

You can produce a listing of all the names of files you have created.

Using a directory/folder structure

You can very quickly build up a sizable collection of working files, such as word processing documents, databases, spreadsheet workbooks etc. If you are using Microsoft Windows® then these will be normally be placed in the

My Documents folder (also known as a directory). You can create as many extra folders as you like within My Documents.

You might think it a good idea to place all your word processing documents in one folder, all your desk top publishing publications in another folder and so on. But many people prefer to organise their work by subject matter instead.

When you are working on a networked PC at your centre or at work then you will only be able to save files in My Documents or possibly in a folder than you share with a group. On a home computer you will find that you can create folders anywhere you like, and you may want to set up new folders elsewhere on the hard disk system.

 Signpost for portfolio evidence

You can produce a screen shot of the directory structure you have used.

Keeping a log of problems

As you carry out your work you will inevitably encounter problems with the computer system. Keep a log of all the problems you get and note down how you solve each problem. The problems could range from simple ones, such as having to change an ink cartridge, to more complex ones like having to reinstall some software.

 Signpost for portfolio evidence

Your log will be useful evidence that you have managed to solve everyday ICT problems.

UNIT 1

ICT and society

Introduction

Information communication technology (ICT) has had a huge impact upon the way in which we communicate, socialise and work. Almost every aspect of society has been affected by ICT developments and to a large extent ICT is an integral part of our lives.

This unit explores how developments in technology have impacted on society, including business and organisations, law and order, entertainment and leisure and personal communications. In addition this unit will also address the impact that ICT has had on people with particular needs, and how technology has provided opportunities for these needs to be addressed.

The growth in ICT use and technology development has also generated the need for more responsive legislation to ensure that users are protected from illegal activity. This unit will identify the legislation that offers this security to employees, employers and individuals that capture, process, store and output information.

Finally this unit will focus on you as a user of ICT and how you should present information using standard formats, and working professionally within an environment that is managed effectively and safely.

What you need to learn

✳ How developments in technology have influenced individuals and society

✳ How to communicate and present information that is suited to its purpose and audience

* The importance of adopting standard ways of working

Resource toolkit

To complete this unit you need these essential resources:

* access to computer hardware and appropriate software that will enable you to produce a range of templates and documents
* access to the Internet
* sufficient storage space for your work
* a range of other resources such as CD-ROMs, newspapers, books, journals and other business documents.

How you will be assessed

This unit is externally assessed through an AQA set assignment under controlled conditions. You will be expected to produce a portfolio that will include:

* A time plan to show how you will complete all the tasks within the time available
* A record of how you spend your time to show that you have followed your time plan
* Evidence of an investigation and an understanding of the effects that the use of ICT has on society
* Identification of ICT-related legislation and evidence of understanding why it was introduced/amended, and how it influences the use of ICT for individuals and society
* A design of a newsletter or set of web pages that is suited to its purpose and audience and includes a range of features
* Evaluation criteria for the newsletter or set of web pages
* A newsletter or set of web pages that you have produced which is suited to its purpose and audience and includes a range of features
* Evidence of testing the newsletter or set of web pages

* An evaluation of your work
* An evaluation of your own performance
* Evidence of use of standard ways of working
* Evidence of appropriate written communication throughout the portfolio.

In preparation for assessment you will be encouraged to research and experience the following:

* How developments in technology and ICT have influenced work styles, individuals and society
* How legislation has impacted upon ICT and the users of ICT
* Styles of presentation – see how different styles and formats are used for communicating different types of information
* How people with different needs and disabilities have been affected by ICT and technology advances
* How to manage your own learning and improve your own knowledge and understanding
* Standard ways of working, working safely and an understanding of how to keep work secure.

How high can you aim?

This unit is assessed through a time-constrained assessment. To facilitate you in the preparation for this, there are 'Theory into Practice' and 'Knowledge checks' sections throughout this unit that have been developed to support you in your understanding of ICT in Society and its impact upon businesses and individuals.

1.1 The effects of technology on society

There are a wide range of technologies available that allow users to access and exchange information. Developments in technology have

IMPACT ON THE BUSINESS	IMPACT ON THE CONSUMER
More streamlined and efficient service. Items can be marketed through a website, transactions can be taken using e-commerce and electronic payment systems.	Loss of personal one-to-one service. Possibly no one to speak to. All transactions are carried out electronically.
More variety in products and services. An organisation can advertise more items online in a virtual shopping environment.	Greater flexibility, e.g. wider payment options; opportunity to shop around for the best deals and compare prices, etc.
Using a website to promote goods and services means that an organisation does not need a physical high street presence, thus saving costs.	Consumers will not have to leave home to purchase items. All transactions can be carried out online.

TABLE 1.1 *The impact of e-commerce*

influenced, and may continue to influence, areas such as:

* business and organisations
* law and order
* entertainment and leisure
* personal communications.

Business and organisations

Developments in technology have had a tremendous impact on businesses and organisations. Organisations have had to embrace new technology, and this has hadboth positive and negative implications.With regards to employees and their work styles, developments in technology have improved communications withinorganisations and generated a more interactive, collaborative environment. In addition, operations have become more efficient and productive.

What does it mean?

E-commerce can be defined as any financial transactions that take place by electronic means. With the growth of commerce on the Internet and the Web, e-commerce often refers to purchases from online stores, marketplaces and auction sites.

The impact of new technology on products and services may be seen as a positive effect for an organisation due to the ability to sell online, reduce costs and increase efficiency. However, the consumer may perceive these changes differently. The growth in e-commerce has contributed to different ways of buying, selling and trading, as shown in Table 1.1 above.

Law and order

Law and order have been affected extensively by developments in technology. Examples can be seen in all areas of policing and law enforcement. In terms of road-traffic control and congestion, changes in technology have led to digital speed cameras being installed that are more robust and accurate.

Advances in technology are also evident in schemes designed to capture motorist information

FIGURE 1.1 *A digital speed camera*

Anybody that drives a vehicle into a zone of central London between 07:00 and 18:30 Monday to Friday is obliged to pay £8. The charge increases to £10 if you have not paid by 22:00. If you haven't paid by midnight, TFL (Transport for London) looks up the number plate with DVLA and sends out a penalty notice for £40. If the penalty is not paid within two weeks, it goes up to £80 and, after four weeks to £120. Failure to pay the charge after this date will result in more serious penalties being imposed that could include the vehicle being clamped, impounded or destroyed.

in relation to congestion charges such as the one imposed in central London.

The latest moves in technology have also resulted in the National DNA Database being expanded to fight crime. Every month 5,000 DNA profiles are taken from crime scenes and matched to names on the database. The expansion will include DNA profiles from prisoners and mentally disordered offenders currently not on the database. Since 2000, DNA samples of offenders are routinely taken, along with their fingerprints and photographs. This database contains samples from around 1.8 million individuals.

Entertainment and leisure

The Internet has provided endless opportunities for people to communicate, play games and be involved in interactive pursuits. It has also enabled people to plan their leisure activities online by allowing people to book tickets for flights, concerts, attractions and holidays.

In addition, the ability to use technologies such as games consoles has contributed to changes in the way in which people are entertained. In February 2003, UK sales in games consoles were:

* Play Station 2: 17,382 unit sales
* Game Boy Advance: 5,481 unit sales
* Xbox: 4,033 unit sales
* Game Cube: 1,938 unit sales.

The growth in ownership of games consoles is due to the vast range of software available for each format, advances in software design, the compactness of the consoles, the price and the addictiveness of playing and completing single- and multi-player games.

Services such as Sky television and the growth in popularity of DVDs and the new associated rental services (delivery to the door) offered by a range of entertainment companies, have all impacted on the way in which people now use their entertainment and leisure time. The need to go out and socialise is

FIGURE 1.2 *MSN Messenger*

FIGURE 1.3 *Yahoo! Messenger*

in many cases being superseded by a culture of 'stay at home' entertainment and leisure pursuits.

Personal communications

Developments in technology have impacted positively on the range of personal communication devices available to consumers. Devices such as laptops, PDAs and mobile phones have enhanced personal communications, especially for people on the move, who need to stay in contact with the office, family or friends.

In terms of advances in software, the need to communicate with people almost 24 hours a day has also given rise to 'virtual communities' and the setting up of newsgroups and chat rooms. The trend of communicating online has seen a growth in popularity for sites such as MSN Messenger and Yahoo! Messenger.

Technologies that are available differ between those that store, search, access, connect, broadcast and organise data and information and enable users to communicate this globally. One of the most widely available and popular technologies is the Internet.

Internet technologies

The Internet was first developed in 1969 as a research and defence network in the USA. It was intended to link together servers used by military and academic personnel at the time of the Cold War. Since then, the Internet has grown into a much more advanced and interactive communications system, allowing users the ability to navigate between information resources through the use of World Wide Web browsers.

Email has become one of the fastest and most widely accessible formats of communication over recent years. The advantages of using email include:

* speed: the facility to send messages at the touch of a button to anywhere in the world

* multiple sends and copies: the option to communicate the same message to multiple users

* cost: minimal costs

* convenience: facility to communicate 24 hours a day, 7 days a week

* sharing data: because information can be transferred to multiple users, these users will have access to the same shared information that can include attached files, graphics and moving images

* ease of use: once familiar with the basic functions of an email package, it is very easy and user friendly (because it is icon driven) to send and receive email.

There are a number of other benefits of having and using email, in that users can keep a historical record (audit) of messages that have been sent and received. Messages can be saved into different formats, updated and printed out if required. Email embraces a range of multimedia elements that allow users to send messages containing graphics, sound, moving images and even hyperlinks to Internet pages, all of which can be viewed, downloaded, imported and saved from the Internet.

The disadvantages of having and using email mainly focus on technical and security issues such as:

* spamming: the receiving of unwanted messages by advertisers, third parties and unknown users that broadcast messages universally to an entire address book

What does it mean?

Spamming is the process of sending junk email to another user/users without them authorising or requesting the send. Spam emails usually consist of advertising materials being sent by companies.

* routing: email is not always sent direct from A to B; it can be routed to other destinations before it finally reaches the receiver. This can cause a number of problems including:
  – more time is taken before the message reaches its destination
  – there are more opportunities for the message be breached and intercepted by a third party
  – the message can become distorted or lost

* security: email can be intercepted easily unless some sort of encryption has been applied to the message

What does it mean?

Encryption is a process of scrambling data to ensure that it is kept secure during the transmission process.

* confidentiality: because email can get lost, intercepted or distorted it is not deemed appropriate to send confidential messages using this format.

When a message is encrypted, a secret numerical code is applied so that the message can be transmitted or stored in indecipherable characters. The message can only be read after it has been reconstructed through the use of a 'matching key'. Many Internet-based companies use encryption software to protect sensitive user information.

FIGURE 1.4 *PIPEX home page*

Internet connections

The Internet is a physical network that links computers globally, enabling communication links that will store and transfer vast amounts of data and information. To access the Internet, a number of factors have to be considered.

Traditionally, the hardware required to gain access to the Internet included a computer and a modem with access to a telephone line (dial-up).

In the early days, the most common method of connection was through dial-up using a modem to physically make the communication connection. A modem would be linked by cables to the computer and also connected to a phone line to enable the data transmission. Issues with speed, however, led to developments being made in other transmission mediums. Alternative methods (such as ISDN and broadband) became more widely available.

What does it mean?

ISDN is an abbreviation for Integrated Services Digital Network which is an international communications standard for sending voice, video or data over a digital telephone line or normal telephone wires.

Broadband is a very high-speed connection to the Internet that, once connected, is always active/on. It has a much larger capacity to receive and send data (up to 50 times faster than a 56K modem, allowing the user to view web content and download files more quickly). The benefits of broadband are that, although a physical connection is required, the speed of transmission and data retrieval is much faster. If a networked system has been set up, although the router would be physically connected to a computer and phone line, additional computers and laptops with wireless capabilities would not need to be physically connected by cables to gain access to Internet services. There are a number of providers that offer broadband services, PIPEX (Figure 1.7) being just one of these.

These newer, more advanced ways of connecting to the Internet have brought a host of benefits including:

* being able to use the landline to make calls while surfing on the Internet

* faster connection speeds

* better reliability in terms of connecting and instant connection

* permanent connection; no need to repeatedly dial-up.

FIGURE 1.5 *Sky Digital*

Mobile phone technologies

Mobile phones that used to be the size and weight of a brick can now be wafer thin, almost credit-card-sized devices. Today's mobile phones are packed full of communication enhancements to allow users to watch video and movie clips, send and receive photographs and images, and send a wide variety of voice data and multimedia communications.

With technologies such as WAP and SMS text facilities the growth in popularity of mobile phones seems to have overtaken more conventional ways of communicating.

Digital broadcasting

Digital television is a replacement technology for existing analogue services. Digital broadcasting provides a better picture quality and reception, plus it offers a variety of new features that enhance the viewing experience. Companies such as Sky Digital have grown in popularity, with the ability to provide a huge choice of digital programmes ranging from movies to children's programmes, history and documentaries through to sports and music.

PDAs and organisers

PDAs have changed the way that many people organise their working and social lives. A PDA is a handheld device that combines computing, telephone/fax, Internet and networking features. PDAs are small enough to be stored in a handbag or briefcase, and they have the capacity to manage your time effectively and efficiently through easy and interactive navigation tools and menu systems.

Storage media

Storage devices are essential to all users that utilise ICT resources. Storage is required to:

* store programs
* store data that is waiting to be processed
* store the output of future information.

The need for portable, convenient data storage devices has dictated that technologies become even more dynamic in design and functionality. Over the years, storage devices have changed from tapes, to floppy disks, CDs and minidisks to DVDs and USB pens.

What does it mean?

USB is an abbreviation for Universal Serial Bus, this is an external bus that supports data transfer. An example of a USB device can be seen in the USB pen (see Figure 1.6) that is used for saving data and information onto a portable device.

Storage requirements differ between user types and organisations. For example, a home user might require 20 gigabytes (GB) as an entry level for storing data. A small organisation with three or four stand-alone computers might require a minimum of 40 GB on each. A small networked organisation with up to ten computers running via a server could have anything up to 500 GB. A large networked organisation running up to 50 computers without individual local drives could require terabyte (TB) storage.

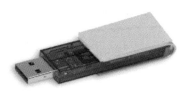

FIGURE 1.6 *A USB pen*

Assessing the effects of ICT

Choosing a topic to research

You should investigate for yourself how the use of specific developments in ICT have changed the way we live and work. Although your normal direct contact with ICT is through a desktop computer, you should recognise the ways in which ICT is embedded in many other systems. For example, the rail network uses information display boards and automated announcements that derive data from the traffic control systems; schools use whiteboards for teaching; hospitals use computer controlled scanning equipment; music and video studios use highly complex recording systems.

You will probably want to select a topic that is of interest to you, but you would also be wise to select a couple of topics that you know nothing about, so that you can develop your research skills and broaden the base of your knowledge.

Watch out for newly emerging technologies. It may be interesting to speculate whether they are going to be taken up by businesses and by the population at large, or whether they will just be used by a small minority. When the WWW was developed in the early 1990s it was difficult to imagine the impact this would have on the way we find information, communicate with each other, and buy goods. At the time of writing 3G phones have been promoted as a major technological breakthrough, but there has been little uptake so far. As you read this, has that changed?

Carrying out research

Your main sources of information are people and resource materials.

You should speak with people who are directly affected by the technology. Do this in a systematic way by making an appointment to speak to someone, planning the questions you want to ask, recording the answers on paper or by taping the conversation (always ask permission first). Write up a summary of what you were told, but keep your original notes as well.

Bit (b)	Smallest unit of measurement	Single binary digit 0 or 1
Byte (B)	Made up of 8 bits, the number required to represent a single character	Value between 0 and 255
Kilobyte (KB)	Equivalent to 1,000 characters	Approximately 1,000 bytes
Megabyte (MB)	Equivalent to 1 million characters	Approximately 1,000 kilobytes
Gigabyte (GB)	Equivalent to 1 billion characters	Approximately 1,000 megabytes
Terabyte (TB)	Equivalent to 1 thousand billion characters	Approximately 1,000 gigabytes

TABLE 1.2 *Storage measurements*

You should note this information about each person you interview:

* age, gender and employment or interests
* how much are they affected by the technology
* how much do they use the technology
* whether they have an opinion about the technology.

Resource materials may include books, magazines, newspapers, reports, broadcast material and websites. Try to include a mixture of resources, and do not rely entirely on the Internet. You should note this information about each resource you find:

* name of publication/website/broadcast
* date it was published
* whether the information is reliable, and how you have checked it.

Theory into practice

A company wants to install a communications network and is unsure about the prices of different types of connection mediums.

1 Compare and contrast three different broadband provider prices.

2 Set up a table to identify monthly costs, speed, functions and the services of each of the three providers.

3 Produce a set of recommendations as to which provider the company should use.

4 There are a range of mobile technologies available on the market. Select three different mobile phone manufacturers, e.g. Motorola, Nokia, Samsung, and produce an information sheet of the range of phones available from each. The phones should include a range of the latest technologies, e.g. video capture, photo messaging, etc.

Theory into practice

Investigate the impact on society at large or on individuals of a specific use of ICT that interests you. Carry out research and then present your findings in an appropriate way, such as a small presentation to a group of students.

Carry out a second investigation into a use of ICT which you know very little about.

1.2 Legislation

Legislation can impact on different users in different ways. Organisations will have to ensure that they operate within certain legislative boundaries, that include informing employees and third parties about how they intend to safeguard systems and any information collected, processed, copied, stored and output on their systems. Personal users need to be aware of the legislation that affects them, what their responsibilities are and the penalties that can be imposed if any laws or regulations are breached.

The types of legislation that an organisation needs to consider affect everyday operations in terms of:

* collecting, processing and storing data
* using software
* protecting their employees and ensuring that working conditions are of an acceptable standard.

Data Protection Act 1998

The Data Protection Act applies to the processing of personal data and information by any source, either electronic or paper-based. The Act places obligations on people who collect, process and store personal records and data about consumers, customers or staff. The main principles include the following:

1 Personal data shall be processed fairly and lawfully.

2 Personal data shall be obtained only for one or more specified and lawful purposes, and shall not be further processed in any manner incompatible with that purpose or those purposes.

3 Personal data shall be adequate, relevant and not excessive in relation to the purpose or purposes for which they are processed.

4 Personal data shall be accurate and, where necessary, kept up-to-date.

5 Personal data processed for any purpose or purposes shall not be kept for longer than is necessary for that purpose or those purposes.

6 Personal data shall be processed in accordance with the rights of data subjects under this Act.

7 Appropriate technical and organisational measures shall be taken against unauthorised or unlawful processing of personal data and against accidental loss or destruction of, or damage to, personal data.

8 Personal data shall not be transferred to a country or territory outside the EU (European Union) unless that country or territory ensures an adequate level of protection for the rights and freedoms of data subjects in relation to the processing of personal data.

What does it mean?

Personal data: Information about living, identifiable individuals. Personal data does not have to be particularly sensitive information and can be as limited as name and address.

The Act gives rights to individuals in respect of personal data held about them by data users. These include the rights:

* to make subject access requests about the nature of the information and to discover to whom it has been disclosed
* to prevent processing likely to cause damage or distress
* to prevent processing for the purposes of direct marketing
* to be informed about the mechanics of any automated decision-taking process that will significantly affect them
* not to have significant decisions that affect them made solely by an automated decision-taking process
* to take action for compensation if they suffer damage by any contravention of the Act by the data user
* to take action to rectify, block, erase or destroy inaccurate data
* to request the Commissioner to make an assessment as to whether any provision of the Act has been contravened.

The Act provides wide exemptions for journalistic, artistic or literary purposes that would otherwise be in breach of the law.

The Information Commissioner is an independent supervisory authority and has an international role as well as a national one. Primarily, the Commissioner is responsible for ensuring that the Data Protection legislation is enforced. In the UK, the Commission has a range of duties which include:

* promotion of good information handling
* encouraging codes of practice for data controllers.

Computer Misuse Act 1990

The Computer Misuse Act was enforced to address the increased threat of hackers trying to gain unauthorised access to a computer system. Prior to this Act, there was minimal protection and difficulties in prosecuting because theft of data by hacking was not considered a deprivation to the owner. There are a number of new offences defined under this Act:

* *Unauthorised access*: an attempt by a hacker to gain unauthorised access to a computer system.
* *Unauthorised access with the intent of committing another offence*: on gaining access a hacker will then continue with the intent of committing a further crime.
* *Unauthorised modification of data or programs*: introducing viruses to a computer system is a criminal offence. Guilt is assessed by the level of intent to cause disruption, or to impair the processes of a computer system.

The penalties for such crimes are given below.

* *Unauthorised access*: imprisonment for up to six months and/or a fine of up to £2,000.
* *Unauthorised access with the intention of committing another offence*: imprisonment for up to five years and/or an unlimited fine.
* *Unauthorised modification*: imprisonment for up to five years and/or an unlimited fine.

Copyright, Designs and Patent Act

The Copyright, Designs and Patent Act provides protection to software developers and organisations against unauthorised copying of their software, designs, printed material and any other product. Under copyright legislation an organisation or developer can ensure that its intellectual property rights (IPR) are safeguarded against third parties who wish to exploit and make gains from the originator's research and developments.

A number of copyright issues exists in regard to computer software:

* *Software piracy*: the copying of software to be used on more machines than individual licences have been paid for
* *Ownership*: if a bespoke piece of software has been developed for an organisation the copyright remains with the developer unless conditions have been written into a contract
* *Transference*: can an employee who has developed a piece of software for their organisation take the ownership and copyright with them to another organisation? Unless this is addressed in the employee's contract, the organisation will have no right to any software developed.

The Federation Against Software Theft (FAST) was set up in 1984 by the software industry with the aim of preventing software piracy. Anybody caught breaching the copyright law can be prosecuted by this federation.

Health and safety legislation

Organisations have a responsibility to comply with health and safety measures. One that has been set up to protect users of information systems is Display Screen Equipment (VDU) Regulations 1992.

Display Screen Equipment (VDU) Regulations 1992

Under these regulations an employer has six main obligations to fulfil. For each user and operator working in his or her undertaking, the employer must:

1 assess the risks arising from their use of display screen workstations and take steps to reduce any risks identified to the 'lowest extent reasonably practicable'

2 ensure that new workstations meet minimum ergonomics standards set out in a schedule to the Regulations

3 inform users about the results of the assessments, the actions the employer is taking and the users' entitlements under the Regulations.

For each user, whether working for this business or another employer, the employer must:

4 plan display screen work to provide regular breaks or changes of activity.

In addition, for his own employees who are users, the employer must:

5 offer eye tests before display screen use, at regular intervals, and if they are experiencing visual problems. If the tests show that they are necessary and normal glasses cannot be used, then special glasses must be provided

6 provide appropriate health and safety training for users before display screen use or whenever the workstation is 'substantially modified'.

In general, health and safety legislation can only benefit users and help to protect them against computer-related injuries such as:

✱ repetitive strain injury (RSI)

✱ back and upper joint problems

✱ eye strain

✱ exposure to radiation and hardware ozone

✱ epilepsy

✱ stress-related illnesses.

Knowledge check

1 Why will legislation have an impact on users of ICT?

2 What are the important features of the Data Protection Act?

3 What does the Computer Misuse Act cover?

4 Why do you need copyright laws?

Health and Safety at Work Act (1974)

The Health and Safety at Work Act was drawn up in 1974 to protect all employees, whatever the nature of their work. This affects someone working in the ICT industry as much as anyone else.

Employers have certain duties towards their employees and their customers, and employees have duties towards each other.

The main elements of the Act are:

✱ an employer has a duty to ensure the health and safety of employees as far as is reasonably practical

✱ an employer must consult employees on any changes to the workplace that might affect their health and safety

✱ an employer must appoint someone with responsibility for implementing health and safety measures, and provide first aid facilities

✱ an employee must take reasonable care of their own and others' health and safety, and must co-operate with the employer

✱ an employee must use any protective equipment provided by the employer.

The Management of Health and Safety at Work Regulations (1999) have added to the Act and require employers to carry out a risk assessment of the workplace, set up emergency procedures and provide information and training for employees.

The Regulation of Investigatory Powers Act (2000)

This Act gives certain public authorities, such as the police or HM Customs and Excise, the right to intercept communications and access data. This is only allowed, and usually requires a warrant, where this is necessary to combat crime or in the interests of public safety. Since most data and communications are electronically based, this is particularly significant for the ICT industry. The Act:

✱ permits the interception and disclosure of postal or electronic communications

✱ regulates the use of covert operations and surveillance, and the use of informants

✱ requires any required data that is encrypted to be turned into plain text.

Internet Service Providers are required to co-operate with all aspects of this when a warrant is issued.

1.3 ICT and people with particular needs

There are a large number of people that require specialist hardware or software in order to interact with ICT.

The range of ICT technologies available is extensive (Table 1.3), and there are a number of organisations that are committed to providing either hardware or software to users that may have a sensory impairment, limited mobility or a language disability. In addition, certain people may have a particular need as a result of an illness resulting from an accident, an inherited illness or general learning disability. These conditions can affect the lack of motor control or dexterity.

People who are visually impaired

Organisations such as Technologies for the Visually Impaired Inc. offer a wide range of adaptive devices, software and accessories specifically designed for use by blind or visually impaired individuals.

The range includes adaptive computers, reading machines, Windows access software, speech synthesisers, refreshable Braille products, voice recognition software, screen magnification software, CCTV products, Braille embossers, Braille translation software, tactile imaging products, various accessories, customised personal computer systems, and much more.

People who are deaf

The Royal National Institute for the Deaf and more specifically the New Technologies team have made huge advancements in the area of facilitating deaf people, and enabling them to communicate and embrace ICT.

The New Technologies department at RNID has two overall objectives:

* to harness information and communication technology to bring tangible benefits to deaf and hard of hearing people and to remove barriers they face in society

* to participate actively in the various technology communities so that both existing as well as emerging technologies become more inclusive for deaf, hard of hearing and speech-impaired people.

CONDITION OR DISABILITY	HARDWARE OR SOFTWARE AVAILABLE
Sensory impairment	Reading machines, Braille products, videophones
Limited mobility	Adaptive computers, videophones
Language disability	Speech synthesisers, text processors
Lack of motor control or dexterity	Adaptive computers
Limited use of limbs	Headsets, text phones and communicators
Short attention span	Signing avatars (virtual humans)

TABLE 1.3 *Hardware and software available for people with particular needs*

TECHNOLOGIES FOR THE VISUALLY IMPAIRED, INC.

Braille and Speech within Easy Reach

http://www.tvi-web.com

Speech amplifiers and induction loops

A wide range of hearing aids support induction loop technology, which has been used for decades in banks, libraries, hotels and other public premises to help deaf people to communicate. Videophones enable deaf people to communicate with others by transmitting and receiving a moving picture in Sign Language.

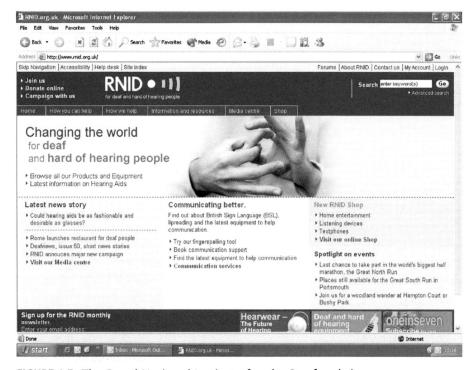

FIGURE 1.7 *The Royal National Institute for the Deaf website*

Speech synthesisers

Speech synthesis has developed steadily over the last decade and it has been used in several new applications. For most applications, synthetic speech has reached an acceptable level. However, in areas such as text processing and pronunciation there is still a great deal of work and development to be done to ensure that synthesised speech sounds natural.

Text telephones

Text telephones are used instead of a voice telephone if you are deaf or if you have problems with your speech. Unlike a standard telephone, a text phone has a keyboard and a display screen. Instead of speaking into a telephone mouthpiece, information is typed in, using the keyboard.

In the UK, the word 'Minicom' is often used to describe any text phone. Minicom is a widely used brand of text phone. When a text phone is used to call someone with a voice telephone, a pre-recorded message such as 'hard of hearing caller, please use a text phone' will be heard, or just silence. If they also have a text phone, they should be able to take the call and continue with the conversation. If they do not have a text phone, then a 'relay service' will need to be used to call them back. At present, the only national relay service in the UK is RNID Typetalk.

1.4 Styles of presentation of information

It is vital that information is presented clearly. Good presentation skills are essential in all environments. The way in which a message, thought or idea is presented can have a strong impact on the recipient of that message. Some messages can be delivered in a written format such as a report, newsletter or formal letter. Others could be delivered in a more visual format through the use of charts, graphs and pictures. The use of presentation tools and software can enhance the oral delivery of information.

To help you understand the different styles and presentation of information, this section will introduce you to a range of templates, tools and techniques that will allow you to customise different documents.

CASE STUDY: VIDEOPHONES IN FINLAND

In the multimedia project of the Finnish Association of the Deaf, new forms of services have been created with the help of modern technology. In the Joensuu region, the videophone is used for long-distance interpreting in Finnish Sign Language and, in the northern part of Finland, for bringing social services within the reach of deaf people.

A deaf person, together with a hearing person, can be seated in front of the same videophone and together make picture contact with the Joensuu interpreter referral service centre. Alternatively, a deaf person can use the videophone to contact a Finnish Sign Language interpreter who can connect him or her to a hearing person with a regular phone, and vice versa.

Page layout

There are a number of ways that you can customise your page layout to incorporate a number of features. Some of these include:

* setting the margins
* using headers and footers
* orientating the page
* changing the paper size.

Setting the margins

Margins are set to leave an edge all around the document to improve its appearance or to make it easier to read.

Margins can be set left, right, top and bottom (see Figure 1.8). They may need to be set up to fit around pre-printed headers, footers or side logos.

Headers and footers

Headers and footers (Figure 1.9) can help to enhance the style and formality of a document. They should provide meaningful information about the author of the document, the date of creation, filename and page numbers, etc.

Page orientation

The way in which a page is set out can have a dramatic impact on how the information will be received by an intended audience. For example, in terms of orientation will the page be 'portrait' or 'landscape' (see Figure 1.10)? Documents such as letters, reports and most business documents are portrait style.

Paper size

Paper size will vary depending on the type of document being created, for example A2, A3, A4 or A5 (see Figure 1.11). The relationship between

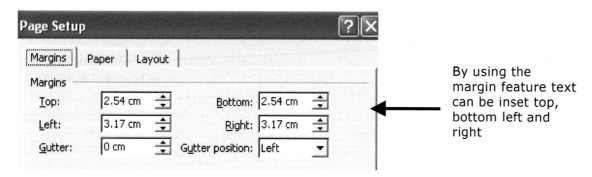

By using the margin feature text can be inset top, bottom left and right

FIGURE 1.8 *Setting the margins*

FIGURE 1.9 *Headers and footers*

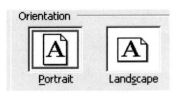

FIGURE 1.10 *Portrait or landscape?*

paper sizes is that A3 is double the size of A4, A4 is double the size of A5, etc. Most standard documents such as letters and reports are A4, although you need to ensure that the letter size is set for UK and not US standards which are different. User guides and newsletters may use smaller or larger paper sizes to emphasise or consolidate the information.

Text and paragraph formats

Fonts

To make a document look more professional and creative, a range of text and presentation styles can also be included. In terms of text styles, consideration has to be given as to what font is going to be used, (see Figure 1.12) and what style, size or format (bold, italic, underline, superscript or subscript).

There are three main styles of font: serif, sans serif and cursive.

* Serif fonts have small extra marks at the tops and bottoms of letters, such as the ones you are reading now. They derive from the marks left by chisels when carving letters in stone. Some of the best known fonts, such as Times Roman, are based on ancient lettering styles. Serif fonts are generally considered to be easier to read for sustained passages of text.

* Sans serif fonts do not have the serif marks, and appear simpler and cleaner. In this book, and many others, sans serif fonts are commonly used for headings. They can also be used for blocks of text although care has to be taken that the font is easy to read at the chosen size. You will probably be familiar with Arial, a sans serif font that has become very popular on computers.

* Cursive fonts imitate handwriting. They are best used for decorative documents, such as invitations, or for mock signatures, as they are not so easy to read.

Heading and title styles

Headings should normally be in a larger size than the body text, and are often made bold as well. It is tempting to use uppercase (capitals) for headings, but in some fonts that can be difficult to read.

You will often want to use more than one heading style – one for the main title, another for section headings and maybe a third for sub-sections. As a general rule, do not use more than two fonts in a document, but experiment with different sizes, colours and weights.

Instead of formatting each heading as you come to it, you can create a list of stylse that you want to use within a document. You can easily define new styles, choosing the font, size, weight and other decoration for each. Then whenever you want to use a subheading you simply highlight the text and apply the style.

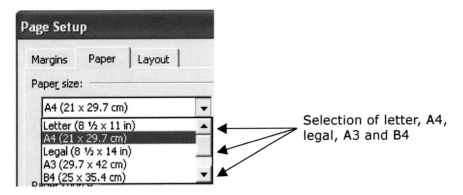

Selection of letter, A4, legal, A3 and B4

FIGURE 1.11 *Selecting the paper size*

Bold, italic and underline

Bold, italic and underline styles are all used to emphasise text. Bold and italics can both be used for headings and for body text. They are more effective if used sparsely so that the emphasised text stands out from surrounding text. Italics can also be used for quotes.

Underlining has now become the standard way of indicating a hyperlink, so it is wise to avoid using it for any other purpose in a document that is going to be viewed electronically. In the past, underlining was used in handwritten text as a substitute for bold.

Superscript and subscript

All text handling software allow you to create superscript (raised characters) and subscript (lowered characters). These are particularly used in scientific notation, amongst others, such as H_2O, cm^2, 4th. Make sure you know how to achieve these effects.

Some superscript characters are simply found already raised in extended fonts, for example, $29°$.

Tabs and indents

Tabs and indents (see Figure 1.13) will enable you to set up predefined sections in any document that you are working on. For example, indents for new paragraphs can be defined to enhance the style of the document.

Paragraph numbering

Paragraph numbering is very useful in certain documents such as reports, where automatic numbering can be used to section out areas of the report. Numbering can be set either manually or automatically.

Bullet points

Bullet points can be used to emphasise certain parts of a document in a list format, for example:

Bullets can be used to:

* emphasise certain text
* put information into an orderly list
* identify key features within certain information.

Hyphenation

Hyphenation can be used to insert hyphens, when needed within a document. Word will automatically fit a long word that appears at the end of a line to the beginning of a new line instead of hyphenating it.

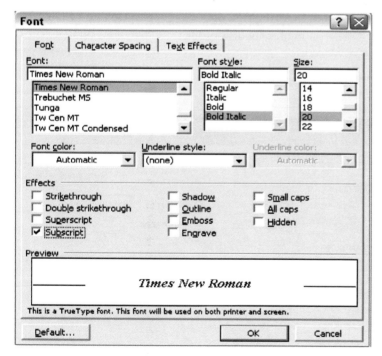

FIGURE 1.12 *Selecting the font*

Special features

Some features can be applied to a complete document, or to sections within it.

Non-graphical borders

You can place a line as a border around sections of text, to separate them from the surrounding text. This is particularly appropriate if you have inset a passage within the body. You can identify this technique within this book.

A border can also be used around each complete page. This style can be effective when it adds a design element to plain text, but should not be used if the text is heavily illustrated.

Contents page

You should always provide a contents page for any document that is at least several pages long. Most word processing and DTP software has a function (eg Index and Tables in Word) for automating this process. To use it you need to be consistent about your use of heading styles, preferably by using a style list. When you use the function, you identify the style that is used for a heading. Then it creates a contents page that includes all the headings in that style, along with their page numbers.

Colours of background and text

The colours you use depend on the way in whether the text will be viewed on screen or on paper. In both cases, background and text colours should be strongly contrasted to aid reading. Dark backgrounds can look very dramatic on screen, and can be quite effective, but should not be used for large amounts of text. Dark backgrounds for printed materials should only be used to make an impact, for example, in a poster, or for a small area of print.

Generally, it is wiser to use no more than two colours for text and headings, although within that you can use several shades of the same colour. Multiple colours on one page can be very distracting.

Index

An index at the back of a book lists all the key words with their page references. Creating an index by hand is a tedious process, but once again you can use the automated functions in your software. You have to mark the words that you want to be indexed as you key them in. Alternatively you can go back through the whole document at the end and mark up the words to be indexed. When the document is complete, the indexing function will generate an index, laid out in alphabetical order.

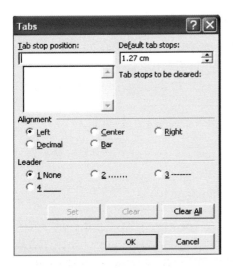

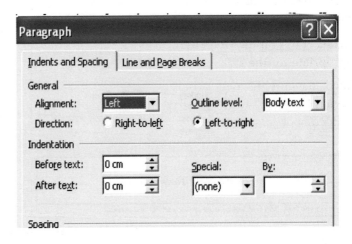

FIGURE 1.13 *Using tabs and indents*

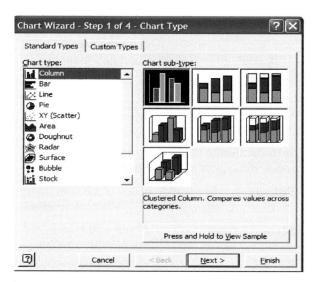

FIGURE 1.14 *Setting up a graph*

Bibliography

You will often find a list of books given at the end of a book. In some academic texts a bibliography will be listed at the end of each chapter. The list all the books that are referred to in the text, or that might be useful further reading.

There are a number of conventions for listing the book titles in a bibliography. The following is a common format:

Reid, K. Mary (ed.), *AS Level for AQA Applied ICT*. Oxford: Heinemann Educational, 2005.

Graphic images

Graphics such as graphs, drawings and scanned images will provide a more visual overview of any data that you have generated. However, if graphics are going to be used, ask yourself these questions:

✱ What sort of graphic will be used, and is it appropriate for the style of the document?

✱ How is the graphic going to be inserted/scanned/downloaded/pasted into the document?

Graphs and charts

Different types of graphs and charts (see Figure 1.14) can be used. Depending on what you need to display, these include:

✱ pie charts

✱ bar graphs

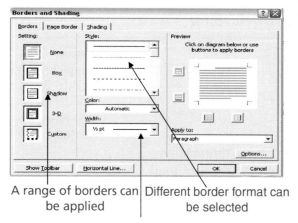

A range of borders can | Different border format can
be applied | be selected

Different widths can also be applied

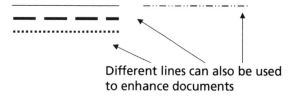

Different lines can also be used
to enhance documents

FIGURE 1.15 *Selecting lines and borders*

✱ line graphs

✱ scatter graphs.

Lines and borders

A range of lines and borders can be applied to your documents, as shown in Figure 1.15.

Drawings and scanned images

Pictures, drawings, clip art and scanned images can all be used to add interest and variety to your documents.

> **Knowledge check**
>
> 1 Identify three ways in which you can change the style of a document?
>
> 2 What feature/tool could you use if you wanted to produce a list of items?
>
> 3 What ways can a page be orientated?

Structure of documents

Different written documents have different styles and layouts, each having a set of essential criteria that makes the document unique. Examples of these templates are shown here

A structure for a letter

Sender's information Mrs Penelope Jordan 56 Briers Cranburn Road Norwich NR7 3DD **Recipient information** SJ Archaeological Group 445 The Glades Hingham Road Norwich NR3 3RD **Date** 22 February 2002 **Reference Number** (if applicable) **Salutation** Dear Sir/Madam **Introduction** **Content** **Closure** Yours faithfully Penelope Jordan

A structure for a memorandum

Memorandum To: From: CC: Date: Re: Body of text would be displayed here

A structure for an agenda

AGENDA **Staff Committee Meeting** Friday 29 October 2004 Room 5 First Floor 1 Re-structuring programme 2 Appointment of new Section Leader 3 Retirement party for J Norson 4 New canteen facilities 5 Staff outing proposals 6 Any other issues

A structure for a report

Title page: front sheet identifying the report title, the author, date and who the report is commissioned for.

Contents page: page referencing the information given on each page.

Introduction: a short summary of the overall focus and content of the report.

Procedures: identification of any procedures used to collect, collate, analyse and present information.

Main findings: the bulk of the report should be broken down into task, action or research areas. Each area of the findings section should put forward arguments or statements supported by research and analysis. This section can be broken down further into subsections.

Conclusions: brings together all of the items discussed within the main findings section and provide a summary of the key areas identified.

Recommendations: this section is solution based, providing the subjects of the report with proposals as to how they can move forward with the report objective.

Bibliography: identifies and gives credit for all information sources used to include; books, magazines or journals, other documents or reports, the Internet, etc.

Appendices: provides supporting documentation, including lists of facts and figures, leaflets, downloaded information, photocopied material, etc.

Index: to create an index you need to mark the 'index entries' in your document and then build the index. Once you mark an index entry, Word adds a special XE (Index Entry) field to your document. After you have marked all the index entries, you can choose an index design and build the finished index. Word then collects the index entries, sorts them alphabetically, references their page numbers, finds and removes duplicate entries from the same page, and displays the index in the document.

Creating a document

Creating templates

You should normally create a template for the document you are preparing. This preserves the underlying style for the whole document. In some software, especially DTP or presentation software, a template is known as a master page.

The simplest way to create a template is to set up a sample page using all the formats that you want to use – page layout, style list, borders etc – and then save it as a template.

Many software packages now include a variety of templates for you to use. You should certainly experiment with these, and they will give you plenty of ideas for styles you might wish to adopt. You can usually modify these templates to get just the look you want.

If you are creating a document for an organisation, you will probably be expected to use the corporate (or house) style. This is a set of rules that govern how all printed and electronic materials are to be designed. They will specify the logo to be used, and its exact size and position on the page, colours for text and background, fonts and decorative elements.

For assessment purposes you would not be advised to use a pre-existing template as it stands. You should create your own from scratch, and then provide evidence to show that you have done so.

Sources of information

The contents of a document may be all your own work, based on the research you have done, or it may incorporate appropriate elements written by others that you have come across. You should read again the section on Respecting Copyright in Standard Ways of Working to remind yourself about the acceptable ways in which you can use other people's material.

If you refer to any books you should list them in a bibliography.

Consistent style

You can maintain a consistent design style throughout a document by using a template. But it is still easy to stray from this, so if you do need to remain alert and ask whether you really do need to introduce any new styles as you go along.

As well as design style, you also have to be sensitive to the writing style that you use. It must be suitable for the audience, so you should think about the age, skills and interests of your readers, and how you want to relate to them.

Design

A complex document may include text, sound, graphics and numeric information. You need to do this in a way that is easy to use and pleasing in appearance. It is very tempting to show your skill in using all the features in your software, but in a way that produces a final result that is confusing and amateurish. The best designs are often quite restrained.

Theory into practice

With a group of students, collect together two examples of each of these types of document. One example in each pair should be, in your opinion, badly designed and the other effectively designed. Try to identify the features that distinguish good design from bad.

* book
* poster
* leaflet
* web page
* presentation
* magazine or newsletter.

Applying techniques

Although we have been referring to documents in the preceding sections, much of what is stated could equally apply to onscreen materials, such as web pages or presentations.

You will be demonstrating your mastery of these techniques in the assessment that you undertake for this unit. You will be set an external task which, amongst other things, will require you to create either web pages or a newsletter. The web pages or newsletter will be for a specific audience.

Target audience

The target audience will determine the design style and the writing style that you adopt. These are the kinds of factors of the audience that you may want to take into account:

* age
* gender
* skills and interests (e.g. whether the audience is already well-informed about the subject matter)
* reason for reading the document (e.g. to get information, to be entertained, to learn)
* internal or external (e.g. whether intended for the members/employees of an organisation).

Presentations

The style of a presentation will depend on the environment in which it is being delivered and the intended audience. Formal presentations tend to be more structured with more time built into the planning and overall delivery. Formal presentations may also be delivered to an audience that is not known to you. Informal presentations are more likely to be casual where the presenter could talk 'ad lib' with little or no preparation.

Presentations can be delivered in a number of ways, with or without the use of ICT, to include:

* reading from cards, sheets, etc.
* free style
* using presentation software
* using aids such as flip charts, overhead transparencies (OHTs), whiteboard, etc.

As well as text documents, styles of presentation can also be applied to visual documents such as slide presentations. Within a slide presentation, sequences of screens can be created to include text, graphics and different page layouts. In addition, sound and moving images can also be inserted to make the presentation style more dynamic.

ICT has played a big role in the way in which presentations are delivered and the overall quality of presentations. Software applications can be used for the specific purpose of delivering a professional presentation. Presentation software today can provide a number of benefits:

* it is easy to use
* it provides step-by-step designs
* it allows for interactivity
* it incorporates sound and images, both static and moving
* it is widely available
* you can customise each presentation.

Theory into practice

Presentations provide the ideal opportunity to communicate an idea, proposal or project etc. to a range of audiences. The use of presentation software will enable you to design professional presentation at the touch of a button.

1 Produce a 15 minute presentation that incorporates at least 10 slides. The presentation must also demonstrate the use of a slide design template, transitions, a graphic, link and a chart.

2 Ensure that you use a master slide to include an appropriate footer.

3 Add some notes pages and print out handouts for the audience.

Newsletters

A newsletter usually has a quite specific audience. It is targeted at the members of a club or interest group, so it can assume a certain level of common understanding and knowledge.

You can create a newsletter using either word processing or DTP software. Although you may like to explore the template provided you should create your own templates and styles for the assessment.

You may note that some newsletters are deliberately modelled on newspaper styles, whilst others look much less formal.

Web pages

Web pages can also be targeted at a specific audience, although you will not be able to limit the visitors to that group.

You can create web pages using standard web authoring software. You create the pages in much the same way as when using DTP software. The software then generates the HTML code that is used by the World Wide Web. As you become proficient at web page design you will want to look at, and maybe modify, the code.

It is possible to create web pages very rapidly using other types of software, such as word processing, DTP or presentation packages. But you would be wiser not to use these as they can become quite difficult to manage if you want to develop and extend the pages.

If you create more than one page you should create links between the pages in the form of hyperlinks. These can be arranged in a row or column to form a navigation bar. Alternatively you can simply create links from words or images on the page.

Web authoring packages do provide you with page templates, and even templates for complete websites. You can modify these to give the exact look and feel that you want to your pages, rather than use them as they come.

1.5 Evaluation

Evaluation is an essential part of any project. Being able to reflect on the work that has been carried out and provide a justified statement outlining what went well, or not so well, can add value to any investigation or research that you have undertaken. There are two areas that need to be addressed under the term 'evaluation'. The first is an evaluation of the solution, and the second is an evaluation of your own performance.

Evaluation of your solution

Before you begin developing a solution for a client you should discuss with them how it will be evaluated. The agreed evaluation criteria will then guide you when doing your work. This approach will apply to the newsletter or website that you will be implementing for assessment.

An evaluation can be based on qualitative or quantitative criteria and information. Qualitative criteria may be generated from any feedback that you have received about your evidence/solution. This feedback may include written comments and observations, and completed fact-finding documents such as interview notes or questionnaires. Quantitative criteria may be generated from numerical or statistical data, for example data relating to any testing that has taken place.

The feedback you receive from other people, in conjunction with any actual results that you have, should all form part of evaluating your work. Throughout the evaluation you must remain objective, and justify any decisions or comments made from evidence collected throughout the period of data collection, analysis, design and testing.

Evaluation of your performance

There are a number of ways that can be used to evaluate your own performance. An evaluation should be based on the following criteria:

* What have you done/produced?

* How have you done it?

* What did you use in terms of resources and know-how?

* What have you learned?

* What issues or problems have you had to address and overcome?

* What went well?

* What would you change and why?

By evaluating your own performance you should be able to identify any strengths and weaknesses that have developed during the project. For example, a strength may be the fact that you have developed new skills and acquired new knowledge that has helped in the final solution. Through evaluation you can set out recommendations that could be used to help with work that you might produce in future projects.

The ability to remain objective in the evaluation stage is sometimes very difficult, especially if you have strong personal views as to why the project did or did not meet expectations. By identifying the strengths and weaknesses of the project, you will be able to view the project more objectively.

1.6 Evidence of quality of written communication

The portfolio that you produce should demonstrate that you are capable of using, and have used, a suitable and appropriate style of writing. All text must be legible, meaningful and organised appropriately. Standard conventions such as applying headers and footers, using page numbers and title pages, etc. should also be applied.

ICT and organisations

Introduction

Organisations throughout the developed world use ICT: large and small organisations, public and commercial organisations. This unit focuses on the information needs of these different types of organisation, how the organisations are structured and how ICT meets their various needs.

In particular, this unit investigates how organisations collect information and how that information flows within and between organisations. It looks at how developments in ICT systems support different activities or functions with organisations, and how these developments affect why and how organisations present information. Finally, the unit focuses on the effectiveness of ICT in helping organisations to achieve their goals.

What you need to learn

* The information needs of organisations

* How organisations, both large and small, public and commercial, are structured

* How developments in technology affect how organisations collect information and how that information flows within and between organisations

* How developments in technology affect how and why organisations present information

* How ICT systems support different activities or functions within organisations

* How to evaluate the effectiveness of ICT systems in helping organisations to achieve their goals

Resource toolkit

To complete this unit, you need these essential resources:

* access to computer hardware and software facilities, including word processing software

* access to the Internet

* a wide range of information sources, such as books, trade journals of the ICT industry, newspapers

* contacts working within the ICT industry.

How you will be assessed

This mandatory unit is centre-assessed and externally moderated.

There are four assessment objectives:

1 Practical capability in applying ICT

2 Knowledge and understanding of ICT systems and their roles in organisations and society

3 Apply knowledge and understanding to produce solutions to ICT problems

4 Evaluate ICT solutions and own performance

To demonstrate your coverage of these assessment objectives, you will produce a portfolio of evidence, showing what you have learned and what you can do:

* You will research the purposes of large and small, public and commercial organisations and their differing data-handling needs.

* Using ICT, you will produce a formal report of your findings, written for an organisation, describing how one ICT system is used to handle the information needs of that organisation, and how developments in ICT have affected working styles in the organisation.

* You will submit a draft of the report showing how you edited the report during its production.

* You will evaluate your finished report and your own performance. This report will offer you the opportunity to demonstrate that you have used a style of writing which is appropriate for the portfolio produced, and will demonstrate the quality of your written evidence.

Your portfolio must meet the requirements set out in the assessment criteria for this unit:

* You must choose a range of different types of ICT systems used to handle data in organisations.

* It will be important to include both large and small organisations, and to cover different types of organisations in your report.

You are also expected to adopt standard ways of working so as to manage your work effectively, and show evidence of this. Standard ways of working are covered in the preliminary pages of this book.

How high can you aim?

The presentation of your portfolio is important. You should aim to present your work in a format that would be acceptable in industry. For this particular unit, how you present your portfolio, and what you include within it will determine the maximum number of marks that you earn.

You should include evidence to show that you have carried out research into several types of ICT system, used by different types and sizes of organisation.

Your formal report will then focus on one specific ICT System in one organisation. Tables 2.1 and 2.2 show how you can gain marks for the structure and content of this report.

	1–5 MARKS	6–10 MARKS	11–15 MARKS	16–21 MARKS
Initial draft	Included but lacking in detail	Includes most aspects of proposed content	Shows proposed content	Shows proposed content and changes to content and layout
Annotation of changes		Yes	Yes	Fully annotated
Structure of final report	Limited	Basic	Formally structured	Well-structured, formal report
Contents page		Yes	Yes	Yes
Introduction			Yes	Yes
Conclusion		Yes	Yes	Yes
Index			May be incomplete or inaccurate	Full and accurate
Bibliography			May be incomplete or inaccurate	Full and accurate
Using proof-reading symbols			Yes	Yes
Standard ways of working	An awareness	Attempts to adopt	Shows ability to follow	Close adherence

TABLE 2.1 *Practical capability in applying ICT*

	1 – 5 MARKS	6–10 MARKS	11–15 MARKS	16–21 MARKS
Background information of the organisation	Some	Detailed	Detailed	Detailed
Describes how ICT systems help to meet data-handing needs	Attempted	Basic description	Yes, and relates these to organisation's purposes	Detailed, and explains in terms of organisations' purposes
Data processing		Basic description	Yes, detailed	Yes, fully
Effect on working styles	Acknowledged	Some described	Described in detail	Describes and explains in detail

TABLE 2.2 *What you need to write about in your report*

	1–4 MARKS	5–9 MARKS	10–14 MARKS
Selection of sources	With variety, including the Internet	Appropriate, with variety	Appropriate, with variety
Justifies appropriateness of sources			Yes
Evidence in report of research into organisations, their purpose and their use of information	Limited research	Yes	Yes
Checking report for accuracy and/or meaningful content	Limited evidence	Yes	Fully, and makes changes where necessary

TABLE 2.3 *Apply knowledge and understanding to produce solutions to ICT problems*

You will be assessed on your ability to carry out research effectively (see Table 2.3). This will be based on your general portfolio evidence as well as on your formal report.

Having produced your report, you will evaluate it and your own performance in producing it (Table 2.4).

So, in working through this unit, remember that the maximum number of marks that you can earn, and hence your grade, will depend on the number and choice of organisations, how you research these organisations, what your report says and how well you evaluate your work.

	1–4 MARKS	5–9 MARKS	10–14 MARKS
Describes actions taken to solve the problem	Briefly	Yes	
Identifies strengths and weaknesses, and areas for improvement		Yes, some	Yes, successfully – and makes appropriate changes as a result
Planning and time management	Limited evidence	Some evidence of meeting agreed deadlines	Strong evidence, and of monitoring and effective use of time
Evaluation criteria	Some	Some qualitative and quantitative criteria appropriate to some client needs	Qualitative and quantitative criteria appropriate to client needs
Testing	Some	Some	Full, taking into account the evaluation criteria
Evaluation of solution	Attempted	Some evaluation done	Full

TABLE 2.4 *Evaluate ICT solutions and your own performance*

2.1 Types of organisation

In all types of organisations, people work together to make a product or provide a service. This unit refers to two case studies to provide illustrations for you:

* Papercourt Sailing Club is a large members-only club run by elected volunteers. For its 200-plus members, it manages a clubhouse and organises dinghy sailing, racing and training on the lake at Send.

* redhouse is a privately owned company that manufactures and sells bespoke furniture.

What does it mean?

An organisation comprises one person, but more usually a number of people who, between them, pool their talents and expertise to provide a service or manufacture a product.

You need to study a range of organisations, ideally at least three, of differing types and sizes, and ask yourself these questions:

* What information do they use?

* How do they process that information?

* What use do they make of that information?

So, to make sure you select different organisations, how can you categorise organisations? What makes one organisation different from another?

Think it over...

In a group of five or six, list as many different types of organisation as you can. Think about the sizes of organisations and what they do.

There are many ways of categorising organisations:

* by ownership type, e.g. private versus public

* by size, e.g. large or small

* by location, e.g. local, national or international

* by function, e.g. a manufacturer, a wholesaler or a retailer.

CASE STUDY: REDHOUSE

Nick runs redhouse, a small private company creating items from metal and wood (Figure 2.1). Part of their revenue comes from private individuals who buy bespoke furniture, i.e. items made exactly to the buyer's specification. They also have corporate clients, and may be asked to fit out a bar with tables and stools, or a borough council may need railings for the local park.

1 In discussion with your friends, list people that you know (parents, neighbours) who work for small private companies. Consider whether any of these contacts might help by introducing you to a relevant person at their place of work who might be willing to provide you with information about how the company uses IT and its impact on their organisation.

2 Think of other types of organisations that are not private. How might they be categorised?

1 Rod being heated up in the fire	2 Rolling the rod

3 Hitting the rod into shape	4 Wrapping the rod around an upright

FIGURE 2.1 *Work in the redhouse studio*

Ownership of organisations

The ownership type determines who owns the wealth of the company and who has the responsibility for decision making. These aspects may influence how IT could have an impact on an organisation.

Most organisations have the primary motive of making a profit for their owners or shareholders. Multinational commercial organisations, national companies and public limited companies like banks and major shopping chains publish their accounts, and their success may be measured by the profit that they make.

However, not all organisations share this primary goal:

* Public service organisations such as hospitals, schools and collages tend to be funded by the state, although private provision may also be available, e.g. private health care or private schooling.

* Utility companies, such as transport, water, electricity and gas, may be subsidised by the government, government-owned or privately owned. Different societies arrange for these utilities to be provided in different ways.

* Non-profit-making organisations such as charities are set up to raise monies to be spent on a good cause. Charities employ a team of people to manage the activities, but rely heavily on volunteers to do much of the work.

Sizes of organisations

Organisations can be categorised according to their size:

* Small firms include sole traders (i.e. one-man-bands). Their use of IT will depend on their line of work, and the ease with which the individual uses IT.

* The next size of organisation covers partnerships between two persons and family-run businesses.

* Small firms can grow into large firms and, in doing so, a more complex multi-layered management structure may evolve.

CASE STUDY: PAPERCOURT SAILING CLUB

Papercourt Sailing Club is an example of a non-profit-making organisation. At Papercourt, an old quarry pit has been filled with water and the surrounding area developed to provide dinghy-sailing facilities. A clubhouse stands on the side of the lake, and the many members of Papercourt Sailing Club enjoy racing their dinghies all year round.

The newsletter editor generates a newsletter four times a year to keep members informed of forthcoming events and the results of racing to date (Figure 2.2).

The club also has a website, accessible by visitors, members of the club and by the committee members.

1 A voluntary organisation like a sports club may make use of IT. It can save the volunteers time and make their duties less onerous. Think of any organisations that you belong to, or those that provide sports facilities local to you, and list the ways they use IT.
2 Visit your local library (in person, or via the Internet) and find out about voluntary organisations that operate in your local area. Look carefully at their advertising material. Has IT been used to good effect in the presentation of this material?
3 Produce a shortlist of voluntary organisations that might be suitable for you to investigate for this unit.

(Continued)

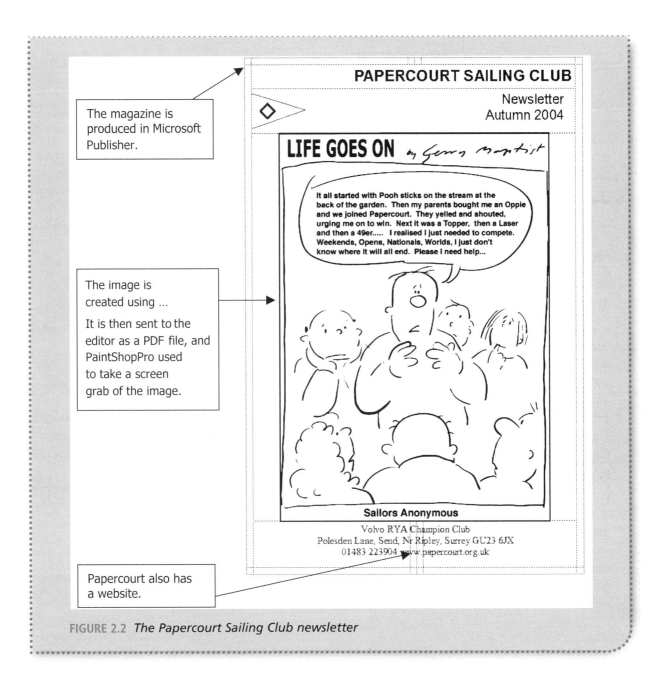

FIGURE 2.2 *The Papercourt Sailing Club newsletter*

Think it over...

In a group of five or six, list as many examples of different sizes of organisation as you can. Think about what each organisation does.

Organisational structure charts

Organisations develop and may change their structure as they grow. Lines of communication become more important as the number of people increases. There are three basic types of organisational structure. The difference between them is the number of levels of management between the most senior manager (the MD or CEO) and the lowest level in the company.

What does it mean?

MD stands for Managing Director.

CEO stands for Chief Executive Officer.

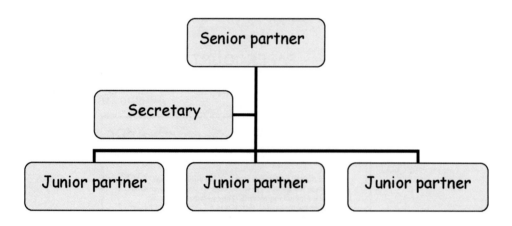

FIGURE 2.3 *Organisation chart for a flat structure, e.g. for a firm of solicitors*

* A flat structure (as shown in Figure 2.3) has only a few levels in the organisation. It can encourage 'team spirit' through the avoidance of 'them' and 'us' feelings. It also, theoretically, improves communication because there are fewer layers of management for information to pass through from the top of the organisation to the bottom. However, as soon as an organisation grows, a flat structure can become unmanageable. There is a limit to how many people a manager can have within his or her team.

* A hierarchical structure (see Figure 2.4) has many layers of management, so the structure works like a pyramid. This is typical of large organisations, but due to the number of layers, it can be difficult for information to flow from top to bottom and vice versa.

* A matrix structure (as shown in Figure 2.5) can suit organisations that have several different divisions. Employees are organised into product teams (e.g. in an electronics company this might be mobile phones, laptops, PDAs, etc.) as well as by function (e.g. R&D, production, sales, etc.). In a matrix structure, a particular group of workers, say television production, will be accountable to both the television division manager and the production manager. Each member of the organisation (below managerial level) is accountable to two or more managers. Marketing, sales and other functional managers will have global responsibility for their functions within the organisation, while divisional managers have responsibility for

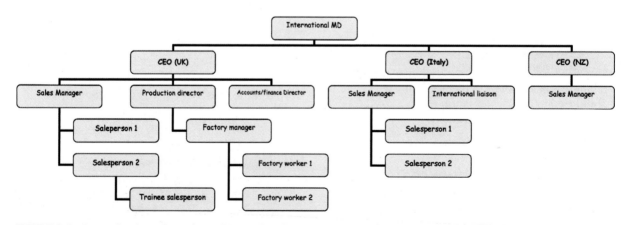

FIGURE 2.4 *Organisation chart for a hierarchical structure, e.g. for an international company*

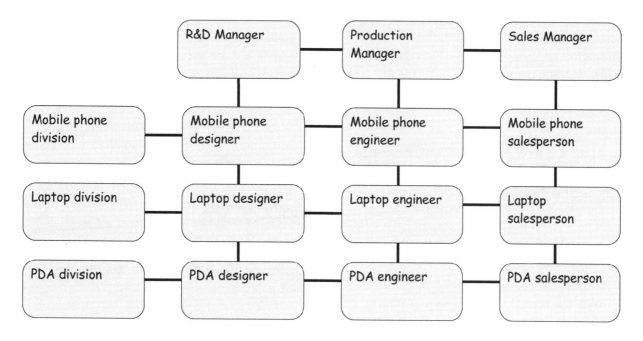

FIGURE 2.5 *Organisation chart for a matrix structure, e.g. for an IT development company*

these functions on a divisional basis. The main problem with matrix structures is that they are complex; some people find it confusing to have more than one manager.

What does it mean?

R&D stands for research and development.

The purpose of an organisation chart is fourfold:

* to show levels of management and their span of control
* to show the chain of command and lines of communication
* to specify levels of responsibility and accountability
* to identify individuals and their promotion/career path.

The structure chart therefore provides information as to who makes decisions, and

CASE STUDY: PAPERCOURT SAILING CLUB

Papercourt Sailing Club (PSC) is managed by its main committee. There are then six sub-committees to deal with issues such as training, social events and sailing. PSC provides sailing facilities for people with disabilities, such as those with limited eyesight or limited physical movement, and so there is also a sub-committee who focus on Sailability. The main committee comprises the Commodore and the chairman of each of the sub-committees. Within the club, there are ten 'class' captains

who organise the sail training and racing events for their own class of boat: Enterprise, GP14, Graduate, Solos and many others. There is one representative of each sailing class on each of the subcommittees.

1 **Draw an organisation chart for PSC.**
2 **For an organisation of your choice, identify the management structure and draw a structure diagram. Find out how those at the bottom of the structure are kept informed by those at the top.**

who is expected to carry out the tasks needed to carry through these decisions. Management means making decisions and directing employees so that these decisions are carried through within the organisation. This happens at three levels:

* At the top level of management, strategic decisions determine long-term organisational planning. These decisions may be unstructured and made infrequently. However, strategic decisions can have a large impact on the whole organisation and cannot be reversed easily.

* In the middle levels of management, tactical decisions relate to medium-term planning. These decisions serve to check the performance of the organisation, monitoring budgets, allocating resources and setting policies. They also move the organisation towards long-term goals set by top management strategic decisions.

* At the lowest level of management, operational decisions focus on the here and now. What needs to be done today? These decisions direct efforts towards meeting the medium-term goals, abiding by the budgets, policies and procedures. They have little impact on the organisation as a whole.

Knowledge check

1 Explain the meaning of these terms: sole trader, partnership, family-run business, organisational chart.

2 Distinguish between flat, hierarchical and matrix structures for organisations.

3 Distinguish between strategic, tactical and operational decisions.

Locating organisations

Organisations may also differ according to their *location*.

* Some organisations exist in urban areas while others only appear in rural settings.

* Some organisations exist in a single location, maybe at a contractor's home. Others are spread across regions, and/or across national barriers. So, an organisation may be categorised as being within the EU – or outside of the EU. An organisation may exist only in one country, or be a multi-national organisation.

Think it over...

In a group of 5 or 6, list organisation local to you that exist in only that location. Identify other organisations that are limited to the UK, and others that are international.

Where an organisation is based can affect its access to other services, and the market it might attract. However, unless the organisation offers something only to the local community, as is the case for a sailing club, with appropriate communication links, nowadays, location need not be such a limiting factor. The option to sell over the Internet also frees up organisations to base their manufacturing and other production efforts to locations where it is most cost-effective, rather than close to target markets.

Function of organisations

Organisations may also be categorised by what they do (their function), as shown in Table 2.5.

Think it over...

Discuss within your group, how would you classify non-commercial organisations such as charities or training organisations?

Different types of organisations fall into a pattern according to the production stage, i.e. where they fit between the raw materials and the end consumer (Figure 2.6).

Industrial organisations make things.	**Extraction organisations** take raw materials from the earth, e.g. coal mining, farming and fishing.
	Manufacturing organisations take raw materials and turn them into products such as clothes or computer hardware. They can be further subdivided into those who make components, and those who take components and assemble them into products.
Commercial organisations sell things.	**Wholesale organisations** act as middle men. They buy from the manufacturers and sell to the retailers. They are most often involved in distribution of goods.
	Retail organisations sell goods to end customers, usually via shops but more often now over the Internet.
	Service industries sell some kind of service, such as insurance cover and banking services.

TABLE 2.5 *Categorising organisations by what they do*

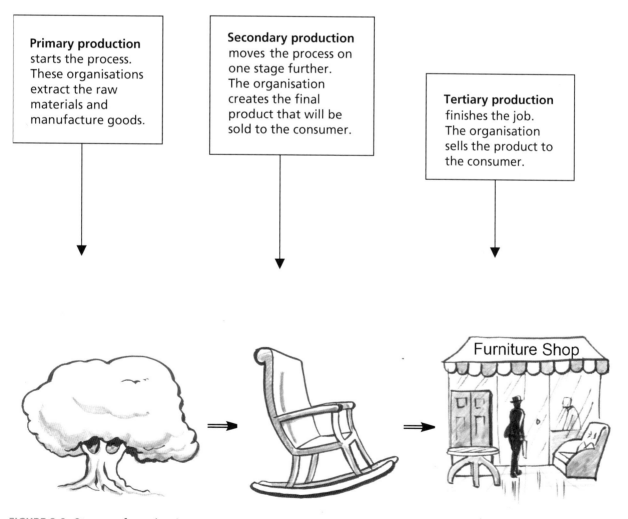

Primary production starts the process. These organisations extract the raw materials and manufacture goods.

Secondary production moves the process on one stage further. The organisation creates the final product that will be sold to the consumer.

Tertiary production finishes the job. The organisation sells the product to the consumer.

FIGURE 2.6 *Stages of production*

You need to identify at least one organisation, and preferably three or more organisations, that you can study.

1 Prepare a proposal for one organisation that you plan to approach. Starting with the organisation's name, write brief notes listing the size and type of organisation, and why you think it would be suitable.

2 Present your proposal to a friend before presenting it to your teacher. Another person provides a different viewpoint, and it may help you to focus your thoughts.

3 Offer to go through your friend's proposal.

4 Review your own proposal in the light of comments received and the other proposals you have seen.

5 Generate more proposals, one for each organisation you intend to study. Make sure that these other organisations differ in some way from the ones already selected.

2.2 Functions within organisations

Within an organisation, different talents are needed to fulfil the various tasks.

* Some people are needed to promote the products and services and secure sales. These people tend to be outgoing personalities, highly motivated to sell more because their earnings are related to their success as a salesperson.

* Some people need to be qualified in specialist areas such as book-keeping and accounts.

* Others need to keep up to date with legislation related to employment and have the talent to interview and select staff.

* More people are needed to plan for future products and services.

Since each of these groups have different training and serve a particular function, they tend to be organised into departments. The tasks each department undertakes is known as a job function.

1 Find out, for one of your organisations, how many staff are employed, and how this is broken down into manageable sections.

2 For a second organisation, find out the size of the sales force. How are these people grouped and managed?

Why are organisations structured into departments?

Any organisation needs to provide management for its employees. If employees are grouped by job function into departments, a manager can be assigned for each department. He or she is then responsible for the work of that department.

Within a small group, discuss what a manager has to do, in order to manage a team of people. Decide how many people one manager could directly manage.

What the organisation does will determine which departments are created within an organisation. Each department will have a specific role and specific responsibilities. Table 2.6 outlines these for a range of departments.

Note that organisations use different names for what are essentially the same departments.

* Accounts and Finance are different names for the same function.

* Human resources is the modern term for Personnel.

Some departments also work closely together:

* The staff within the Marketing department usually work closely with those in the Sales

Accounts or finance	Monitors all aspects of the company's money including incoming and outgoing payments.
	Pays the company's suppliers, employees (payroll), bank and stockholders. Sets customer credit limits, taking references where necessary, and deals with bad debtors.
	Obtains finance funding (e.g. a bank loan) to support the development of the company.
Sales	Creates and manages a sales force to contact potential customers.
	Negotiates contracts, takes orders and processes them.
	Performs follow-up work with customers, handling complaints.
	Deals with customer relationships: discounts, new product upgrades, etc.
Purchasing	Selects the most suitable supplier, ensuring price competitiveness.
	Negotiates contracts with suppliers, including prices, discounts, delivery times, etc.
	Buys all the raw materials, components and other goods that the company requires.
Warehousing	Receives delivered goods, storing them in the warehouse and collecting them to send them to manufacturing or dispatch.
	Maintains goods to be sold and materials for making products, keeping accurate and up-to-date records of exactly what is in stock.
	Reorders items if the number in stock falls below a preset level (the reorder level).
Distribution	Packages and sends goods to customers.
	Manages own transport fleet to deliver goods or arranges to contract out deliveries to specialist companies.
Marketing	Identifies potential customers.
	Understands market demand through the use of market surveys, and other activities.
	Promotes and advertises the company's products.
Research and development	Dreams up new products.
Human Resources or personnel	Responsible for staff welfare, contracts, pay, medicals, appraisals.
	Maintains employees' records, information on job applicants, on employee benefits and compensation and discipline.
Design	Concentrates on deciding how goods might be produced or presented to clients.
Production (or service provision)	Manufactures the goods that are sold.
	Schedules the manufacture of goods, either to meet specific orders (e.g. of large-value items that are made to order) or to ensure sufficient goods are in stock to meet the anticipated demand (for lower-value items that are sold 'off the shelf').
ICT services	Provides suitable hardware and software for employees.
	Selects and purchases hardware.
	Decides provision of user support services, and provides it or arranges for external support provision.
Administration/ Operations	Responsible for day-to-day running of the office: reception, security, post room, stationery supplies, kitchen supplies, car parking facilities.

TABLE 2.6 *Roles and responsibilities of different departments*

department. Sales staff can give useful feedback on what does and what does not sell.

* Marketing will also liaise with R&D to decide on what new products or features consumers may want.

* R&D will liaise with the manufacturing department, who must make the products that the R&D department develops.

How is ICT used in the various departments?

Often an ICT system in one department holds data that is of use to another department, so the two need to work closely together and/or their systems need be integrated. For example, a stock control system could operate as a stand-alone system. However, if an EPOS system is linked to it, the recording of the movement of stock could be automated.

What does it mean?

EPOS stands for electronic point of sale.

Theory into practice

1 For one of your chosen organisations, draw an organisation chart to show which departments exist.

2 For another of your organisations, focus on one department and identify how ICT is used within that department.

3 For a third organisation, look at how ICT is used to communicate between two departments.

2.3 Information and its use

Having identified some different organisations and found out a bit about how they are

structured, you must now turn your focus to the information that is important to your organisations. During the course of this unit, you need to answer these three questions:

* What information does an organisation use?

* How does the organisation process that information?

* What use is made of that information?

Why is information exchanged?

To profit, an organisation needs to sell its products or services.

* To have products to sell, the vendor must make them or buy them from suppliers.

* To offer a service, the organisation must have staff who can provide the service.

What does it mean?

A vendor is the person or organisation that sells the customer a product or service. The word comes from the French *vendre*, to sell.

These activities involve the exchange of information:

* Advertisements are placed to attract custom.

* Invoices are sent and received, and paid.

* Staff are given contracts of employment, write letters of acceptance and receive regular payslips.

* The tax regime requires the return of forms to show profit and loss over an accounting period, and PAYE tax and NI contributions are collected on behalf of the Inland Revenue or VAT for the Customs & Excise.

What does it mean?

PAYE stands for pay as you earn, and is a tax on earnings.

NI stands for National Insurance.

These contributions fund the National Health Service and state pensions. VAT stands for value added tax, an indirect tax applied to most products and collected by the vendor on behalf of the government.

So, on a day-to-day basis, organisations need to communicate with people outside the organisation, such as suppliers and customers, as well as those within.

that all organisations need, regardless of what the organisation does. Table 2.7 lists four main departments and some key information that these departments will need to carry out day-to-day operations. Other departments, provided the information is held centrally, e.g. in a relational database, need only store the reference numbers and use these to find out information from other departments. For more information about how relational databases work, see Unit 3, page 68.

Theory into practice

1 For one of your chosen organisations, identify the people outside the organisation that communicate with the organisation.

2 For another of your organisations, focus on one department and identify how ICT is used within that department to communicate with people outside the organisation.

Theory into practice

1 For one of your organisations, obtain documents from each of the four departments listed in Table 2.7 and check what information is key to each department's day-to-day operation.

2 For another organisation, find out what is considered to be key information for the R&D department.

3 For a third organisation, identify information that is maintained by one department but is useful to other departments.

Key information

For a given organisation, the information that is important to them (the key information) may relate specifically to what the organisation does. However, there are many items of information

With whom do organisations communicate?

Communication can be classified as either internal or external.

DEPARTMENT	DATA ITEMS
Personnel and training	**Employee ref number**; employee name; employee contact details. **Job code**; job title; job description; salary scale; location. **Training course number**; venue; start date; trainer details.
Accounts, finance and payroll	**Customer ref number**; customer name; customer contact details. **Supplier ref number**; supplier name; supplier contact details. Employee ref number; job code; salary level; bank sort code; bank account number.
Sales and purchase orders	**Sales invoice number**; customer reference number; items purchased; total cost. **Purchase invoice number**; supplier reference number; total cost; payment due date.
Stock control	**Product ref number**; supplier reference number; minimum stock level; number in stock; warehouse bay number.

TABLE 2.7 *Key information held by major departments*

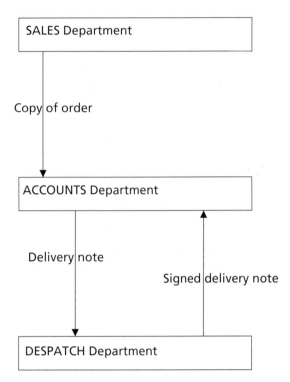

FIGURE 2.7 *Information flow diagram of the internal documentation for a sale*

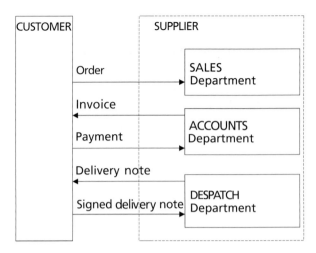

FIGURE 2.8 *Information flow diagram of the external documentation for a sale*

* Internal communication happens within an organisation. People within an organisation need to pass information so that it can be processed. Figure 2.7 shows the flow of information within an organisation that may result from the sale of goods to a customer.

* External communication happens when an organisation communicates with other organisations or individuals outside the organisation. Figure 2.8 shows the external communication that may result from the sale of goods to a customer.

Who needs information within an organisation?

To understand how information is used within an organisation, you need to find out who needs what information, who sends it, who receives it, how it is processed and how ICT is used to support these activities. This will tell you a lot about how the organisation works.

Some organisations work well, co-ordinating their information in the most efficient way. Other organisations, over time and in a piecemeal way, may have developed a number of different ICT systems, each designed to manage or process a different type of information.

* Several of these systems may be linked to each other within the same organisation, e.g. personnel and finance.

* Some systems may be linked with other systems in a different organisation, e.g. the stock control within an organisation may be linked to the supplier's system.

Separate systems are fine, so long as the data is consistent between them. This means keeping all systems up-to-date simultaneously. A better option, usually, is to have a single system, accessed by all departments.

1 For one of your chosen organisations, identify the ICT systems used. Do the departments share information, or do they have separate, isolated computer systems?

2 For another of your organisations, focus on one department and identify how it might benefit from access to information maintained by another department.

Within a small group, discuss the list of documents given in Table 2.8. Can you think of any other documents that are used for communication between a vendor and the customer?

What information is exchanged between organisations?

Although it might seem that there is an infinite list of documents that may be exchanged between organisations, over time and mostly for legal or tax reasons, organisations have adopted standard documents as the best way to conduct business. Table 2.8 lists a few of these documents.

The terminology used for some documents depends on whether you are the sender or the recipient, i.e. whether you are the vendor (or seller) or the customer (or purchaser).

* The purchase order is generated by the customer. When received by the vendor, it is called a sales order.

* The sales invoice is generated by the vendor. When received by the customer, it is called a purchase invoice.

Notice also that products move along a chain of buyers and sellers, so an organisation may buy from a supplier, but is then the supplier to its

DOCUMENT	GENERATED BY	RECEIVED BY	NOTES
Order	Customer organisation	Vendor organisation	Gives details of the intended purchase; signals an intention to buy, subject to terms being agreed, e.g. a delivery date.
Invoice	Vendor organisation	Customer organisation	Confirms contractual arrangements for a purchase, including a tax point, and terms of payment.
Credit note	Vendor organisation	Customer organisation	Confirms release of contractual arrangements for a purchase, and arrangements to repay any monies received in payment.
Delivery note	Vendor organisation	Customer organisation	Confirms what is being delivered, and to where and when. Often a multi-part document, requiring a signature to confirm safe receipt of the goods.
Remittance advice	Customer organisation	Vendor organisation	Confirms how payment is to be made. May accompany a cheque, or warn of a credit transfer that is scheduled to take place.
Statement	Vendor organisation	Customer organisation	Confirms transactions that have taken place during the previous accounting period, e.g. one month. Balance shows how much is still owing.

TABLE 2.8 *Standard business documents used for external communication*

own customers. Figure 2.9 shows how this incorporates organisations such as manufacturers, distributors, wholesalers and retailers.

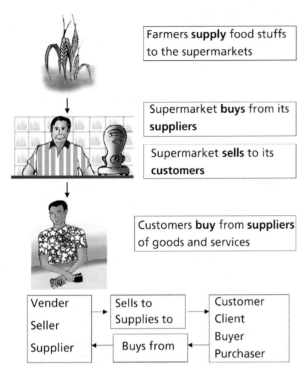

FIGURE 2.9 *The chain of supply*

Knowledge check

1 Figures 2.7 and 2.8 show the general information flow within an organisation and between an organisation and an external contact (a customer who purchases a product). You were asked to produce an extended version of this information flow diagram. Review this diagram and redraw it if you feel you can improve on it.

2 Look at the information flow diagrams of others in your group, and compare them with your own. Do you all agree on the information flow? Are your diagrams identical?

To construct an information flow diagram, you will have to find out who needs what information, and draw connections to show how this information is passed. The information flow diagram should then help you to describe the movement of information inside an organisation. It should include information that flows into and out of an organisation and between its departments.

Theory into practice

1 For an organisation of your choosing, find out what documents are used for external communication. Draw an information flow diagram to show how they are generated and processed within the organisation.

2 Make a list of internal documents (such as payslips, itineraries, agendas, minutes). For each one draw a flow diagram to show how it is generated and processed.

3 Collect sample documents from an organisation of your choosing. Note the information that is communicated using each document.

Theory into practice

1 For one of your organisations, focus on one document and draw an information flow diagram to show how and where the document is created, who handles it and what it is used for. Check that you understand exactly when and how each item of data is added to the document.

2 For another organisation, focus on one department and identify at least three documents that it handles. Draw an information flow diagram for that one department, showing the source and destination of each of the three documents.

Information flow diagrams

One way to show how information is used in and by an organisation is to draw an information flow diagram.

Types of information

Another way of looking at information is to focus on an activity and to consider what documentation is used to record this. Table 2.9 lists some types of information and some of the questions that the information has to answer.

TOPIC	DETAILS
Customer orders	Who has ordered what? At what price? To be delivered when?
Design and production drawings	How is the product to be constructed? What materials are needed and in what quantities?
Invoices paid	Who has paid which invoices, and when? Which invoices remain unpaid?
Items in stock	How much of each product is available for sale?
Monthly income	How much has been received this month, from whom and for what reason?
Monthly outgoing	How much has been spent this month? What was it spent on, and for what reason?
Monthly profit or loss	How much profit has been made this month? Or was a loss made?
Names and addresses of employees	Who works for this organisation? Where do they live?
Purchase orders to suppliers	What has been ordered, from whom and for how much?
Records of staff training	How qualified is each employee? What staff training have they been given? What extra training do they need?
Wages and tax payments	How much has been allocated in wages to each employee? What deductions have been made? How much net pay has been paid?
Website publicity pages	What information appears on the website? When was it last updated?

TABLE 2.9 *Types of information*

For each of the entries in Table 2.9, ICT could be used to process the data.

✳ Customer orders may be recorded in a database, or on a spreadsheet, so that they can be tracked. A customer order made over the Internet may be acknowledged by an automatic email (Figure 2.10). Some organisations provide the customer with a tracking number, so that the progress of their order can be tracked over the Internet.

✳ Purchase orders to suppliers form the first step in a chain of actions which should result in the receipt of goods and payment for these goods. Some organisations require all suppliers to quote a purchase order number on each invoice; otherwise, the invoice will not be paid. This system means close budgetary control may be kept over the spending of individual

FIGURE 2.10 *Acknowledgement email*

departments, and the likely cash flow requirements can be identified when goods or services are ordered, rather than when an invoice is received. Some organisations will also require a delivery note to be signed to show safe receipt of the goods, together with sight of the invoice, before payment of the invoice will be approved.

* Design and production drawings can be generated using CAD/CAM.

* Wages and tax payments have to be recorded to comply with PAYE taxation regulation within the UK. Most organisations use a specialist payroll package that performs all the necessary calculations and prepares all documentation automatically. There are many statutory forms to be completed: payslips, P60s, P11Ds.

* Employee details, including their names and addresses, will be retained within the human resources (HR) system. This information is necessary for tax returns, and would be needed when mailing a contract of employment to a prospective employee. Records of staff training may be included within an HR system. For some organisations, salary levels are tied to the qualifications held by an employee, and training may form an essential part of obtaining those qualifications. Training may be organised in-house, or it may involve sending employees on external courses. The suppliers of this external training will be recorded, together with feedback from delegates to ensure the quality of the instruction received.

* Goods in stock and the number of items available will be recorded in a stock control system. Incoming goods will increase the stock level. Sales, e.g. through an EPOS system, will automatically reduce the number of items in stock. The number of stock will need to be kept above a minimum stock level and reordering may be automatic, especially if an external link to a supplier is in place. The actual stock level will need checking manually regularly to ensure that discrepancies (caused by theft, breakages, spillage, etc.) are accounted for, and the stock levels shown on the computer system match what is actually available on the shelves or in the warehouse.

* Invoices paid (or more importantly, invoices unpaid) may be a by-product of a sales accounting package. The credit controller within an organisation will be responsible for chasing late payers, and keeping a tight rein on cash flow. When invoices are sent, the credit period will be stated as part of the terms, e.g. 28 days. The accounting system may produce statements which are sent to show which invoices have been paid and which are now due (or overdue) for payment.

* Monthly or quarterly accounts will itemise all income and expenditure and arrive at a profit or loss figure for the period. Income should be recorded within the main accounting system, being the sum of the invoices paid and any other monies that may be received by the organisation. This should be reconciled against how much is in the bank account, and how much is still owed to the organisation by its customers. Outgoings will need to be analysed by the type of expenditure: fixed overheads (such as rent), running costs (such as electricity, telephone costs, salaries of head office staff), costs directly attributable to production (purchase of raw materials, wages of assembly workers) and those attributable to sales (such as advertising and marketing costs, and salaries of sales staff). Analysing expenditure can be done automatically by entering a cost centre code against every expenditure. This then means budgetary decisions can be made based on accurate information of actual costs. Profit or loss is then a by-product of the accounting system. It is a requirement that an organisation should cease trading if it is insolvent. It is not acceptable to run up huge debts that cannot be met by income. So, keeping track of profit or loss on a regular basis is an essential part of managing the finances of any organisation.

* Publicity material has to be prepared and kept up-to-date. This material may be printed and/or available on a website. If publicity is via a website, there may be links to external sites which need to be tested on a regular basis.

Theory into practice

1 For one of your organisations, focus on one of the above information types and draw an information flow diagram to show what documents are created, who handles them and what they are used for.

2 Repeat Question 1 for another organisation, focusing on a different type of information.

Methods of communicating information

Communication involves two or more persons: the person sending a message and the person or people receiving the message. Within an organisation, messages can be conveyed in different ways:

* Verbal communication can be done face-to-face as in a conversation. It can be done long-distance, using a telephone, or an Internet link, e.g. via Messenger and using a webcam. Verbal communication is fine for informal discussions, but verbal agreements are tricky to enforce by law. Some companies record telephone conversations for the purposes of training; they may also record verbal instructions so that a record is available in case of dispute at a later date.

* Written communication can be a letter sent in the post, or a memo between colleagues, or an email or a fax. Written material may be text-based but may also include images. When audio messages and/or moving pictures are included, e.g. on an intranet, this becomes a multimedia form of communication. This can be ideal for training purposes. Material may be published in newsletters or in manuals and this provides a way of communicating with many people at the same time.

Today a lot of communication is done electronically.

* Fax machines provided the first opportunity to send copies of diagrams as well as hand-written text. A fax machine scanned the hard copy and transmitted it along the telephone line, and it was printed out at the receiver end. Early fax machines used thermal paper and were slow in scanning and receiving faxes. Modern fax systems work through a PC. A printer doubles up as a scanner and photocopier. The fax is sent via the PC and a telephone line to the recipient's PC or fax machine.

What does it mean?

Fax is short for facsimile, which means copy.

* Email now offers the option to send informal internal messages (instead of memos) and may be via internal email on a LAN (local area network) or intranet. Emails are also used for more formal communications with suppliers and customers, through the Internet. Emails may be sent to more than one person, so this provides a one-to-many communication. Attached files may contain details of a product, the confirmation of an order, an itinerary for a training day, or an agenda for a meeting.

* A centralised database may provide a communication tool for all the employees within an organisation. Any one person updating the database in one part of the organisation will provide everyone else with up-to-date information when they need it.

* EDI is an essential element of e-commerce. Figure 2.11 shows how one organisation offers EDI services to its clients.

What does it mean?

EDI stands for electronic data interchange.

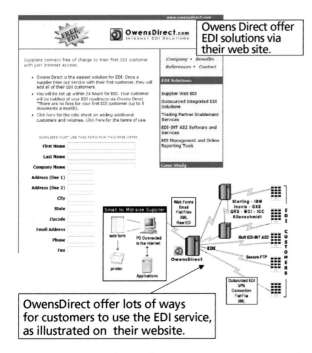

OwensDirect offer lots of ways for customers to use the EDI service, as illustrated on their website.

FIGURE 2.11 *EDI through OwensDirect*

The effectiveness of communication can be measured by checking whether the person (or persons) to whom the message was being sent received it, understood it and acted on it as hoped.

2.4 ICT systems

Organisations rely on ICT to process data in a number of job functions. Most organisations could use the standard applications – word processing, spreadsheets and databases – to process their data, but most adapt these applications, by customising them. Some organisations have specialist systems, according to their own needs.

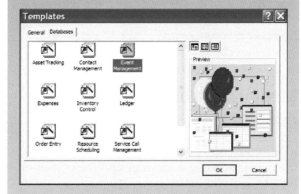
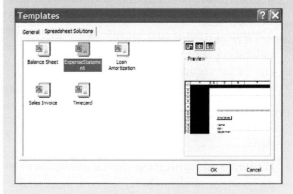

HR: personnel, training and payroll

The HR department will have a personnel database containing information about employees, such as name, address, employee number and position. It will record performance such as number of sick days and punctuality. This database is often extended to cover payroll and training, or will have links to these systems.

Theory into practice

1 Visit the Snowdrop website through the link at www.heinemann.co.uk/hotlinks and read about their work for Ofcom. Make notes.

2 Look for other organisations which offer a similar service to HR departments.

Training records are either integral to the personnel system or an extension to it. Large organisations will record training plans for employees, and note any special skills such as a First Aid certificate. Then, if particular skills are required, a search of the database can produce a shortlist of suitable employees.

In a joint training/personnel system, the job history of an employee will be recorded, with details of any promotions and salary increases. The database will also record any appraisal discussions and agreements, and disciplinary action that has been taken.

Payroll is often an extension of personnel records, although historically, payroll was one of the first applications to be computerised. Each employee will have his or her own tax code and rate of pay from which his or her salary can be calculated. A computerised mailing system can print payslips or (for BACS payments) remittance advices, with details of wage payments.

HR is one area in an organisation that deals with many changes. Staff leave, new staff join, staff move house, get married, and so on. Also, details such as hours worked may vary from week to week, and pay rates and tax codes may change regularly. HR is also an area in which accuracy is essential and confidentiality of information is particularly important.

An important external link for an HR system is with the Inland Revenue. The DTI encourages employers to use electronic submission of data, and this includes Inland Revenue returns (Figure 2.14).

Reports on payroll information must also be available to accounts managers to contribute to statements of profits and losses.

Theory into practice

1 For one of your organisations, identify how ICT is used for HR data processing. Who has access to this data?

2 For another organisation, focus on how training records are maintained using ICT.

3 For a third organisation, find out what external links exist for the payroll system.

4 Compare your findings with others in your group.

Research, design and development

The R&D department keeps records of new products on trial or being investigated. It will be important to forecast how long existing products will remain saleable. Then R&D need to define new areas of productivity for the organisation. To ensure an organisation has products to offer, and ones that meet market demands, the R&D department needs to plan far enough into the

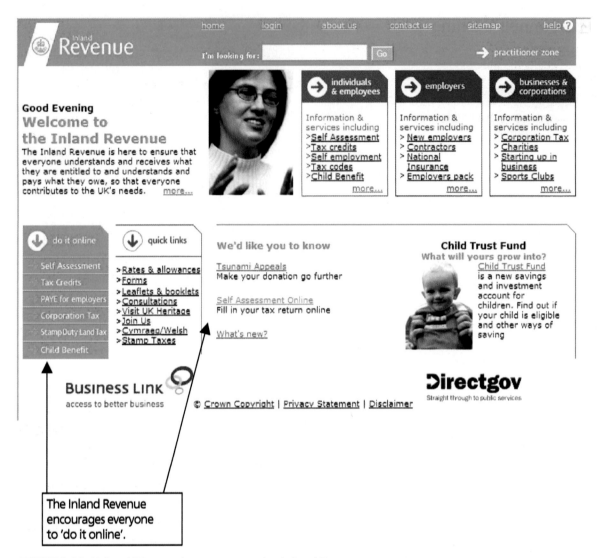

The Inland Revenue encourages everyone to 'do it online'.

FIGURE 2.14 *Using ICT to make returns to the Inland Revenue*

future to allow for development time and production schedules so that the product flow is maintained.

* The time it takes to commission an author to write a textbook, plus the time it takes for the author to write the book, plus the time it takes to edit, set, proofread, and print the book, all adds up to quite a long time before the book is available in the classroom. Publishers need to be planning what students will be reading about 18 months before the books will be needed for new courses.

* A holiday company has to work at least a year ahead of time, planning which trips to offer, in order to prepare publicity material and to

reserve accommodation and secure flight deals with airlines.

* A monthly magazine that offers recipes to its readership has to plan next Christmas' menus and test the recipes many months ahead of time.

The R&D department will keep records of changes to product design or to new products. They will also produce specifications for all products. The product specifications may include production drawings and instructions that accompany the product or appear on the packaging.

The R&D department may use specialised software like CAD/CAM and/or other drawing tools, or specially devised software.

Accounts

Accounting software dates back to the early use of computers. There are many organisations offering tailored software to meet the needs of organisations.

An accounts department can incorporate many functions: finance, sales, purchasing and stock control or inventory systems.

* If the organisation needs to raise funds by take out loans, or issuing shares, a section of the Accounts department, or the Finance department, will be responsible for the arrangements. Lists will be kept of shareholders, and their holdings in the organisation.

* The Accounts department, or a section within it, will maintain the stock control and inventory systems, tracking items held in stock by serial number. These systems record the number, cost and location of items held in stock. Often there will be an automatic reordering process. Sometimes, there will be links with robotic systems in warehouses, and these systems can automate much of the restocking necessary.

* The Sales department keep records of all customer orders. They initiate the internal requests for provision of services or goods. These may be sent to a Despatch or Delivery department.

* The Purchasing department links with stock control, accounts, production and most other departments. It will generate purchase orders and contracts for goods and services.

Financial systems are needed to keep track of cash receipts and payments. It is important to keep track of money paid and money owed, and the Accounts department will prepare a general ledger summarising accounts. This allows the preparation of balance sheets and income statements, and can be used to forecast cash flow.

FIGURE 2.15 *Sample output from CAD*

1 Sage supply accounting software and claim that one in three UK businesses are using their software. Visit the Sage website through the link at www.heinemann.co.uk/hotlinks (express code 994XP) and find out what products they offer that might meet the needs of the organisations that you have been studying.

2 Look for other organisations which offer a similar service to HR departments.

FIGURE 2.16 *The Sage website*

CASE STUDY: PAPERCOURT SAILING CLUB

Members of PSC have the option to send a message to all other members, via one central person, Caroline. When someone sends Caroline the message to be circulated, she forwards it to all members on a distribution list. In this way, only one person needs to have up-to-date information of the email addresses of all members and the email addresses are kept confidential, thus reducing the likelihood of spam.

A quarterly newsletter is sent to all members through snail mail, but the PSC website also provides a channel for communication, and a version of the newsletter is posted on the site.

1 **For one of your organisations, identify how email is used for internal communication.**

2 **For another organisation, focus on how email is used for external communication. What kinds of external communication happen through email alone?**

3 **For a third organisation, find out who maintains the email accounts for all employees.**

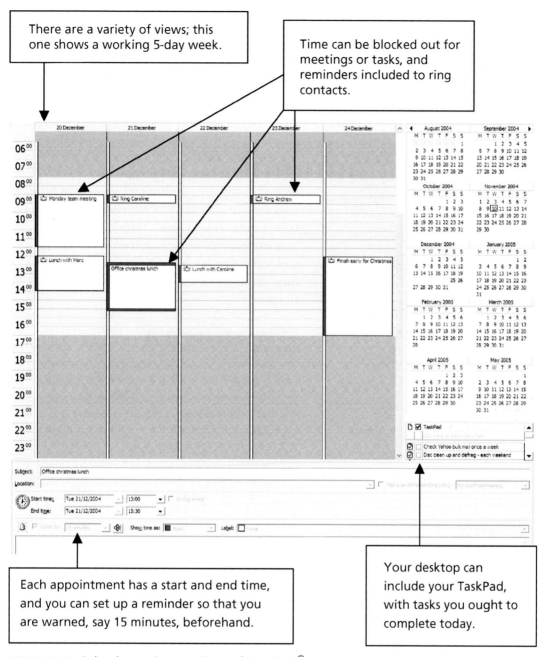

There are a variety of views; this one shows a working 5-day week.

Time can be blocked out for meetings or tasks, and reminders included to ring contacts.

Each appointment has a start and end time, and you can set up a reminder so that you are warned, say 15 minutes, beforehand.

Your desktop can include your TaskPad, with tasks you ought to complete today.

FIGURE 2.17 *Calendar option on Microsoft Outlook®*

Email, the Internet and intranets

Today, email is used extensively to communicate information within the organisation and with external contacts.

Software such as Microsoft Outlook® provides a calendar facility (Figure 2.17) and this is useful for organising meetings. Staff can post their availability on the system, and book meeting rooms and invite people to attend the meetings.

If email is used for internal communications, copying in to lots of staff can result in email overkill. Staff who are faced with too many emails to process may not be able to identify the ones that need their urgent attention. Problems can therefore arise if too little care is taken to decide who receives what information. Some organisations create an intranet, for access by employees only. This provides a useful vehicle for communicating essential information to all staff.

The Internet provides the opportunity for organisations to use a website to promote products and attract custom. One other important aspect of using the Internet is e-commerce, which is used to buy and sell goods and services online.

Data capture, processing and presentation

All organisations use information, but where does this come from? The source of all information is data.

What does it mean?

Data is the raw information that is collected: lots of characters of text, digits and images.

Information is the interpretation of data by applying some meaning to the data.

Data has to be found, captured and processed, and then presented in a way that makes sense to those who need to understand it.

Data overload (or information overload) is a common complaint. With the growth of online transactions, organisations must store, capture and analyse thousands of customer transactions every day, from email to e-commerce. The availability of more data provides these organisations with greater opportunities to learn about their customers. The process of extracting useful information from data is called data mining.

What does it mean?

Data mining is the analysis of data in a database using tools that look for trends or anomalies without knowledge of the meaning of the data.

An organisation needs to know who its customers are and their profile. Then, all marketing efforts can be directed towards prospective customers with the same profile. With the growth of Internet usage and e-commerce, it has become very easy to collect data on web users. Data mining of website logs can provide information on who has visited a site, what they have purchased, and can provide a huge database of information to use for marketing purposes.

Data capture

Data has to be captured before it can be input to an ICT system and processed to produce useful information for an organisation. There are many different data capture methods, each one suited to particular circumstances.

✳ Data can be captured on a form, and this form may be a hardcopy or one that is provided on screen (Figure 2.18).

It is important to warn the person who has to fill in the form, roughly how long it might take.

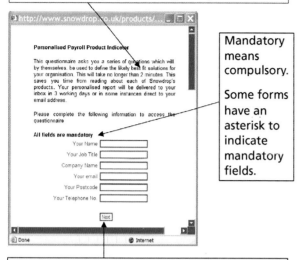

Mandatory means compulsory.

Some forms have an asterisk to indicate mandatory fields.

The Next button lets the visitor navigate to the next screen. At this point, the data entered so far will be validated. If any fields have not been completed, an error message will politely ask for all mandatory fields to be completed.

FIGURE 2.18 *Data capture using an on-screen form*

❋ Data may also be captured automatically, by a scanning process or input in a format that is readable by a computer.

Think it over...

Within a small group, ask yourselves: what restrictions are placed on organisations regarding the methods used to obtain data?

Data that is captured on a form still needs to be input to the ICT system:

❋ For a hardcopy form, this may involve manual keyboard input, which is a time-consuming process. Depending on how the form has been created, part of the input may be automated.

❋ For an on-screen form, the form filler does the keyboarding while completing the form, and while this still takes time, it tends to be someone outside the organisation who is filling in the form, so costs to the organisation are minimised. However, the data that is entered has to be transferred to a safe storage place, e.g. within a database. So, for form filling online, the organisation has to set up a website with all the necessary functions to allow the form to be completed and the data to be downloaded to the organisation's database.

There are many options for automatic data capture. The data can be scanned using one of a range of scanners:

❋ A bar code is scanned using a handheld wand or by passing the bar code in the line of sight of an infrared ray. This is an example of OMR.

What does it mean?

OMR stands for optical mark recognition.

❋ Another example of OMR is the scanning of lottery tickets (Figure 2.19) or multiple choice examination answer grids. The form has time tracks to ensure the form is placed within the scanner with the correct orientation, and the completion of the form involves making marks in certain positions to mean certain choices.

❋ A special type of mark is made on cheques to allow automatic data entry of essential information (the sort code, account number and cheque number). This scanning technique uses MICR; the marks are printed in a magnetic ink that allows the characters to be recognised.

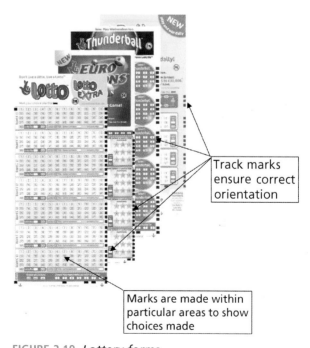

Track marks ensure correct orientation

Marks are made within particular areas to show choices made

FIGURE 2.19 *Lottery forms*

MICR stands for magnetic ink character recognition.

OCR stands for optical character recognition.

1 Explain these terms: OMR, MICR, OCR.

2 Explain the need for a time track on an OMR document.

3 Why is a turnaround document so called?

4 List some examples of uses of OCR on official documents.

✳ MICR was the first of the OCR systems. OCR can be used for reading forms that have been partly completed by a computer, before full completion and being returned to the computer. This type of form is called a turnaround document, and was used mainly for reading meters (gas and electric) before other automated ways of reading these devices was introduced.

OCR involves two stages:

✳ The text is scanned.

✳ The image that has been scanned is then interpreted.

Today, the software that interprets the image is more sophisticated than early versions which were limited in the range of fonts they could recognise with accuracy. You can now buy a printer/scanner/photocopier which comes complete with OCR software (Figure 2.20), very cheaply.

Interpretation of captured data is an essential part of voice-recognition systems. Your voice

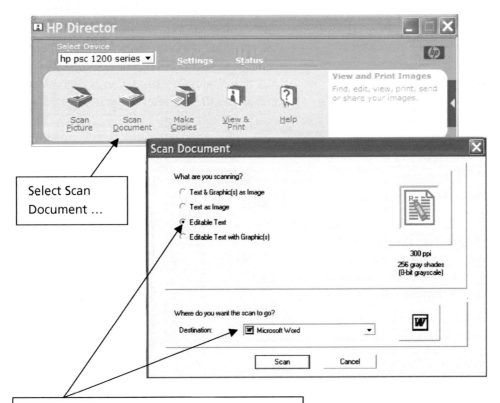

Select Scan Document ...

... and then indicate that you are scanning text to be transferred into a Word document.

FIGURE 2.20 *Scanning text into a Microsoft Word file*

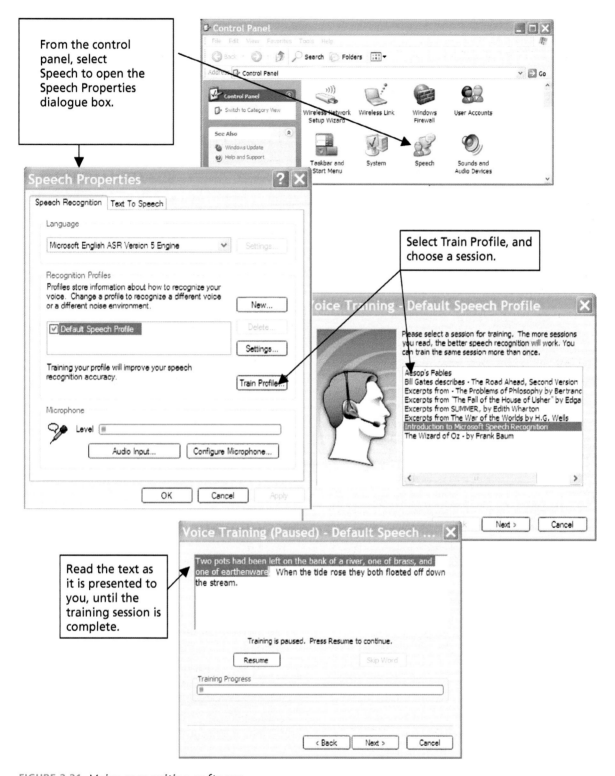

From the control panel, select Speech to open the Speech Properties dialogue box.

Select Train Profile, and choose a session.

Read the text as it is presented to you, until the training session is complete.

FIGURE 2.21 *Voice-recognition software*

– and what you say – can be captured using a microphone. For most voice-recognition systems, you have to train the software (Figure 2.21) to recognise what you say. This is because, when you speak, you could say anything, and there are millions of words you might use. Your accent and tone can alter how each word sounds, so this means an almost impossible task for the computer.

Some automated telephone services let you speak your instructions. Because the software matches what you say with a very limited range of words, it can quite successfully interpret what you say. When you are offered options like 'to change your personal options, press or say 2, or for callers who left no message, press or say 4', the software only has to distinguish between your saying 'two' or 'four'. These two words are easily distinguished.

One of the more recent advances in automated data entry is the invention of the chip reader for credit and debit cards. These cards have a magnetic strip which holds sufficient data for your card to be recognised when it is swiped through a card reader or placed in the slot in an ATM. However, this strip can become damaged, and is easy to duplicate for credit card fraudsters. Chip technology may therefore help in the fight against credit card fraud, as a chip embedded within the card can be used instead of the magnetic strip.

The most recent advance has involved the use of biometric data for authentication purposes. Characteristics such as fingerprints, eye retinas and irises, voice patterns, facial patterns and hand measurements can all be used to check a person's identity, for example, of someone trying to gain entry to a building or cross a national boundary. The checking process involves comparing biometric data, e.g. your fingerprint, with a database of many other examples, and looking for match points.

Data processing

Data processing is what happens after the data has been input and before it is displayed.

* Calculations may be needed to produce summary statistics, such as a total or an average.

* The data may need to be sorted into an order, or grouped.

* The data may need to be merged with other data to form an up-to-date picture of a situation.

The data processing stage is sometimes referred to as data handling (see Unit 3). There are two methods of data processing: now and later.

* Some data needs to be processed straight away. If you access your bank account online and transfer money between your current account and a savings account, you expect the subtraction from one account to happen at the same time as the addition to the other. When your bank reacts straight away to your request to transfer funds, this is called transaction processing.

* Some data need not be processed straight away. Transactions that can wait tend to be grouped together and processed together. This is called batch processing. Nowadays, payments in and withdrawals from a bank account are processed immediately, but standing orders and direct debits are processed in a batch overnight.

Real-time processing is a term that may be applied to instant reactions to what is input. Real time, as a term, should be applied only when the events happen in real time, and this tends to apply only with data control systems. When the delay between input (say a burglar setting off a sensor) and output (an alarm sounding) is so short that the processing time is negligible then the computer is working in real time.

What does it mean?

A data control system is a computer system which relies on data collected automatically through sensors to make decisions and thus to control an environment, for example a central heating system or a greenhouse watering and ventilation system.

Think it over...

In a small group, discuss examples of real time and batch processing.

Data presentation

Once the data has been captured and processed, it will be presented to the user as information. Information can be classified into three distinct types:

* Textual information is necessary, for example, for contact details such as the name and address for each customer, supplier and employee. Note that telephone numbers are usually treated as text, because they include spaces to aid legibility.

* Numerical data includes amounts of money (e.g. on an invoice), other measurements (such as time clocked on and off for workers) and reference numbers. Reference numbers such as invoices are treated as numeric because, to decide the next one to issue, the software will add 1 to the previously issued number. Any data that needs to be used in a calculation should be treated as numeric data. Presenting numerical data numerically is essential on documents like invoices but, sometimes, it is better to present numerical data graphically.

* Graphical information includes charts and diagrams. Often a huge table of numbers is far better presented as a bar chart or a line graph.

Think it over...

Discuss in a small group, under what circumstance you might use a pie chart to present numerical data. When would a bar chart be used instead of a pie chart? When would a line graph be used instead of a bar chart?

The information can be presented, physically, in two ways:

* The user may view the information on-screen.

* The information may be printed on paper, called a hardcopy report.

Hardcopy reports have the advantage of providing a permanent record of the information. A report can be taken with you and read without access to a computer. You can annotate the report, and read it several times over, at times to suit you. The downside of hardcopy reporting is the time needed to print it out, and the cost of paper and ink.

On-screen presentation will suit users who are at their computer and are interacting with it. They may need some information to help them to decide on their next course of action. It gives immediate feedback, and, just in case a hardcopy is needed, there is usually an option to print out a page, or a screen.

Theory into practice

1 For one of your organisations, and focusing on just one department, identify how data is collected, processed and presented.

2 For another organisation, focus on how the organisation controls the presentation of material that will be sent to external organisations.

3 For a third organisation, consider how on-screen forms are provided for completion by prospective customers. What happens to the data that is keyed in?

4 Compare your findings with others in your group.

Think it over...

Hot-desking means employees have no personal space in a office provided by their employer. How do you think you might feel about this?

2.5 Effects of ICT on working styles

Over a period of time, the reduction in costs of mobile equipment (laptops and mobile telephones), and the increased speed of transfer of data through broadband connections, has made it viable for more people to change their working styles.

Where people work

Instead of being based in an office with everyone else who works for the organisation, using mobile and communications technology, employees can be based at home, and be more mobile generally.

Think it over...

Working from home sounds wonderful. Discuss with others the possible downside of such an arrangement. Are there any disadvantages from the employer's point of view?

Having staff work from home has benefits for the employee: it also has benefits for the employer (such as not desking) and for society as a whole (Table 2.10).

What does it mean?

Hot-desking is a system where employees do not have a personal space within an office, but share any spare desk whenever they come into the office.

Theory into practice

1 For one of your organisations, identify how employees are encouraged to work from home.

2 For another organisation, ask the employees what benefits they see in working from home.

3 For a third organisation, identify any aspects of home working that disadvantage the employees and/or the employer.

4 Compare your findings with others in your group.

For the employee	No commuting so more time available; savings in costs of travel.
For the employer	Reduction in desk space; hot-desking an option; cost-savings because overheads are proportional to amount of office space needed.
For society	Reduced commuting resulting in reduced pollution and reduced congestion on the transport system.

TABLE 2.10 *Benefits of people working from home*

Work patterns

The traditional office hours used to be from 9 till 5. As organisations expand their market to include overseas customers, and have offices located in different time zones, the 'normal' working day has become blurred. Three advances in ICT have helped this to happen:

✳ The use of email to replace telephone calls has meant it does not matter what time it is where you are, or where the person you need to communicate with is. The recipient can check the incoming mail box when he or she turns on the computer at the start of his or her day, and reply when it suits them. If your work involves writing a report, or preparing a presentation, you can work whatever hours suit you (or your employer!) and send your work in when it is done, as an attachment to an email. For electronic mailings, there is no need to work around postal collection times, or how long it takes to deliver something. So long as your work reaches your client by the deadline, you can work anywhere in the world and at any time of the day or night.

✳ The use of mobile phones means that people can be contacted anywhere, they do not have to be in the office to receive business calls.

✳ A lot of commerce happens on the Internet, and there are no opening hours (unless the Internet connection is down). So, you can check your bank balance, pay bills, order goods, write emails wherever you are, at whatever time suits you. Many of the follow-up activities (such as confirming an order) are automated, so the customer receives immediate feedback, via email, and the goods arrive soon after.

✳ Many organisations offer a 24/7 service and, in the past, this has meant shift working for many employees. Now that telephone costs have fallen dramatically, especially when routed though Internet connections, it is possible to locate call centres all around the world.

Think it over...

1 Having the option of a 24/7 service sounds wonderful. Discuss with others the possible downside of such an arrangement.

2 Discuss any disadvantages for a customer if routed through to an overseas call centre.

Theory into practice

1 For one of your organisations, identify how work patterns have changed due to the use of ICT.

2 Compare your findings with others in your group.

ICT skills and training

Nowadays, most students leave school able to use the standard ICT software packages: word processing, spreadsheets and databases. Some students have additional skills related to customer support and the maintenance of ICT systems. However, there are many people in the workplace for whom computers were not the norm when they were students. For them, learning how to use the new technology can be daunting, and they need lots of support and training to make the best use of ICT.

Jobs in the IT industry call for vocational skills:

✳ Design: dreaming up solutions to problems, within the constraints of the software and hardware available, the client's budget and time available.

✳ Analysis: finding out exactly how things have been done in the past, how things need to be done in the future and documenting this so that a solution can be implemented.

✳ Programming: using programming languages to turn the ideas of the designer and plans of the analyst into reality, i.e. programs that will meet the needs of the client.

✳ Hardware maintenance: maintaining hardware regularly, and diagnosing and fixing hardware faults so that the computer system runs smoothly with minimal downtime.

* IT use: using applications such as word processing to produce documents; spreadsheets to process numerical data, statistical charts and diagrams; databases to store records and produce reports; presentation software to produce slide shows; and so on.

As with any other industry, people working within the IT industry need personal skills: team work, problem solving, numeracy, communication and IT user skills.

Think it over...

In groups of six or eight, brainstorm a list of the skills needed by a systems analyst and those needed by someone who works in the user support team of a large organisation.

IT user skills are essential in any job:

* At the lowest level, these skills include using the keyboard and a mouse while working with the user interface so that you can very quickly communicate with the PC or Apple Macintosh. This includes understanding the screen layout; how to use the scroll bars to see different parts of a document; how to use hotlinks to move from one page to another in a website, etc. Being able to touch type is an advantage, but not essential. As time goes on, the interface with PCs may utilise voice recognition (see page 57), and this will revolutionise how data and instructions are communicated to the PC.

* Then there are file-handing skills: keeping your documents safe in folders and choosing sensible names for the files so that you can find them easily when you next need them. These organisational skills will help a user to make more effective use of a PC.

* The next level of skills involves using particular software applications – word processing, spreadsheets, databases and so on – to achieve a particular objective. It may involve using just one application, e.g. presentation software. It may involve using several applications and combining information from more than one source. A newsletter created using a DTP package may include images scanned into a painting package and text files from a word processor that have been saved as RTF files.

What does it mean?

DTP stands for desktop publishing. RTF stands for rich text file, a format which excludes many formatting features and is therefore more successfully imported into some software.

* Users might not be expected to fix hardware faults, but should be able to do minor things like cleaning a mouse and changing a print cartridge.

Think it over...

In groups of six or eight, brainstorm the skills that you consider to be essential for an IT practitioner.

Theory into practice

1 For one of your organisations, identify what training is provided to support the use of ICT in the workplace.

2 Compare your findings with others in your group.

Interaction at work

Before desktop computers were introduced into the workplace, people sat at desks and all their work was hand-written or typed on a typewriter, probably by a secretary who took dictation and wrote in shorthand.

Almost overnight, secretaries have become a thing of the past, with all managers being expected to use a word processor to write their own letters. There is now a computer on every desk, and instead of pushing pens, the workforce uses a keyboard. Colleagues use email to communicate with each other, even when they are in the same office. This may lead to the loss of interaction between people, with less face-to-face discussion and debate from which ideas might spring.

Jobs

ICT has automated many traditional jobs:

* The typesetting of a book like this used to be done by a printer who placed the lead characters into place, one by one. Nowadays, DTP packages mean that anyone, well almost anyone, can produce the material for a book.

* In car factories, robots do many of the assembly and paint-spraying work.

* In warehouses, robots are used to transport materials from one point to another. Robots can also be programmed to do precise and dangerous jobs, like disposing of bombs and mines or inspecting nuclear reactors.

ICT has also created new jobs, for those with ICT skills:

* Software engineers devise the code for the programs that run on computers.

* Hardware engineers maintain computer systems and fix them when they go wrong.

* Website designers design websites.

UNIT
3

Data handling

Introduction

Relational database management software is used by organisations to handle data. The data handled may concern items such as appointments, orders and invoices, reservations or hire/rental applications.

This unit focuses on how relational database management software can be used: to find, select and manipulate data; to process numerical data; to develop and present information; to communicate information in the most suitable way.

You will create a solution involving a relational database, one suited to a particular organisation, which demonstrates your skills in constructing tables, creating data entry forms, creating queries, producing printed reports and screen output – and using wizards and other built-in database facilities appropriately.

This unit will help you to understand the purpose and use of databases in organisations to handle data and to evaluate the suitability of information provided for a client.

What you need to learn

* How to find, select and manipulate data

* How to use numerical data in large and small data sets

* How to develop and present information

* How to communicate information in a way that is suited to the audience

* An understanding of the use of databases in organisations

* How to evaluate the suitability of information for a client

Resource toolkit

To complete this unit, you need these essential resources:

* access to computer hardware and software facilities, including word processing software and relational database software

* access to the Internet

* a wide range of information sources, such as books, trade journals of the IT industry, newspapers

* contacts working within the IT industry.

How you will be assessed

This unit is internally assessed.

There are four assessment objectives:

1 Practical capability in applying ICT

2 Knowledge and understanding of ICT systems and their roles in organisations and society

3 Apply knowledge and understanding to produce solutions to ICT problems

4 Evaluate ICT solutions and own performance.

To demonstrate your coverage of these assessment objectives, you will produce a portfolio of evidence, showing what you have learned and what you can do:

* You will write a description and justification of how a computerised relational database could be used by a particular client.

* You will create a relational database solution to meet your client's needs. This database will contain at least two related tables that have been created to meet the identified client needs.

* In designing your database, you will consider the data types, formats, structures, input, processing and output requirements of your client.

* You will annotate queries and reports that you have created to search for and present information to meet the client needs.

* You will establish evaluation criteria and a test plan and will use the results of testing to evaluate your solution against the client's needs. You will also evaluate your own performance.

You are also expected to adopt standard ways of working so as to manage your work effectively, and show evidence of this. See the preliminary pages for more information about standard ways of working.

How high can you aim?

The presentation of your portfolio is important. You should aim to present your work in a format that would be acceptable in industry. For this particular unit, how you design your database solution will determine the maximum number of marks that you earn (Table 3.1).

Your report must show that you have knowledge and understanding of ICT systems and their roles in organisations and society. Table 3.2 shows how important it is to study the needs of your client carefully, and to match your solution to these needs.

In developing the inputs and outputs for the client's database, you will apply knowledge and understanding to produce solutions to ICT problems. The extent to which you take into account validity and correctness of data inputs, and how user friendly your solution is, will determine your marks (Table 3.3).

Having designed your solution, developed it and tested it, you will evaluate the solution and your own performance in producing it to your client's satisfaction (Table 3.4).

So, in working thorough this unit, remember that the maximum number of marks that you

	1– 5 MARKS	6–11 MARKS	12–18 MARKS
Use of data types, formats and structures . . .	Some	Yes	Effective use
. . . to produce a solution where input data are processed to produce output	Some suitable output	Some output meet client needs	Output fully meets clients needs
Use of queries and reports to search for and present information	Yes	Good use	Effective use of range of queries, fully meeting needs of client
Standard ways of working	Awareness of	Adopted	Close adherence to, at all times

TABLE 3.1

	1–3 MARKS	4–6 MARKS	7–10 MARKS
Describes the organisation/background	Partially	Yes	Fully described
A list of tasks for which the solution is developed	Simple description of the tasks	Simple description of the tasks	Detailed description of the tasks
Description of client needs	Some	Yes	Detailed
List of selected software	Yes	Yes, and attempts to justify	Yes, and fully justifies

TABLE 3.2

	1–7 MARKS	8–14 MARKS	15–21 MARKS	22–28 MARKS
Consideration of input needs of client	Some	Yes	Yes	Full, and justifies
Consideration of validity and correctness of data inputs	Some	Yes	Yes	Full, and justifies
Use of user-friendly error responses			Yes	Yes
Consideration of processing and output needs in relation to client needs . . .	Yes	Yes	Yes	Yes, and justifies
. . . including data structures, formats and types needed to solve the problem			Yes	Yes, and justifies

TABLE 3.3

	1–4 MARKS	5–9 MARKS	10–14 MARKS
Descriptions of actions taken to solve the problem	Brief	Yes	Yes
Identifies strengths, weaknesses and areas for improvement		Yes	Yes, successfully
Makes appropriate changes as a result			Yes
Time management and planning	Limited	Some evidence	Strong evidence
Monitors progress		Partially	Fully
Meets deadlines		Some	Yes, giving reasons for any that are missed
Evaluation criteria	Some produced	Some qualitative and quantitative criteria identified appropriate to client's needs	Qualitative and quantitative criteria identified appropriate to client's needs
Testing	Some done	Some done	Takes full account of evaluation criteria
Evaluation of the solution	Attempted	Yes	Yes, and draws meaningful conclusions
Use of written expression	Adequate to convey meaning	Coherently so that meaning is clear	Suitable in form and style, conveying meaning within complex subject matter

TABLE 3.4

can earn, and hence your grade, will depend on how well you understand the needs of your client, and how well your database design meets these needs.

3.1 The use of databases

Using software to design data-handling solutions

Database software is used to produce data-handling solutions. Exactly which software best suits a situation depends on the problem that has to be solved, and what is available to you. The problem to be solved will lie with your client, so part of your task will be to find out what your client needs.

The specification for this qualification lists some examples that you might study, before deciding on the task you might tackle:

* Appointment systems, such at that used at a doctor's surgery, would involve data about the people who are to meet (the doctor and his or her patient) plus details of where they are to meet and at what time. The outputs for this system could include lists of appointments for a particular doctor.

* Orders systems which would record products

and suppliers of those products, and any orders placed. The output could include the order itself, to be sent to the supplier, and perhaps an exception report showing which orders have yet to be delivered.

* Invoicing systems might include the production of invoices, or the tracking of their payment and the production of statements. The data would include details of customers to whom invoices are sent.

* Hire/rental systems could apply to a number of different organisations: the hire/rental of videos or DVDs overnight, the hire of bicycles, cars or boats for a holiday period and many other products that some people prefer to hire than buy, like TVs and washing machines.

Whatever the line of business, to demonstrate your skills in designing and developing a data-handling solution, you will use a relational database management software (RDMS) to design, develop and test a solution for your client, specifically to meet his or her needs in the completion of a task.

What does it mean?

RDMS stands for relational database management software.

A database is a collection of data items and links between them, structured in such a way that allows access by a number of different application programs.

Think it over...

Working within a small group, list some other ideas for systems that would involve the use of a relational database.

In producing your solution, you will follow a process:

* Knowing what is available to you as a designer, and what software the client has, or

intends to install, will limit what you might offer as a solution.

* Considering the needs of the client is the first step in any design process. There is no point in producing a database that suits you and shows how clever you are; it has to meet the needs of your client. So, you need to discover these needs.

* You can then start the process of designing a solution to match the needs of the client and produce a prototype for your client to see what you have in mind.

* Once your client is happy with your overall design ideas, you can set about the implementation of your solution.

* The next stage is testing your solution and making sure that it works.

* Once your solution is ready to hand over to your client, you will start the evaluation process. When evaluating your solution, if you have completed all the previous steps with due consideration for your client, you should be pleased with what you have done, and so should your client. You also need to evaluate your own performance, and will be assessed, not just on what you have produced and how you have managed the process, but also your evaluation of it.

What is a relational database?

Databases are used to solve data handling problems. The type of database – a flatfile database or a relational database – depends on the problem and the type of data that is involved.

For this unit, you are directed to find a problem, the solution to which is a relational database. Relational databases are a relatively modern invention.

To understand what they replaced, consider the 'shape' of a spreadsheet database.

A spreadsheet file comprises one or more worksheets, each worksheet being a two-dimensional table with rows and

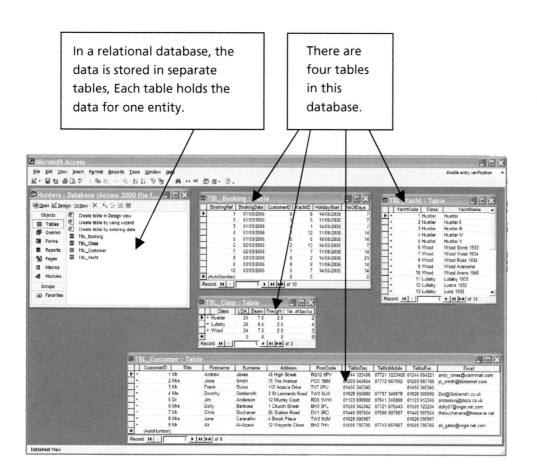

In a relational database, the data is stored in separate tables, Each table holds the data for one entity.

There are four tables in this database.

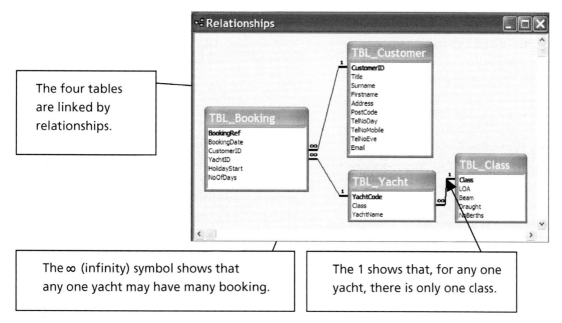

The four tables are linked by relationships.

The ∞ (infinity) symbol shows that any one yacht may have many booking.

The 1 shows that, for any one yacht, there is only one class.

FIGURE 3.1 *The shape of a relational database*

stored, but this also provides greater security in that the design is clearer and less likely to include errors and, most important, data can easily be validated.

✳ It is possible to sort the data in one column of a spreadsheet, while leaving the rest of the data in place. If each row represents a record and each column a field, then sorting in this way destroys the integrity of the data (Figure 3.2). Within a relational database, such sorting is not permitted, so data that belongs together stays together, even when it is stored in what looks very much like a spreadsheet table.

columns. For this reason, it is called a flatfile database.

A relational database is also a database, but of a different shape, and it is constructed in a more rigid way. In a relational database, the data are collected into two-dimensional tables, each table holding the data for a particular entity.

For your relational database, you need to provide a solution that involves at least two tables, but this should not cause you any problems. Most relational databases have many more than two tables. The rows of the table are similar to records, but as you will see in the case study on page 73, they may only hold part of a record. The columns of each table are the fields (also called attributes) but may also hold links to other tables; these are called foreign keys. You will see how to use foreign keys to create relationships that form the links between tables on page 90.

Apart from this difference in shape, how else do spreadsheet (flatfile) databases and relational databases differ?

✳ In a spreadsheet column, it is possible to store data of different data types. In a database table, each field (or column) is defined as being a particular data type. So, relational databases offer less flexibility as to what data can be

Traditionally, spreadsheets have been used for data that is mostly numerical. They offer powerful features for functions and formulae. They also offer simple-to-use chart creation wizards. Relational databases are more geared towards holding textual data, manipulating that data via queries and the preparation of reports.

✳ If a client's data leans towards being more about numbers (such as costs and revenues and other statistical data) you might choose to use spreadsheet software for a solution.

✳ If it leans more towards textual data (names and addresses and other non-numerical data) you would find RDMS more appropriate.

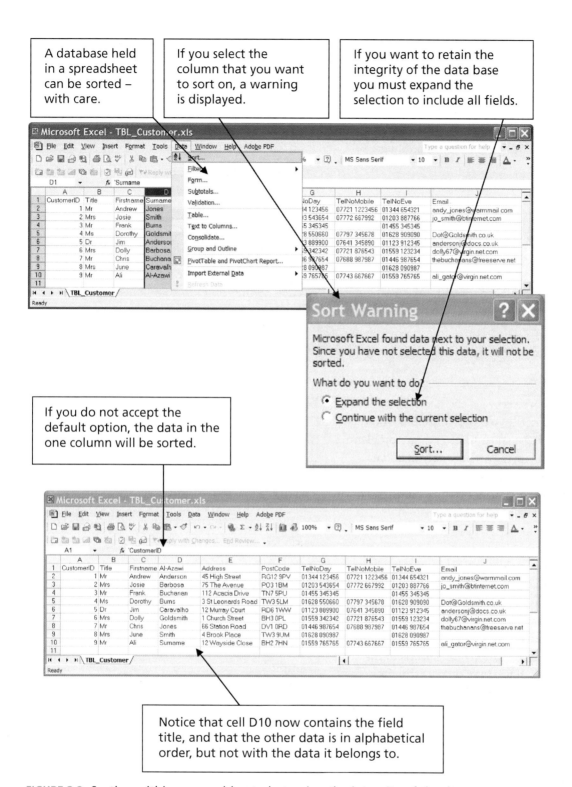

A database held in a spreadsheet can be sorted – with care.

If you select the column that you want to sort on, a warning is displayed.

If you want to retain the integrity of the data base you must expand the selection to include all fields.

If you do not accept the default option, the data in the one column will be sorted.

Sort Warning

Microsoft Excel found data next to your selection. Since you have not selected this data, it will not be sorted.

What do you want to do?

○ Expand the selection
○ Continue with the current selection

Sort...   Cancel

Notice that cell D10 now contains the field title, and that the other data is in alphabetical order, but not with the data it belongs to.

FIGURE 3.2 *Sorting within a spreadsheet: destroying the integrity of the data*

For this reason, in selecting a client and a problem to solve, you need to avoid problems that would be better solved using a spreadsheet, i.e. any problem that relies heavily on numerical analysis of data.

So, how can you identify the needs of your client, and how would you design a solution to meet their needs by producing a relational database?

The Hunter's Yard case study shows how a database to keep track of their bookings could be designed from scratch.

Sometimes, a client already has a system in place, but it does not fulfil all their needs. Your task would therefore be to identify the shortfall and then decide how to solve this problem for them. Sometimes, it is a case of extending the current system or, as with the redhouse case study, a complete change of application may be advisable. You should be able to use the data from the current system to reduce the workload in setting up the solution. You should also be able to run both the old solution system and new solution in parallel for a while to make sure the solution works as required.

Considering the needs of a client

Before you can arrive at a solution for your client, you must understand his or her needs:

Working within a small group, start to think about clients that you might approach, offering to produce a relational database to solve a problem for them.

* What is their vision of what the solution will do for them?

* What does their current solution do that still needs to happen?

* What should the solution offer in addition to what is already done?

* What data is to be processed? How could it be input?

* What processing is required? What special calculations or rules have to be followed?

* What outputs are needed? What reports are required? Showing what information? In what order?

When discussing the problem with your client, you will need to make notes, and collect sample data. You need to know what data is available for input, and what information the client expects as output. You should gather as much evidence as you can about the current system: documents that they receive, documents and reports that are

CASE STUDY: REDHOUSE

Currently, orders are recorded in a spreadsheet (Figure 3.3), with details of the customer (first name, surname, etc.), what they have ordered (code number, footboard style, size, mattress size, if any, finish type, etc.) and so on. This spreadsheet is used to track the progress of an individual order. It can also be used to schedule work and to identify priorities for those working in the studio.

1 Within the data fields in the spreadsheet, some items of data represent decisions made by the customer (such as the method of paying the deposit), some are decided by redhouse staff on receipt of the order or at some later date (who is going to deliver the bed) and some are calculated or might be generated automatically (such as the date of the order). Identify one more example of each from Figure 3.3.

2 In Unit 2 (page 42), you learned about information flow diagrams. Using only the information shown in Figure 3.3, start to produce an information flow diagram for the order information within redhouse. Make a list of the questions you would need to ask, to fill in the gaps in your diagram.

3 For your own client, identify one document that is essential to the solution (such as an appointment card, an order, or an invoice) and, within it, identify the source of every data item.

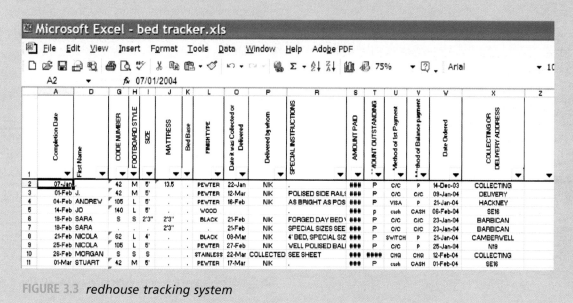

FIGURE 3.3 *redhouse tracking system*

generated and files that are kept. You should then present your findings as a report, summarising what you see as the problem, and what the solution is expected to do.

In the real world, where such an analysis would be a costly exercise and necessitate a contract between the client and the analyst, this feedback to the client would be called a feasibility report. It should state the problem and give an estimate for how a solution might be developed with costs, both in money terms and the time it would take to develop and implement. The client can then make a decision as to whether to proceed to the next stage: commissioning you to design the solution in more detail.

Designing a solution to match the needs of the client

In designing a solution for a client, your challenge is to match the software facilities available to the functions that the client needs.

* The client may need to store data in such a way that finding it again, perhaps in a different order, is quick and easy.

* The client may need to select particular records from a large database of records.

* The data may be collected in one form but needed in another form, so some manipulation may be required to produce the desired results.

* The data may require analysis and presentation in a graphical way, for example as a chart or graph to show trends from volumes of numerical data.

Think it over...

In a small group, think of user needs that match the four categories of functions listed above.

You then need to express the solution in a way that you can communicate it to your client. Since development of databases is conveniently done using the software itself, it would be normal to show the client a prototype of the proposed solution.

What does it mean?

Prototyping is used for evolutionary development of a product. An initial version is presented to the client and then refined in line with their reaction.

A prototype is a simplified version of the finished product. It will have limited functionality but will convey the general concepts sufficiently for the client to accept it, or to identify what has to be changed.

* The navigation through the solution for basic operations should be evident, even if the screen it leads to displays dummy data.

* The way in which data will be input should be clear, although the validation routines may not be in place, so it will not be robust.

* The way reports will appear, or screens will be displayed, will be clear but may depend on dummy data being used, instead of real live data.

The benefit of prototyping is that the time it might have taken to document the design is spent actually building the prototype, and it is more easily understood by the client. Further refinements also benefit, subject to cost constraints, from input by the client. Prototyping is an aid to meeting the client's needs.

Knowledge check

1 Explain these terms: RDMS, database, record, field.

2 What is the main difference between the structure of a flatfile and that of a relational database?

3 Explain these terms: entity, instance, attribute.

4 What is determined by the data type of a data item?

5 What is a feasibility report?

6 Gives examples of finding, selecting, manipulating and presentation activities for a database.

7 What is a prototype? What should a prototype show? What will it not show?

3.2 Input, processing and output needs

In analysing any data-processing system, the system should break down into three easily identifiable stages: input, process and output (Figure 3.4).

It helps to draw a table listing all the data items and deciding when these are input, what processing is done on them, and when they are output. Table 3.5 shows a very simple example, showing how the system keeps track of how much a customer owes on a single purchase.

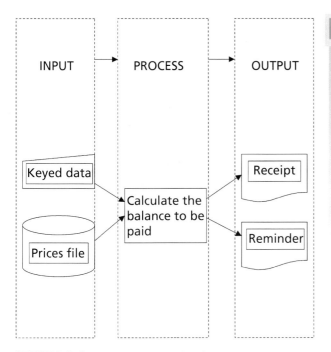

FIGURE 3.4 *Input, process, output*

Theory into practice

You analysed a document for Question 3 of the redhouse case study on page 73.

1 Review this document to check that you are confident with the source of every data item.

2 Obtain another document that is linked to it, e.g. a statement that is produced when a customer has not paid all outstanding invoices. Identify data items that are common to both documents.

3 Draw a table that shows how the data items originate and appear on both documents.

There are some essential points to gain from producing such a table:

✳ If you start with the data items that you need to display on-screen or print out, each one has to come from somewhere. They are either input (like the DepositPaid) or have already been stored for later use (like the PriceOfItem) or they are calculated as a result of some processing (like BalanceToBePaid). Some data items can be generated automatically (like today's date).

✳ If you start with the data you intend to input, you should check that everything is needed. There is no point in keying in data that is never used in any processing, and never output again.

✳ If you know what calculations your client needs the software to do automatically, this will tell you all the input data items that will be needed and the output data items that are produced.

Once you have a clear idea of what data items are needed in your solution, you need to think about how these will be stored (the data type) and how they will be presented (the data format).

Data types

As shown on page 59, data can be divided into textual data and numeric data. Based on these two general data types, there are at least five basic data types that will be common to all RDMS (Figure 3.5) which you are expected to have studied for this qualification.

✳ In Access®, if you choose the **Number data type**, you are then offered many more options: **byte, integer, long integer, single, double, replication ID** and **decimal**. Each type suits a particular range of numbers and level of accuracy, so you need to match this against the data that your client needs to store and use.

DATA ITEM	INPUT	PROCESSING	OUTPUT
Price Of Item	From PRICES file		
Deposit Paid	Keyed in, from cheque		Printed on RECEIPT TO CUSTOMER
Balance To Be Paid		Price Of Item MINUS Deposit Paid	Printed on REMINDER TO CUSTOMER

TABLE 3.5 *Tracking input, processing and output*

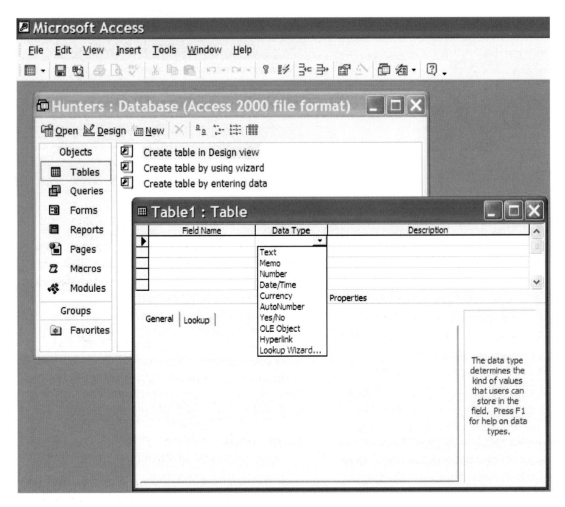

FIGURE 3.5 *Microsoft Access® data type options*

* Currency is not strictly a data type; it is a data format for money amounts, and is stored just like a number. However, it is offered as a default numeric data type with two decimal places which suits most users.

* The text (or string) data type is the simplest; you just decide on a length (field size). A text field can be used to store up to 255 characters but the default (in Microsoft Access®) is set at 50. If you need more than 255 characters, Access® offers a Memo data type which accepts up to 65,356 characters, although you can sort on only the first 255 characters.

* Dates are stored as the number of days since an arbitrary start date. This allows differences in dates to be calculated, so it is straightforward, for example, to work out whether an invoice is overdue for payment.

* The Boolean data type is named after a mathematician called George Boole, who approached logic in a new way, reducing it to a simple algebra, incorporating logic into mathematics. He also worked on general methods in probability by considering only two states: a pass or a fail. His Pass/Fail, Yes/No concept is used to good effect in the logic circuits of computers, and make the two values of a bit (on or off) work wonders. So, the Boolean data type is one that requires only one bit of storage; to represent the values Yes or No.

What does it mean?

Bit stands for binary digit.

Theory into practice

1 Explore your database software to find out
   what data types are on offer.

2 Review your lists of data items and consider what
   data types you might decide to use for each one.

Theory into practice

1 Explore your database software to find out
   what data formats are on offer for the various
   data types.

2 Review your lists of data items and consider
   what data formats you might decide to use
   for each one.

Data formats

When you define the data type of a data item, you should also specify the format you would like to see for its display on-screen and/or on paper.

✳ The format of text data type fields can be controlled using special symbols. For example, if a telephone number is entered as 00441234567890, you can set its format as @@-@@-@@@@-@@@@@@ and it will be displayed as 00-44-1234-567890 which may be easier for the reader to remember. The less-than symbol (<) forces all characters in the string to be lowercase, regardless of what is entered. Similarly, the greater-than symbol (>) forces the following text into upper case.

✳ For number data types, there are a range of formatting options: currency, euro, fixed, standard, per cent and scientific. Between them, these provide just about every option your client may want you to use. However, if you want something special, as with text formatting, you can set up a custom format using special characters.

✳ There are many alternative formats for a date:

   — Long date: Sunday, January 1, 2006

   — Medium date: 1-Jan-06

   — Short date: 1/1/06

   — Custom formats: such as dd/mm/yy

Where and how the field of data appears on the screen or within a report can also be controlled by setting the alignment: left, right, centred or justified. The field is given an amount of space, and the data appears within that, using the alignment that you choose.

The use of databases

The database that you are setting up will relate to your client's line of business. Whatever solution you are providing, you need to have an overview of what it is expected to do.

✳ If your client is a doctor, a hairdresser or a private tutor, you may provide part of an appointments system that will help them to keep track of their work schedule (Figure 3.6).

✳ If your client is involved in trading that includes the taking of orders and creating invoices, like redhouse, you might provide part of an orders and invoicing system (Figure 3.7).

✳ If your client sells holidays, theatre tickets or train journeys, you might provide part of a reservations system (Figure 3.8).

✳ If your client hires out bicycles, cars or yachts (like Hunters Yard), you might provide part of a hire/rental system (Figure 3.9).

Notice that each overview diagram identifies the people or things that are of interest, and the transactions that take place. It also indicates the inputs, processing needed and the outputs to the system.

Theory into practice

1 Produce an overview diagram to explain the
   systems needs of your client, and from which
   you will design your database solution.

2 Compare your diagram with others in your
   group. Talk through what you propose, and make
   sure that your diagram fully explains an overview
   of the system that you propose to produce.

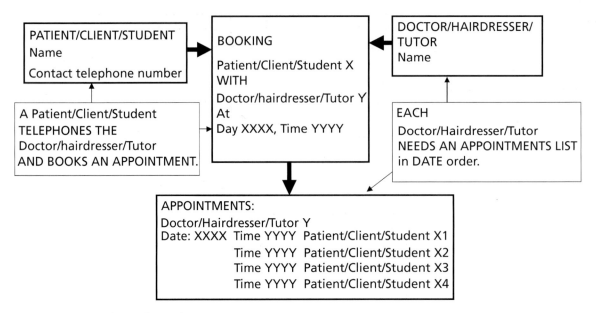

FIGURE 3.6 *Overview of appointments system*

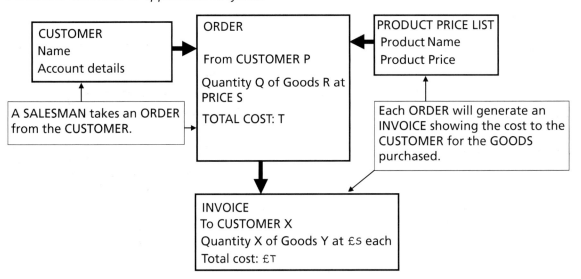

FIGURE 3.7 *Overview of orders and invoicing system*

3.3 Basic database facilities

Relational database software allows you to build and interrogate a database. There are a number of steps or stages in the development of the database:

* The very first step is to construct the tables, one for each item of interest. This may be a person such as the customer, or a document such as an invoice, or a physical object such as a yacht, or an event such as a booking. Each of these items is called an entity, and the general rule is to have one table per entity.

* Having decided on your entities and hence your tables, for each one you need to decide how to define each attribute or field of data within that table. You will identify the primary key fields. The primary key is used to uniquely identify that particular record; or instance of an entity, within the table. You will also set up any links between the tables using foreign keys. Having set up the design of your tables and the relationships between them, you will populate the tables (see page 92) and create any data entry forms that your client needs (page 93).

* The next stage is to set up a query (see page 96) which will create an additional table. The

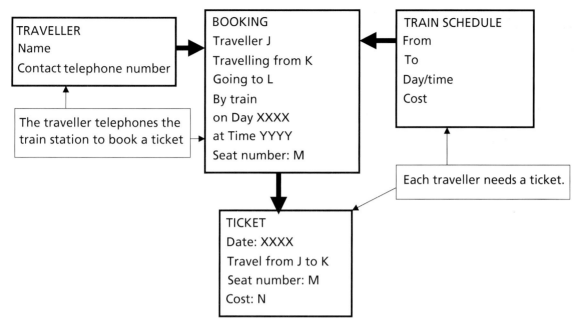

FIGURE 3.8 *Overview of reservations system*

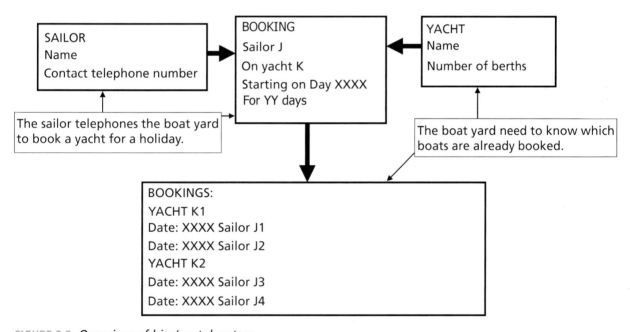

FIGURE 3.9 *Overview of hire/rental system*

query table created holds the data fields that will provide the answer to some question that your client needs answering. Your client's system may require one or more queries.

* You will design a report (see page 97), so that the client can see (or have a printed copy) of the answers to his or her question. This may involve some manipulation of data (see page 102) and, as with creating queries, you will

have the option to use a wizard (see page 103) to help you to set up the report.

What does it mean?

A wizard is a step-by-step aid that can help the designer. Wizards are provided with *Access* for many activities like setting up a table, setting up a query or setting up a report.

* Finally, you may decide to use built-in database facilities (see page 103) such as buttons and macros to set up a menu (Figure 3.10) so that your client is presented with a user-friendly interface.

Welcome menu : Form
HUNTERS YARD BOOKING SYSTEM
NEW CUSTOMER
NEW YACHT
MAKE BOOKING
VIEW BOOKINGS
QUIT
Each button leads the keyboard operator to the appropriate form for data entry – or to view booking – or to close the application.
Each button needs to be set up so that when clicked, a macro is actioned. The macro opens a form, shows a report or closes down the application.

FIGURE 3.10 *Menu for Hunter's Yard*

What does it mean?

The opening menu for a database system provides an interface between the database data and the user.

Constructing tables

The first stage in developing a relational database is to construct the tables to hold the data. Each table is used to store data that relate to a particular entity. So, this task involves

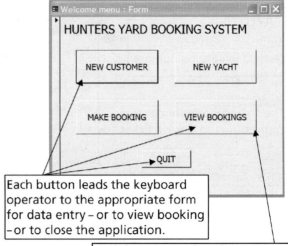

CASE STUDY: HUNTER'S YARD

The hire/rental system for Hunter's Yard involves three entities: YACHT, CUSTOMER and BOOKING.

* For each yacht, there is the boat class (Hustler, Wood, Lullaby), the yacht name (Anemone, Sorrel, Violet, Rose), number of berths (2, 3, 4) and costs at the various rates according to the time of year and the number of days booked. This information is shown in the brochure.
* For each customer, the booking form shows the customer's name, address, contact telephone number and so on. For customers who have hired yachts before, these data may be on file already.
* For each new booking, there is a customer (the skipper), the yacht they want to hire, and the date of the holiday.

Figure 3.11 shows how this data can be arranged into three separate tables.

A single customer may sail on a number of different yachts in any one year, because he or she may make multiple bookings; the relationship between CUSTOMER and YACHT is one-to-many.
A particular yacht will be sailed on by many different skippers; the relationship between YACHT and CUSTOMER is one-to-many.
The relationship between CUSTOMER and YACHT is actually many-to-many- and this won't work in a RDMS.
CUSTOMER
BOOKING
YACHT

FIGURE 3.11 *The entities for Hunter's Yard: YACHT, CUSTOMER and BOOKING*

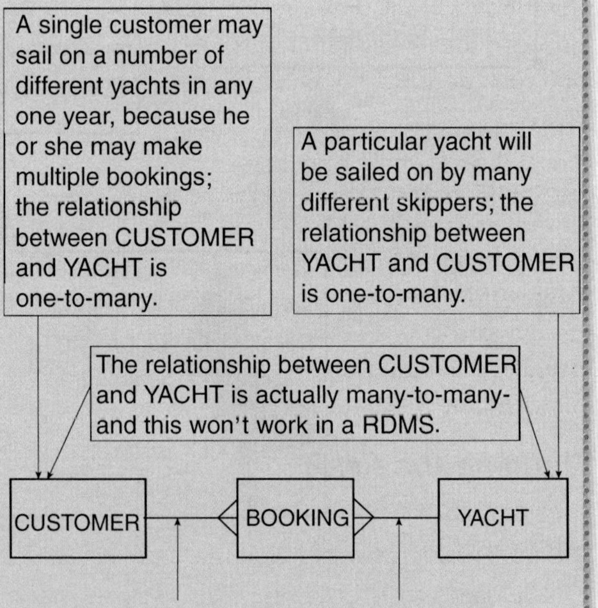

1 For your client, review the overview diagram that you produced. From this, identify the separate entities, and list the data items that go in each of the data tables.

2 Working in pairs, check that your separation of data into tables avoids any unnecessary repetition of data, and that each table contains only the data that relates to that particular entity.

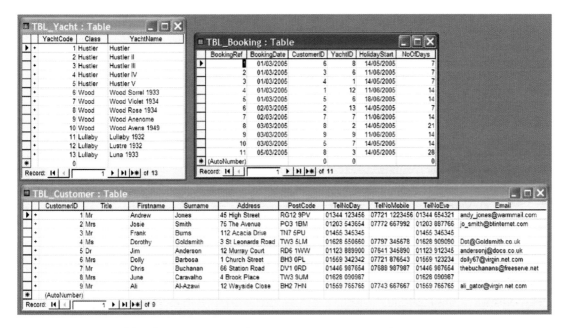

FIGURE 3.12 *The tables for Hunter's Yard: YACHT, CUSTOMER and BOOKING*

identifying which data items can be sensibly grouped together with minimal repetition of data and then deciding which fields are to be key fields.

Notice the convention to use capital letters for the entity names. Also the fields within a table have no spaces but, to aid legibility, capital letters are used to start what would have been a new word. Alternatively, you could use the underscore as in Customer_no. Once you have decided what goes where, you can set up each table (Figure 3.12).

Defining the fields in each table

Microsoft Access® provides three options for setting up a table of data:

✳ Creating a table in Design view assumes that you understand how to specify the data type for each field.

✳ The Table wizard (Figure 3.13) tries to help you through the process of creating the table. It offers some standard tables with the fields you might expect to include already set up with data types, etc. already in place. If you were producing a standard system, this might save you time, and/or

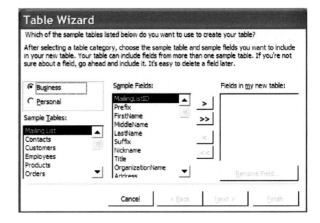

FIGURE 3.13 *Table wizard*

give you some idea as to how you might set up your table.

✳ The third option involves keying data straight into a table, in Table view (Figure 3.14). The software assumes a data type according to the data that you key in. If you already have the data set up elsewhere, e.g. in a spreadsheet, you might import the data and let the software do a lot of the design work for you. You could then go to Design view and rename the fields, and make any other adjustments that you feel are necessary.

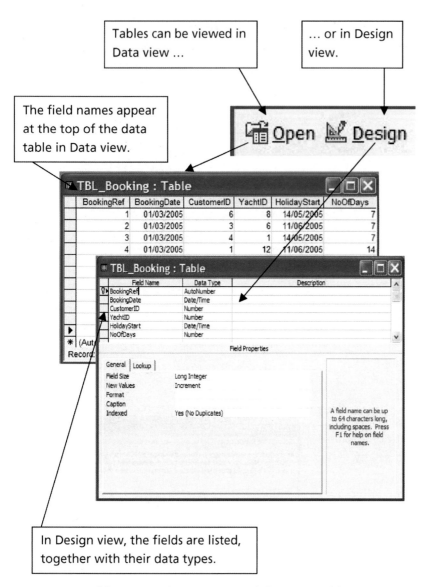

Tables can be viewed in Data view ...

... or in Design view.

The field names appear at the top of the data table in Data view.

In Design view, the fields are listed, together with their data types.

FIGURE 3.14 *Table view and Design view of the same table*

1 Explore your RDMS to see what options you have for creating a table.

2 Find out what standard tables are on offer, and what fields they include.

3 Check that you understand how to toggle between Table view and Design view.

4 Experiment with entering data straight into a table. Work out how the software decides the data type to apply to each field. (Hint: it takes notice of the first character you type, and the structure of the data.)

Validation and verification of data

Validation and verification are two terms that are easily confused; and, to confuse you further, they have different meanings according to the context.

When you are testing your solution (or anything else that you design for a client) these two terms can be distinguished as follows:

* Validation: Have I built the right product?

* Verification: Have I built the product right?

So, in a testing context, the validation stage checks that whatever you have produced does what the client expects and meets with his or her approval. The verification tests check that it matches what the client said that he or she wanted. The two are not necessarily the same!

In a data entry context, these two terms take on different meanings:

* Validation checks that data entered into a system is valid, i.e. what is input is reasonable and in the correct format.

* Verification checks that the data entered on to the system is the same as that on the original source.

Both validation and verification are essential to ensure that the system is processing data that is useful and that the information the system generates is to be trusted. There are then a number of ways of achieving both types of checks.

Validation tests

For validation purposes, there are at least three options, and more than one could be used on any item of data:

* A type check restricts the acceptable characters for a field of data. Some input values may only contain certain types of characters, for example, people's names cannot contain numbers, while their ages cannot contain letters. A National Insurance number contains both numbers and letters in a certain format, e.g. YH105247A and the system would need to check for two alpha characters followed by six numerical digits followed by a single alpha character. In some database applications, the type check can be carried out using an input mask. The mask is set to allow all acceptable patterns to be entered (Figure 3.15).

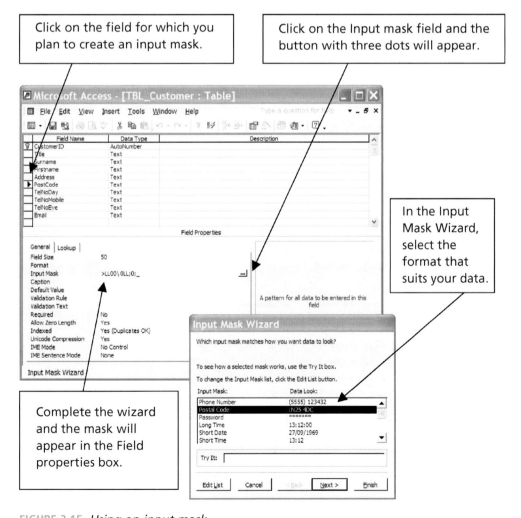

FIGURE 3.15 *Using an input mask*

* A length check is used to check that the correct number of characters are entered. Data items such as account numbers are usually a certain number of characters. If more or fewer are input, then an error must have been made. The required length can be specified when defining the field (Figure 3.16).
* A range check is used when an attribute has boundary limits set. For example, if for insurance purposes, Hunter's Yard can only accept bookings from people who are over 17 and under 70 on 1 September 2005, then each date of birth must be after 1/9/1988 and before 2/9/1936 (Figure 3.17).

If there are a limited number of input options, one way to prevent input errors is to offer the user a list box (or drop-down menu or combo box) listing all the options (Figure 3.18). The user could still choose the wrong one, but at least that option is a valid one, i.e. the data is inaccurate but not unreasonable. In Microsoft Access®, this type of field is created with the table lookup data type.

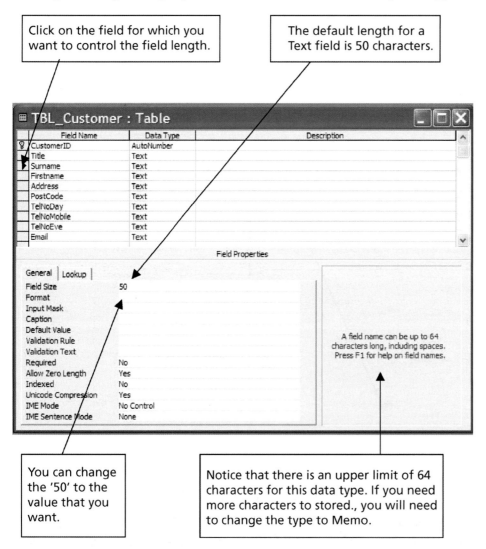

> Click on the field for which you want to control the field length.

> The default length for a Text field is 50 characters.

> You can change the '50' to the value that you want.

> Notice that there is an upper limit of 64 characters for this data type. If you need more characters to stored., you will need to change the type to Memo.

FIGURE 3.16 *Setting a field length*

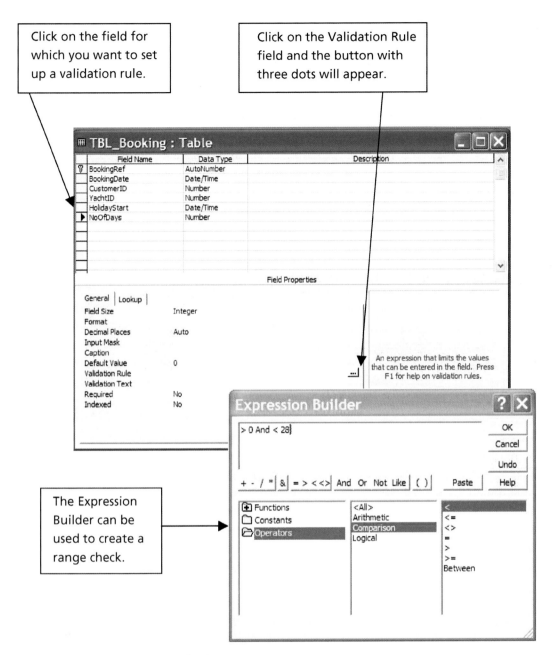

Click on the field for which you want to set up a validation rule.

Click on the Validation Rule field and the button with three dots will appear.

The Expression Builder can be used to create a range check.

FIGURE 3.17 *Setting a range check*

1 Explore your database software to find out what validation techniques are on offer for the various data types. Look particularly at how you might set up an input mask.

2 Review your lists of data items and consider what validation you might decide to use for each one.

Verification tests

Verifying data involves some sort of comparison:

* The user may be asked to enter important data, like an email address or a password, twice. The system can then check if the two match, and reject the data if they don't (Figure 3.19).

* Another verification method is to display some data that depends on what was entered – such

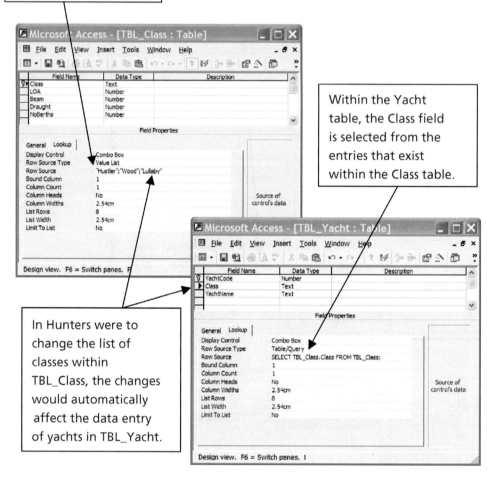

Within the Class table, a list of the acceptable classes is set up as a Value List.

Within the Yacht table, the Class field is selected from the entries that exist within the Class table.

In Hunters were to change the list of classes within TBL_Class, the changes would automatically affect the data entry of yachts in TBL_Yacht.

FIGURE 3.18 *Using the table Lookup data type*

Knowledge check

For each of these items of data, list the validation and/or verification checks that could be made:

* a car registration number

* a house address (break it down into different parts)

* a student ID number

* the price of an item in a shop.

as the name of the account holder that matches the account number keyed in – and to ask the user to check it visually and to confirm that it is correct by pressing another key.

Validation and verification checks serve to filter out data that is invalid or inaccurate. If the user inputs a value that the system rejects, it is important to explain why, otherwise the user will not understand what is expected and what may be acceptable. An error message, accompanied by a beep to stop the user in his or

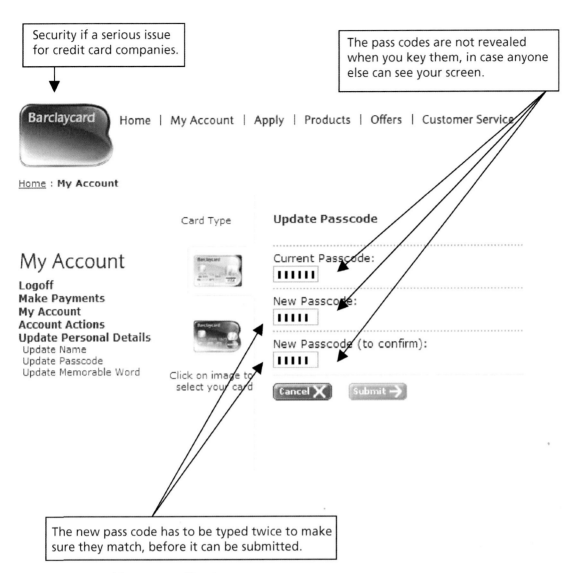

Security if a serious issue for credit card companies.

The pass codes are not revealed when you key them, in case anyone else can see your screen.

The new pass code has to be typed twice to make sure they match, before it can be submitted.

FIGURE 3.19 *Double entry verification*

her tracks, will help (Figure 3.21). This can be set up as part of the field specification in Microsoft Access (Figure 3.22).

Theory into practice

1 Build in validation routines for the most crucial fields.

2 Make notes on any other validation you might incorporate, if the client accepts your initial designs for the tables.

Defining key fields

Having separated the data into tables, one or more fields within each table should be identified as the key field(s). There are two types of key field:

* A primary key field uniquely identifies data within a table. This could be a reference number, a membership number or some other code.

* A foreign key is a data field which holds a number or code that points to the primary key field in another table. In this way, the data in the two tables can be linked.

When the keyboard operator keys the CustomerID, the Surname and PostCode appears, so the operator can see it is the correct customer.

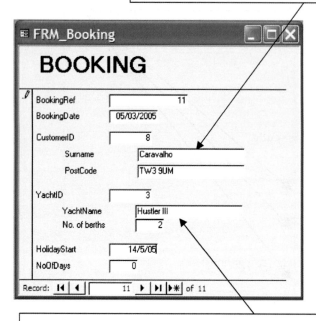

When the keyboard operator keys the YachtID, the YachtName and No. of Berths appears, so the operator can see it is the correct yacht.

FIGURE 3.20 *Table lookup verification*

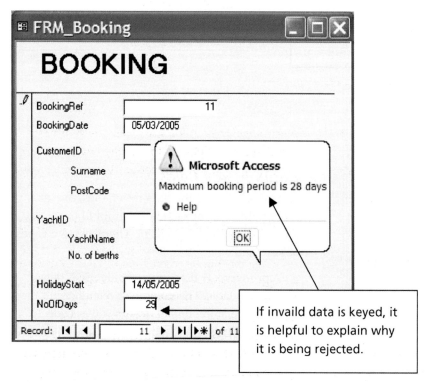

If invaild data is keyed, it is helpful to explain why it is being rejected.

FIGURE 3.21 *An error message on data entry*

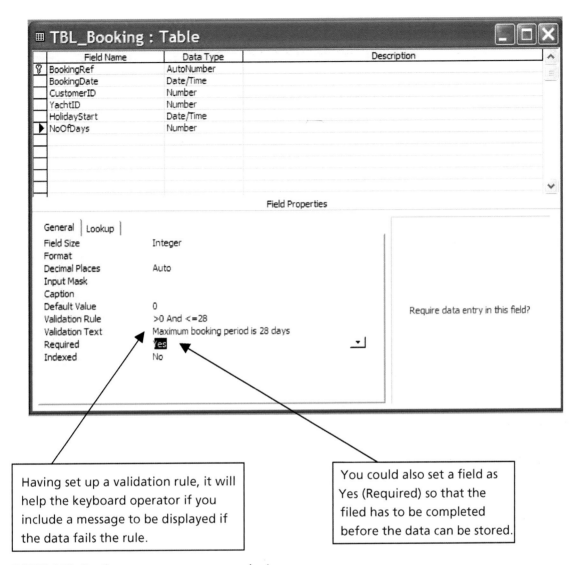

FIGURE 3.22 *Setting up an error message in Access*

Text in image callouts:

Having set up a validation rule, it will help the keyboard operator if you include a message to be displayed if the data fails the rule.

You could also set a field as Yes (Required) so that the filed has to be completed before the data can be stored.

1 For your client, using whichever method you prefer, create one table. Choose meaningful names for each field, and make sure the data type for each field is appropriate for the kind of data that will be entered.

2 Identify the primary key field for your table.

3 Repeat Questions 1 and 2 for the other table(s) in your solution.

In Microsoft Access®, the primary key field is identified by a key icon. If you try to set up a table without defining a primary key field, the software offers to set one up for you. This can involve creating a new field, and that may not be what you want. It is usually a better idea to set up your own primary key fields.

Linking data tables using relationships

Using RDMS, two tables can be linked by setting up a relationship between a field in one table (the foreign key) and another field in the other table (the primary key). In the design of a relational database, the entities and the relationships between those entities are shown in an ERD. Figure 3.24 shows the ERDs for an appointments system, order and invoicing system, reservations system and hire/rental system.

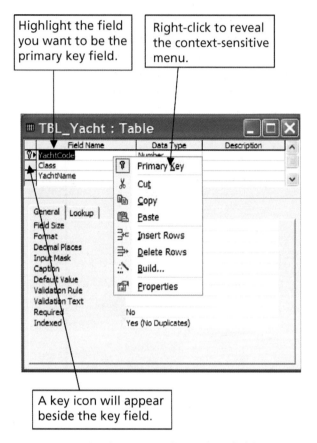

Highlight the field you want to be the primary key field.

Right-click to reveal the context-sensitive menu.

TBL_Yacht : Table

Field Name	Data Type	Description
YachtCode	Number	
Class		
YachtName		

- Primary Key
- Cut
- Copy
- Paste
- Insert Rows
- Delete Rows
- Build...
- Properties

General | Lookup |
Field Size
Format
Decimal Places
Input Mask
Caption
Default Value
Validation Rule
Validation Text
Required   No
Indexed   Yes (No Duplicates)

A key icon will appear beside the key field.

FIGURE 3.23 *Setting up a primary key field*

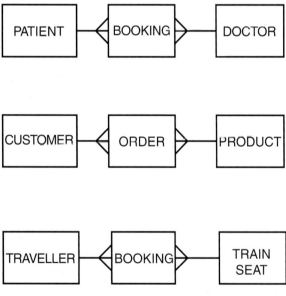

PATIENT — BOOKING — DOCTOR

CUSTOMER — ORDER — PRODUCT

TRAVELLER — BOOKING — TRAIN SEAT

FIGURE 3.24 *ERDs for an appointment system*

What does it mean?

ERD stands for entity-relationship diagram.

There are three degrees of relationship that may be found between entity types:

* One-to-one relationships are rare, because if the data in one table links to the data in another in this way, perhaps the data should be within the same table.

* One-to-many relationships (or many-to-one relationships) are the ones you will meet all the time. The infinity sign (Figure 3.1 on page 69) shows which end of the relationship is the 'many' end.

* Many-to-many relationships will not appear within a RDMS because most database models (including Microsoft Access®) cannot accommodate many-to-many relationships! The good news is that there is a standard way of resolving them in the relational database model: you create a third entity set to act as a link and the relationships are always one-to-many from the original entity to the link entity. Figure 3.25

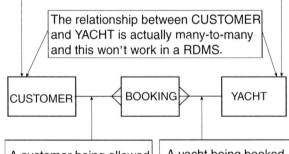

A single customer may sail on a number of different yachts in any one year, because he or she may make multiple bookings; the relationship between CUSTOMER and YACHT is one-to-many.

A particular yacht will be sailed on by many different skippers; the relationship between YACHT and CUSTOMER is one-to-many.

The relationship between CUSTOMER and YACHT is actually many-to-many and this won't work in a RDMS.

CUSTOMER — BOOKING — YACHT

A customer being allowed to have several bookings in any year, means the relationship between CUSTOMER and BOOKING is one-to-many; but each booking will relate to only one customer.

A yacht being booked many times during the year means the relationship between YACHT and BOOKING is on-to-many, but each booking relates to only one skipper.

FIGURE 3.25 *Introducing a third entity to cope with many-to-many relationships*

shows how the BOOKING table can be used to link the CUSTOMER table to the YACHT table in the Hunter's Yard system; the net result is that all the relationships are one-to-many (or many-to-one if you view them from the other side).

The overall aim of separating the data into tables is to minimise data duplication. If you find you have to repeat data for several records in one table, then perhaps there is a need for an additional table.

If you needed to store details of each boat's dimension, rather than include it in the table for

every single boat, it would save repetition to create a new table – with one record per class – and then use YachtClass as a foreign key within YACHT to point to the data related to that class.

Having designed your data tables, the next stage is to enter some data.

What does it mean?

A yacht's draft is its depth below water. If you venture into water shallower than the draught, you will go aground!

Theory into practice

1 Review your data tables. Are there any examples of repeated data? If so, think about how you might create an additional table to minimise this data duplication.

2 Working in small groups, look at each others' database designs, and suggest any improvements that will minimise data duplication.

CASE STUDY: HUNTER'S YARD

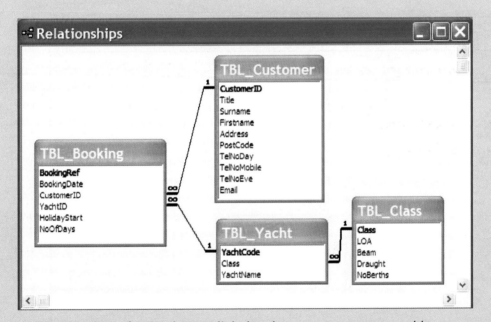

FIGURE 3.26 *Using foreign keys to link data between two or more tables*

1 For your system, consider the relationships between your tables and, if need be, create extra tables to link any that would otherwise need many-to-many relationships.

2 Notice that the BOOKING table needs three fields – the YachtID and the CustomerRef and the HolidayDate – to uniquely identify a booking. For this

reason, an extra field – Booking ID – is invented. Identify the primary key fields in your tables.

3 Notice that CustomerRef is a foreign key in the BOOKING table; it points to the customer who has made the booking, in the CUSTOMER table. Identify the other foreign keys in the Hunter's Yard system.

CASE STUDY: HUNTER'S YARD

Each class of yacht is built to a particular design. All Wood yachts, for example are 24 ft long, 7ft 6in wide and have a draught of 2ft 6in, and have 3 berths. Each class of yacht also has a particular layout (Figure 3.27).

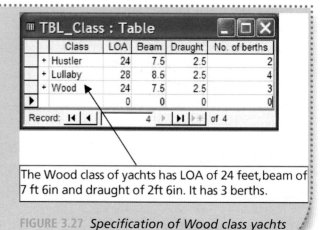

The Wood class of yachts has LOA of 24 feet, beam of 7 ft 6in and draught of 2ft 6in. It has 3 berths.

FIGURE 3.27 *Specification of Wood class yachts*

Populating a data table

Where does the data come from?

* For some tables, you will create the data entries by keying them in, prior to passing the database to your client.

* Most tables are populated (filled in) in the normal course of processing. For this activity, it will help the user if you design a data entry form.

* If you are setting up a database to replace some other system, and the data already exists,

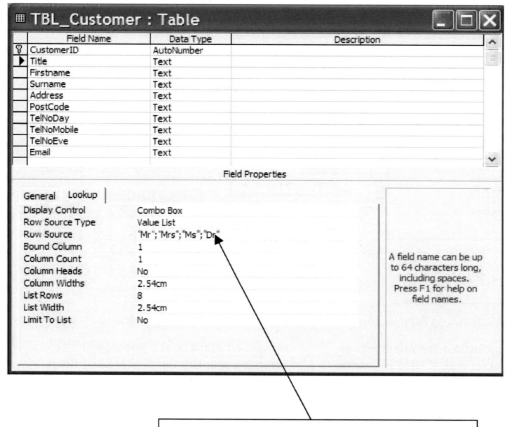

The choices for the Title field need to be keyed in to set up the combo box for the data entry form.

FIGURE 3.28

for example, in a spreadsheet, you will save time and effort if you import the data into the database tables.

If the data is supplied in a table in another Access® database (.mdb), you can import them straightaway. Otherwise, you will need to identify a format that you can import. The two most common are .xls (from a Microsoft Excel® spreadsheet) or .csv.

Creating data entry forms

Microsoft Access® provides a wizard which makes the creation of a data entry form very straightforward (Figure 3.30). You could choose

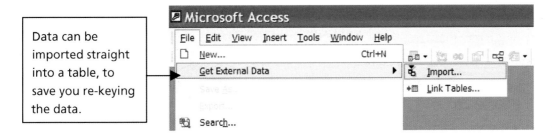

Data can be imported straight into a table, to save you re-keying the data.

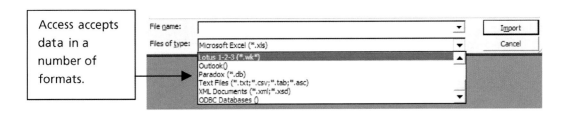

Access accepts data in a number of formats.

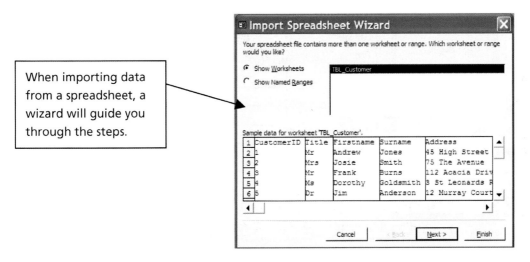

When importing data from a spreadsheet, a wizard will guide you through the steps.

FIGURE 3.29

the option to create the form in Design view, but it makes more sense to use the wizard and then fine tune the form in Design view if you need to.

The field labels are taken from the field names that you used when you first set up the table. If you prefer an alternative caption, you can set this up from the Design view of the table (Figure 3.31).

Each item on a form is called a control, and each control has properties which you can set to suit your client. Figure 3.32 shows the properties of a label, and how to change its alignment.

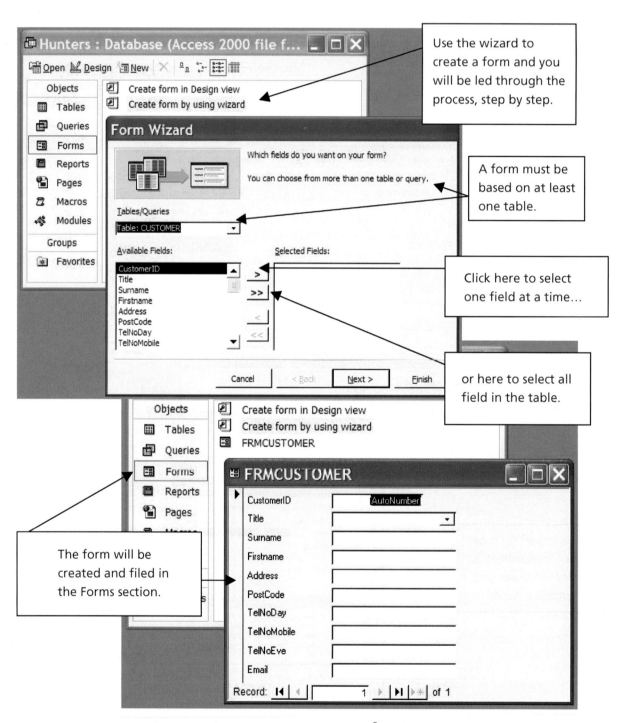

FIGURE 3.30 *Creating a data entry form using Microsoft Access®*

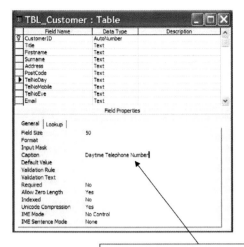

Notice that the Properties box offers a drop-down menu of alignment options. The title data field also shows the downward arrow which indicates a table lookup data type has been defined.

Every control has properties, so you can change these individually, or – if you select several objects at the same time (holding down the Shift key as you click on each one) – you can apply the same properties, such as the background colour, to several controls simultaneously.

Having set up a form, you should test it by entering some data. Make sure that the length of the box into which you enter data matches, i.e. is not too short or too long. When the form is set up by the wizard it offers default widths, but you may prefer to amend these. The field width should be enough to display the longest data item, and this is controlled through the data field specification.

> Text entered in the Caption field will be used, instead of the field name, on reports and forms.

FIGURE 3.31 *Setting up a caption for a form within Design view for a table*

> The Detail section of this form has two types of control: labels (in the left-hand column) and data fields (in the right-hand column).

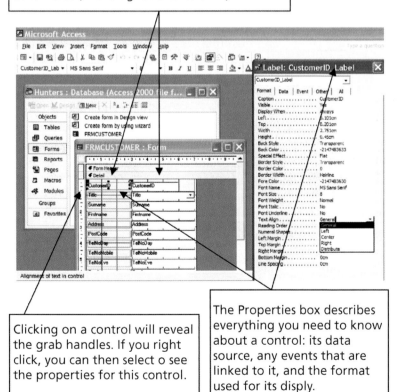

> Clicking on a control will reveal the grab handles. If you right click, you can then select o see the properties for this control.

> The Properties box describes everything you need to know about a control: its data source, any events that are linked to it, and the format used for its disply.

FIGURE 3.32 *Setting the properties of an object on a form*

You should include a title for the form within the FormHeader section of the form, and, later, you may decide to include some navigation buttons (see page 103) as part of a more user-friendly interface (Figure 3.33).

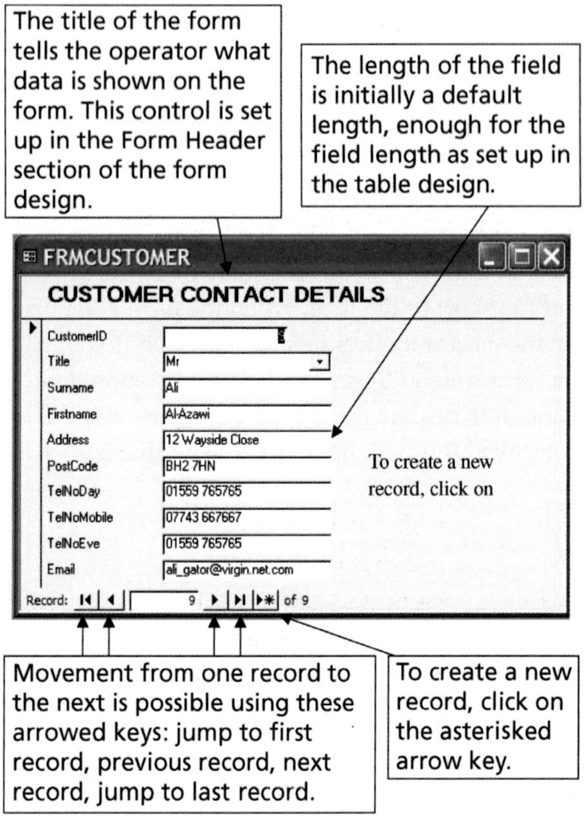

The title of the form tells the operator what data is shown on the form. This control is set up in the Form Header section of the form design.

The length of the field is initially a default length, enough for the field length as set up in the table design.

CUSTOMER CONTACT DETAILS

CustomerID	
Title	Mr
Surname	Ali
Firstname	Al-Azawi
Address	12 Wayside Close
PostCode	BH2 7HN
TelNoDay	01559 765765
TelNoMobile	07743 667667
TelNoEve	01559 765765
Email	ali_gator@virgin.net.com

Record: 9 of 9

To create a new record, click on

Movement from one record to the next is possible using these arrowed keys: jump to first record, previous record, next record, jump to last record.

To create a new record, click on the asterisked arrow key.

FIGURE 3.33 *Titles and navigation*

It is possible to create a form that accepts data that will be held in more than one form; for this you can either select a second table and the fields from it, or you could set up a query which creates a table that combines the fields from both tables, and then creates a form for that query table. When you select the table from which to create the form, the query tables are listed as well as the data tables that you have set up. You might also create a form within a form; the sub-form may present data from a different table.

Creating queries

A query selects data from one or more tables and pulls together relevant fields of data within one new table, so that the query table

Theory into practice

1 Using your RDMS, set up a form for one of your tables using a wizard. Then, amend some of the properties for some of the controls.

2 Experiment with setting up a sub-form. Your RDMS may offer a tutorial in how to do this, and/or sample databases that you can study.

represents the answer to the query. The data tables need to be linked, but if you have not already set up the relationship between the two tables, the query wizard will do this for you.

There are two options in setting up a query:

✳ If you feel very confident in your own skills, you could choose *Create query* in Design view option. This will lead you through the various steps of adding tables, selecting the fields you want to include and so on.

✳ The smarter choice may be to use the wizard; you can let the software do most of the work and then fine tune in Design view if you need to (Figure 3.34).

In Microsoft Access®, the query is set up as a QBE. This creates the code, written in a language called SQL (pronounced see-quel) and visible using View/SQL view. The QBE view shows exactly what is important for your query, in an easy-to-understand way.

What does it mean?

QBE stands for query by example.
SQL stands for structured query language.

For each field of data specified, you can tell the software what criteria you need the data to match, and it extracts these data fields for those instances in the tables that you have chosen – to create a new table full of instances that match.

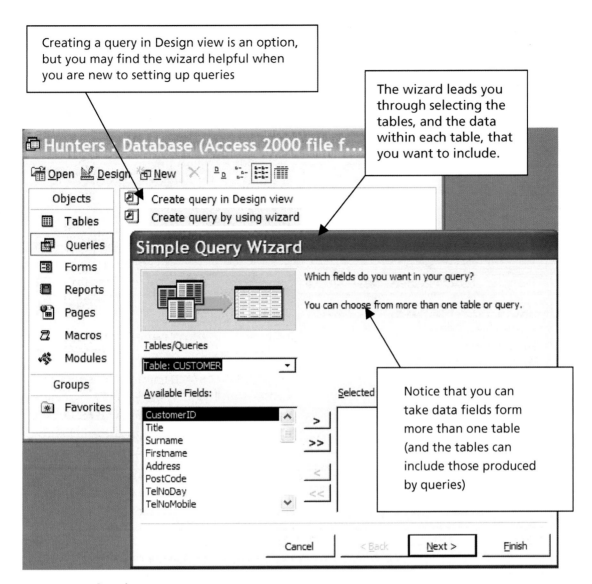

Creating a query in Design view is an option, but you may find the wizard helpful when you are new to setting up queries

The wizard leads you through selecting the tables, and the data within each table, that you want to include.

Notice that you can take data fields form more than one table (and the tables can include those produced by queries)

FIGURE 3.34 *Creating a query*

1 Using your RDMS, set up a query to answer a question that makes sense for your client.

2 Check the data that is created in the query table. Does it answer the question correctly?

Figure 3.35 shows the query used to answer the question 'Which customers have booked to sail aboard the Hunter yacht called Anemone?'.

This yacht has been badly damaged, and cannot be repaired this season. Therefore, these customers will need to be offered an equivalent yacht – or a better one; otherwise, they should be offered the option to cancel or postpone their holiday.

Producing printed reports and screen output

Having set up tables, entered data and set up queries, the next stage is to provide a way for the client to see the results on screen or on paper.

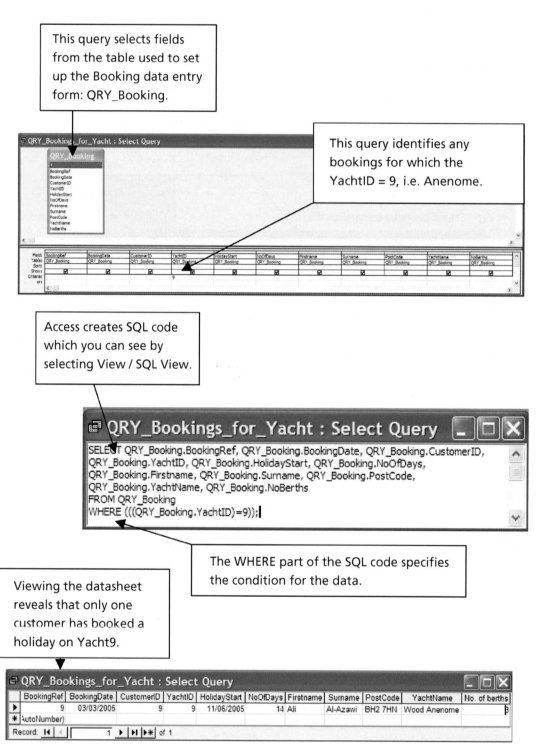

This query selects fields from the table used to set up the Booking data entry form: QRY_Booking.

This query identifies any bookings for which the YachtID = 9, i.e. Anenome.

Access creates SQL code which you can see by selecting View / SQL View.

The WHERE part of the SQL code specifies the condition for the data.

Viewing the datasheet reveals that only one customer has booked a holiday on Yacht9.

QRY_Bookings_for_Yacht : Select Query

```
SELECT QRY_Booking.BookingRef, QRY_Booking.BookingDate, QRY_Booking.CustomerID,
QRY_Booking.YachtID, QRY_Booking.HolidayStart, QRY_Booking.NoOfDays,
QRY_Booking.Firstname, QRY_Booking.Surname, QRY_Booking.PostCode,
QRY_Booking.YachtName, QRY_Booking.NoBerths
FROM QRY_Booking
WHERE (((QRY_Booking.YachtID)=9));
```

FIGURE 3.35 *QBE to extract data*

The Reports tab offers the usual two options: creating in Design view or using a wizard. As with forms and queries, the wizard provides a quick and easy way of setting up a report; you can then fine tune using Design view.

✳ The first step is to identify the tables (original tables or those created using queries). This dialogue box is very much like the one used for creating a query (Figure 3.34 on page 97). If in doubt as to what fields you might need, select all of them (using the double chevron key); you can easily delete them once you are in Design view.

* The next step is to decide what grouping, if any, you need.

* Then, the wizard asks if you want the instances sorted in any particular order. You can sort up to four fields. If you sort on more than two fields, it makes sense to group on the highest level. This will make your report more structured and it will be easier to locate information within it.

* The wizard then has enough information to set up headers and footers for your report, and now needs to know what layout and style you would like (Figure 3.36).

When choosing a title for your report, decide on a name that fully describes the report. The default name offered by the software may just be the name of the table on which the report was based, but this may not be meaningful enough. Use the prefix RPT or something similar to stand for 'report' – it will make your databases easier to maintain at a later date.

The report that is generated by the wizard can be viewed in Design view or previewed (just like Print preview in Word®).

The Design view displays all the controls: labels and fields of data within the various sections of the report. These controls all have properties – just like those seen on a form – so you can set the alignment and other properties for each control, or group of selected controls. Notice the basic structure of the report shown in Figure 3.37.

It will help the reader of your report to include, somewhere on the report, the date that the report is prepared. Similarly, page numbers, which should be

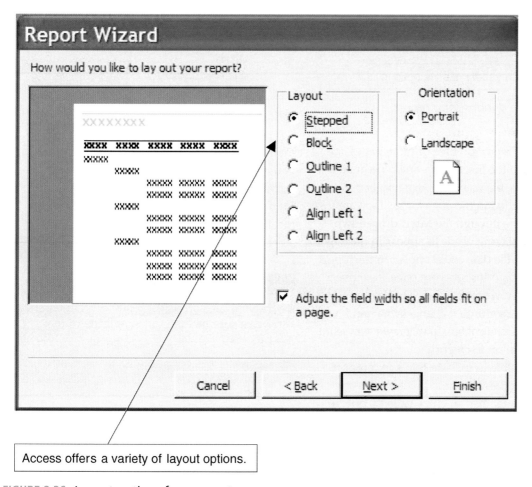

Access offers a variety of layout options.

FIGURE 3.36 *Layout options for a report*

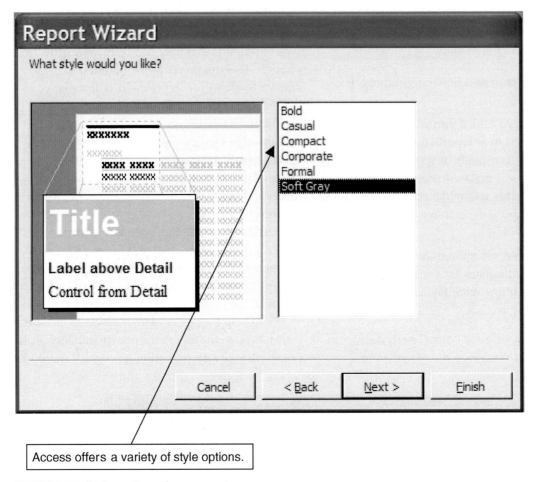

Access offers a variety of style options.

FIGURE 3.37 *Style options for a report*

included for any report of three or more pages, are available through the Insert drop-down menu. By default, in Access, the date and page number controls are included in the page footer; they are also both available through the Insert drop-down menu. Page numbering needs to appear in the page header or footer; the date could appear in the report header or footer, and/or on every page. To move a control, click on it so that the grab handles show, then move the cursor until it changes to a hand; you can then drag the control box to wherever you want the data to appear on the report.

It is also possible to include totals in a report. Within the Properties dialogue box for a given control, the Data tab has an entry called Control Source. Clicking on the three dots reveals an Expression Builder. The Functions folder includes

many built-in functions like Sum and Count, so, you could add up the value of all invoices outstanding on a particular date, or count the number of people who are booked to attend a meeting on a particular day.

Theory into practice

1 Explore the software for producing a report. Make sure that you fully understand the process.

2 Generate one report to suit the needs of your client. Include page numbering, the date and a total.

The **report header** section shows what will be displayed (or printed) once only, at the start of the report.

The **page header** appears at the top or every new page. This may need to include column headings.

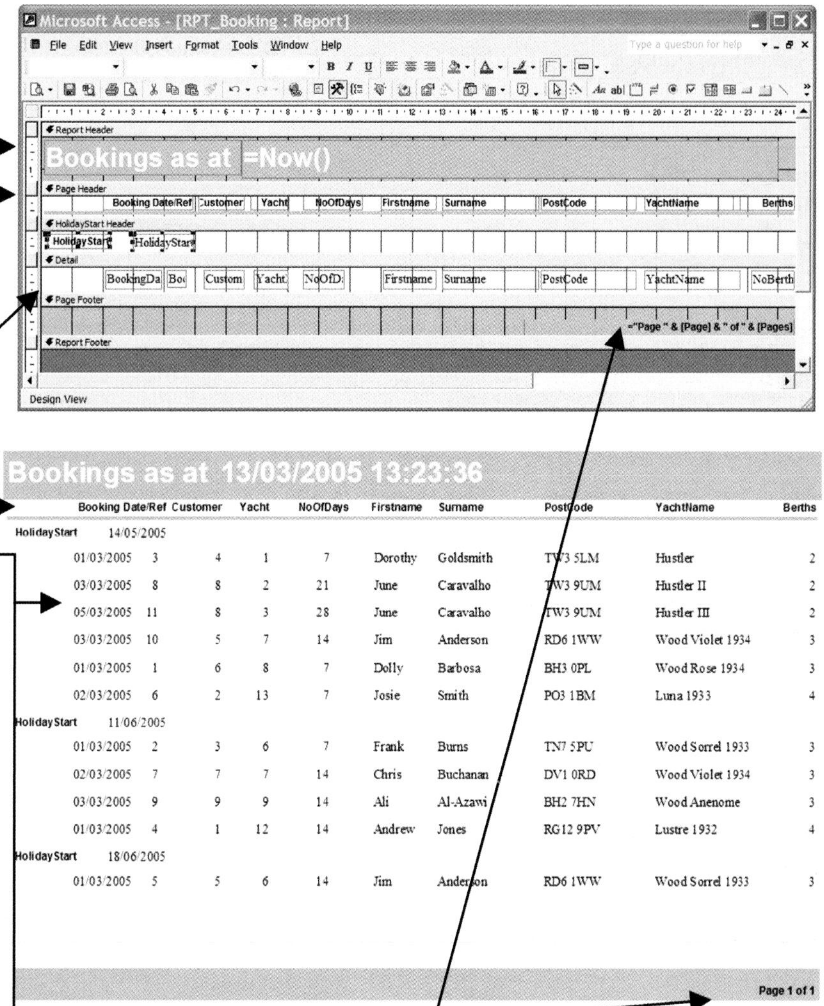

The **detail** is what is printed for each instance in the report table. These will be printed in the order that you have specified - and may also be grouped.

The **page footer** appears on every page, but at the foot of the page. The **report footer** appears once only, at the end of the report.

FIGURE 3.38 *The basic structure of a report*

Using and manipulating data

If your report includes any more than, say, 30 detail lines, then finding useful information within the report will prove tricky unless you include some sorting, and possibly grouping of the data.

Using Access®, you can specify the grouping and sorting requirements during the set up of a report, using the wizard. Alternatively, in Design view, you can select View/Sorting and Grouping. From the Sorting and Grouping dialogue box (Figure 3.39),

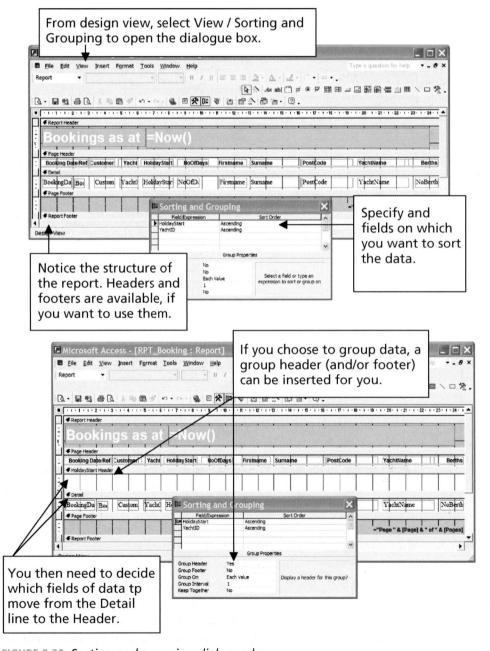

FIGURE 3.39 *Sorting and grouping dialogue box*

you can identify the fields to group and sort, and whether you need group headers and footers.

Using wizards effectively

Wizards are provided to make life easier for the designer of the database. When you set up your first database, you may rely heavily on the wizards. As time goes on, you may find that you work in Design view more instead.

However, it still makes sense to let the wizard do much of the design work, automatically, for you. The questions that it asks you are the questions you will have to ask yourself during the design process. You can then use Design view to make any slight changes.

Apart from the wizards introduced in this unit so far, there are many other wizards available within Access® that you may be find useful.

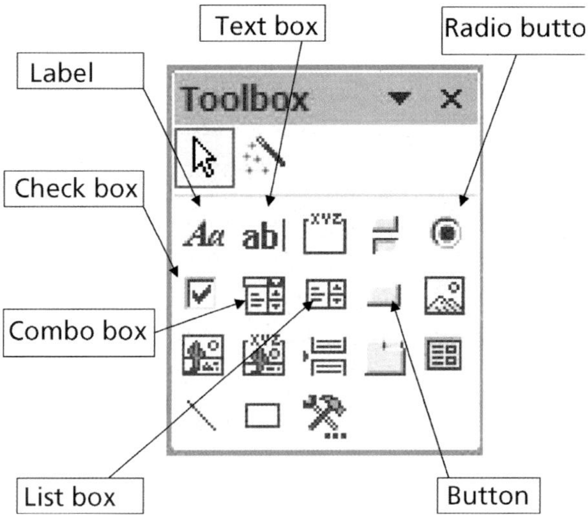

FIGURE 3.40 *Access toolbox*

Theory into practice

1 Using Microsoft *Access* Help, search 'wizard' to locate the list of wizards. Working with others in a group, identify wizards that you have not used, and share the exploration of these wizards between you.

2 Present your finding to others in your group, so that you all have an appreciation of what the many wizards can do for you.

Theory into practice

1 Set up an opening menu and insert buttons on each form to allow the user to navigate the database appropriately.

2 Explore other built-in facilities that are available with your database software. Compare your findings with others in your group.

Using built-in database facilities appropriately.

In Microsoft Access®, a toolbox (Figure 3.40) offers the option of additional controls such as an extra label or text box, or a button that you might use to help the user navigate through the database screens.

To set up an opening menu, you need to create a form in Design view. Open the toolbox (there is an icon, or you can access it through View/Toolbox). Double-clicking on the Command button and then clicking on the form will generate a rectangle that looks like a button. The properties of this object can then be set, so that its label is not the default 'Command' but something meaningful like 'Take a booking' or 'Bookings report'.

3.4 Implementation

Implementation involves developing the prototype to the point where it is ready to hand over to the client.

✳ Your data tables, of which there must be at least two, must match the data requirements of your client: the right fields with minimum data duplication, and appropriate data types and data formats.

✳ For each data table, you should have produced an input form to make the data entry as straightforward as possible for your client. You will need to complete all the validation of as many fields as possible on every form, to make the solution as robust as possible.

* You will need to have imported test data into your solution, and generated queries and reports to meet the needs of your client. This will probably mean sorting and grouping the data to manipulate it in some way

* You will have done some testing of your solution.

* Finally you need to produce some documentation.

3.5 Testing solutions

It is essential that you write a test plan, and then, having carried it out, record the outcomes. This will provide full documentation of the testing process for your portfolio. In deciding on what to test, you might consider the input-process-output concept:

Theory into practice

1 Explore your database software to find out the options to give feedback to the user when an incorrect or invalid data entry is made.

2 Review your lists of data items and consider what error messages you might use for each one.

* Does the solution cope with the data that the user tries to *input*?
Does it accept the data input values that it should, i.e. normal data, including maximum and minimum values (i.e. boundary test data)? Does it automatically reject unacceptable data values (i.e. invalid data)?

* Does the solution *process* the data as required? Do all the facilities provided by the database work? This includes data entry forms, queries and reports. Do all these facilities and/or formulae produce the correct results?

* Is the *output* what the client expected? Does the solution meets the needs of the client?

Alternatively, or perhaps as well, you might identify that there are two types of testing, each of which warrants its own test plan:

* Data testing checks that the database solution copes with the data. For this type of testing, you need to invent normal, boundary and invalid data, and systematically test all input routines to make sure your solution is robust.

* Event testing checks that the database solution copes with whichever route the user takes through the system. When the user presses a particular button or makes a particular choice, does the solution do what it is supposed to do? For this type of testing, you could use valid data, and 'walk through' your solution, doing the kinds of thing the user will do.

Theory into practice

1 Write a test plan, including the test data that you will use and the results that you expect to get.

2 Carry out the test plan, and record the outcomes.

3 Identify any discrepancies and try to solve any problems that arise.

Testing the solution against the needs of the client

When you think you have produced your finished database, the client will look at it from his or her own point of view and, when you receive feedback from your client, you will discover whether you have produced the correct database.

* Does the solution meet the needs of the client, from his or her point of view?

* Does your database accept all the data that the client tries to use on it? This may be slightly different from what you anticipated!

* Is the database robust or can it be made to crash? The acid test really is to let the client loose on your solution. Even if you think you have fully tested your solution, any faults that you missed are bound to show up when the client tries to use it.

3.6 Documentation

For your portfolio, you must document the design, implementation, testing and evaluation of your solution to prove that you have met the assessment objectives for this unit.

Your portfolio documentation should be annotated and could include material that you have produced during the course of competing this unit:

* At the very start of the project, you should have produced a copy of the agreed designs, including the agreed data types, formats, structures, inputs, processing and outputs.

* You will have decided what validation to include, and should print out proof of the validation procedures that you have implemented. These could be screen grabs.

* There should be printouts of all data entry and output screens with appropriate data, plus a printout of all calculations, formula and facilities used.

* You should annotate your printouts of test results so that it is clear what you expected to see, and what you produced.

* Your report printouts should demonstrate the results of data manipulation: grouping and sorting.

* Finally, you will have evaluated your solution and test results.

When a database is produced for a business client, it will usually include two other types of documentation. These are:

* For the user, at the implementation stage, the documentation should include a guide so that the user has something to refer to, if he or she is not sure how to do something.

* For whoever will have to maintain the system, there should be sufficient technical documentation so that, should the client request an amendment, whoever has the task of implementing the amendment can see how the original design was planned.

3.7 Evaluation

There are two separate aspects of evaluation:

* How effective is the solution in meeting the needs of the client.

* How effective were you in producing the solution.

Evaluating the final solution against needs of the client

You need to evaluate the final solution for its suitability, purpose and audience, and this needs to be done in a critical, but constructive way. Before you started the design aspect of this database project, you should have made notes on what the client said he or she wanted. Then, during the course of completing this unit, you should have produced evidence of the database you designed. The results from testing the solution fully, plus the feedback from your client from his or her own testing, should also help you to evaluate the solution.

In comparing the final solution with what the client needs, you need to devise both qualitative and quantitative evaluation criteria:

* Qualitative data relates to the quality according to the user, such as how easy a piece of software is to use. It tends to be subjective and relies on the judgement of people.

* Quantitative data involves counting or measuring, such as the number of keystrokes or mouse clicks needed to achieve something. It tends to be factual; its accuracy depends only on the person counting or measuring.

In real life, if you are producing a solution for a client, you would agree the evaluation criteria with the client, as well as a price, a time-scale and deadlines, etc. Then, once the solution has been created, the evaluation criteria can be used to evaluate the solution, and if it matches, and your performance is deemed satisfactory, then the client should be willing to pay you for your efforts.

For the purpose of this unit, the results of your evaluation should be used to identify the strengths and weaknesses of the solution.

Evaluating your own performance

Part of the benefit of a project such as designing a database to meet a client's needs is that you have the opportunity to reflect objectively on your own performance. From this, you should learn how best to tackle the next project. Consider how successfully you solved the problem:

* How well did you plan your work?

* How well did you manage your time in order to keep to deadlines?

* Did things work out to plan, within the time-scale that you set yourself?

* Were there any areas of the work that did not go according to plan?

* Were there any missed deadlines? You should explain these.

The results of this evaluation should be used to identify your strengths and weaknesses so that you can say, in conclusion, how you might improve your performance in the future.

Theory into practice

1 Gather together all the evidence that you need to evaluate the final solution against the needs of the client.

2 Write an evaluation of the solution, referring to the evaluation criteria that you are using, and incorporating feedback from your client.

3 Identify any strengths and weaknesses of the solution, and make recommendations for improvements that could be made.

Theory into practice

1 Look back at how you tackled this project. Gather together any evidence of your planning and monitoring of your performance.

2 Write a report evaluating your performance. Make sure that it does not evaluate the system, but rather your approach to tackling it, and your success or otherwise.

3 Include, in conclusion, the strengths and weaknesses in your approach and how you might avoid any of the pitfalls in future projects.

UNIT 4

ICT solutions

Introduction

ICT technicians need to have a good understanding of hardware and software and a range of ICT issues. In this unit you will learn to carry out practical installations and configuration, and also to understand the basics of software development. The principles of ergonomics, safety and security procedures, user rights, backup procedures, file permissions and management issues will also be covered. The range of material will be used to support you in the building of a portfolio on which you will be assessed.

What you need to learn

✳ How to carry out research into available hardware and software

✳ To produce a specification for the hardware and software required for a stand-alone ICT system for a specified user

✳ The principles of ergonomics as applied to hardware and software, work station layout and furniture and what the implications are for a specified user

✳ How to collect evidence that demonstrates an understanding of the implications for security and backup, user rights, file permissions and management issues for a specified user

✳ How to install and configure hardware and software

✳ The basic principles of software development

✳ To evaluate my work and my own performance

✳ The importance of using standard ways of working

✳ The importance of appropriate written communication throughout the portfolio.

Resource toolkit

To complete this unit you need these essential resources:

✳ access to computer hardware and software facilities, including word processing software

* access to a computer system on which you can install and configure hardware components, install and configure applications software, and configure the operating system

* a wide range of information sources, such as books, trade journals of the IT industry, newspapers

* access to the Internet.

How you will be assessed

This unit is internally assessed.

There are four assessment objectives:

1 Practical capability in applying ICT

2 Knowledge and understanding of ICT systems and their roles in organisations and society

3 Apply knowledge, skills and understanding to produce solutions to ICT problems

4 Evaluate ICT solutions and own performance.

To demonstrate your coverage of these objectives; you will be expected to produce a portfolio.

* you will carry out research into available hardware and software

* you will produce a specification for the hardware and software required for a stand-alone ICT system for a specified user

* you will consider the principles of ergonomics as applied to hardware and software, work station layout and furniture, understanding their implications for the specified user

* you will collect evidence that demonstrates you have understood the implications for security and backup, user rights, file permissions and management issues for a specified user

* you will provide evidence of the ability to instal and configure hardware and software

* you will provide evidence that you know the basic principles of software development

* you will evaluate your work and your own performance. This section of the report will offer you the opportunity to demonstrate that you have used a style of writing that is appropriate for the portfolio, and will provide evidence of the quality of your written evidence.

In preparing the portfolio you will be expected to know, understand and demonstrate a range of skills including:

* how to select, install and configure hardware and software

* an awareness and consideration of the principles of ergonomics

* a knowledge of the basic principles of software design

* a knowledge of data types, data structures, operators and control structures

* the use of structured English (pseudo-code) to describe processes

* an awareness and consideration of the importance of security

* backup, user rights, file permissions and management issues.

You are also expected to adopt standard ways of working so as to manage your work effectively, and to show evidence of this. Standard ways of working are covered at the beginning of this book.

How high can you aim?

This unit is assessed through the development and building of a portfolio. The portfolio should contain evidence which may be in a variety of formats, including logsheets, checklists, witness statements, diagrams and reports. To obtain the highest marks you should plan your work carefully, carry out the practical tasks successfully, explore the implications of changes that you have made to a system, justify the choices you have made, and evaluate your work in some depth.

What does it mean?

ISO/OSI Reference Model: the International Organisation for Standardisation was founded in 1946, an international organisation represented by over 75 countries all bound together by 'national standards'.

The OSI (open system interconnection) is an ISO standard for worldwide communication based on a networking framework for implementing a format/protocol through seven layers.

4.1 Hardware

This section will provide you with an overview of how to select, install and configure hardware, by introducing you to the components required to facilitate this. You are expected to choose a range of components that meet a required user's needs. To do this you will need to know what each component is, its function, and how it contributes to the systems development process. Over the next few pages you will be introduced to a range of devices that are used to create an ICT system. Some of these include:

* Central processing unit (CPU)
* video or sound card
* network card
* parallel and serial ports
* disk drives and optical drives
* SCSI controller
* connectors.

Central processing unit (CPU)

The CPU is the main chip or processor that connects onto the motherboard in a computer – it is the brain of the computer. The CPU processes data that it fetches or receives from other sources. Currently there are two mainstream manufacturers of CPUs that are used in PCs: AMD and Intel.

The central processing unit is made up of three different parts:

* The arithmetic and logic unit (ALU) that performs calculations and comparisons.
* The control unit (CU) that controls the rest of the computer hardware.
* The registers part that acts as a temporary storage area within the processor.

Video or sound card

These cards will output video or audio data/information. Without a video card a computer will not function, unless there is an on-board integrated card. A computer will function without a sound card, as computers have integrated speakers (although these are very crude in sound output).

Sound cards will enable the computer to output sound through speakers connected to the motherboard, to record sound input from a microphone connected to the computer, and manipulate sound stored on a disk. Nearly all sound cards support MIDI, a standard for representing and transferring music electronically. In addition, most sound cards are Sound Blaster-compatible so that they can process commands that have been written for a Sound Blaster card, the standard for PC sound.

Network card

A network card is sometimes referred to as a Network Interface Card (NIC). The network card plays a very important role in connecting your cable modem and your computer together. It will enable you to interface with a network through either wires or wireless technologies. The network card allows data to be transferred from your computer to another computer or device.

Parallel and serial ports

A parallel port is an interface for connecting an external device such as a printer to a computer. Most computers have both a parallel port and at least one serial port.

* A parallel port uses a 25-pin connector to connect with printers and other devices requiring a relatively high bandwidth.
* A serial port is a general-purpose interface that can be used for almost any type of device including modems, mice and printers (although most printers are connected to a parallel port).

Disk drives and optical drives

Disk drives read data from and write data onto a disk. They can be either internal or external to a computer. There are different types of disk drives for different types of disks. For example, a hard disk drive (HDD) reads and writes hard disks and a floppy disk drive (FDD) reads floppy disks. A magnetic disk drive reads magnetic disks and an optical drive reads optical disks.

Hard disks were invented in the 1950s. They started as large magnetic disks of up to 50 cm in diameter holding just a few megabytes of data. These were originally called 'fixed disks' or 'Winchesters'. They later became known as hard disks to distinguish them from floppy disks. The performance of a hard disk can be measured in two ways: by the data rate and seek time. The other important parameter is the capacity of the drive, which is the number of bytes it can hold.

What does it mean?

The data rate is the number of bytes per second that the drive can deliver to the CPU. Rates between 5 and 40 megabytes per second are common.

The seek time is the amount of time between when the CPU requests a file and when the first byte of the file is sent to the CPU. Times between 10 and 20 milliseconds are common.

In terms of optical drive and disks, the storage capacity of an optical disk is vastly superior to other portable magnetic media, such as floppy disks. The types of optical disks available include CD ROM, WORM (write once read many) and Erasable.

SCSI controller

Small computer system interface (SCSI) is a parallel interface standard that is used by a host of computer systems including Apple Macs, PCs and many UNIX systems for attaching peripheral devices to them. Unlike a parallel or serial port, a SCSI interface has a faster data transmission rate (up to 80 megabytes per second) than standard. In addition, you can attach many devices to a single SCSI port.

Connectors

A connector is the part of a cable that plugs into an interface or port to connect devices together. Connectors can be classed as being male or female. Male connectors contain one or more exposed pins and female connectors contain holes in which the male connector can be inserted.

Selecting Components

You will learn how different systems are suitable for different purposes, and also the importance of particular components. You should also be capable of judging the effectiveness of systems designed for similar purposes – for example, how a different sound card and speakers can affect the quality of sound coming from a multimedia system.

Some of the terms that you will need to become familiar with relate to:

* memory
* main processing unit
* disk drive storage systems
* printers, plotters and VDUs
* connector plugs and sockets.

Memory

When software is loaded it must be stored somewhere inside the computer. The main storage space for programs inside the computer is called 'memory'. Main memory is divided into a number of cells or locations, each of which has its own unique memory address.

What does it mean?

A memory address is a number that is assigned to each byte in a computer's memory that the CPU uses to track where data and instructions are stored. The computer's CPU uses the address bus to communicate which memory address it wants to access, and the memory controller reads the address and then puts the data stored in that memory address back onto the address bus for the CPU to use.

There are two types of computer memory inside the computer: RAM and ROM. RAM (Random Access Memory) is the main store. This is the place where programs and software are stored. When the CPU runs a program, it fetches the program instructions from RAM and executes them. RAM can have instructions read from it by the CPU and can have numbers or other computer data written to it by the CPU. RAM is volatile which means that the main memory can be destroyed, either by being overwritten as new data is entered for processing, or when the machine is switched off. Therefore it is not practical to store data files and programs permanently in the main memory. There are a two types of RAM – static and dynamic:

* Static RAM (SRAM) is incredibly fast and expensive. It is used as cache.
* Dynamic Random Access Memory (DRAM) is used in most personal computers. DRAM chips are available in several forms. The most popular are:

- DIP (dual in-line package) that can be soldered directly onto the surface of the circuit board, although a socket package can be used in place of soldering.
- SOJ (small outline J-lead) and TSOP (thin, small outline package) which can be mounted directly onto the surface of the circuit board.

What does it mean?

Cache is a portion of memory made of high-speed static RAM (SRAM) instead of the slower and cheaper dynamic RAM (DRAM) which is used for main memory. Memory caching is effective because most programs access the same data or instructions over and over. By keeping as much of this information as possible in SRAM, the computer avoids accessing the slower DRAM.

ROM (Read only memory) will allow the CPU to fetch or read instructions from it. However, ROM comes with instructions that are permanently stored inside it and these cannot be overwritten by the computer's CPU. ROM memory is used for storing special sets of instructions which the computer needs when it starts up. When a computer is switched off, the contents of ROM are not erased.

The more memory (RAM) a computer has, the better it works. To measure how much a computer's memory will store we need to think of memory as a series of little boxes, referred to as memory locations, each location being able to store a piece of computer data. The number of locations a computer's memory has provides the key to its overall size. Computer memory is measured in units of 'thousands or millions of locations'.

There are temporary storage areas, built in RAM, known as buffers. They act as a holding area, enabling the CPU to manipulate data before transferring it to a device.

Main processing unit

The main processing unit consists of a case; either a floor standing tower or a desktop unit that a monitor would usually rest on. The case protects the internal components such as the motherboard and acts as the interface between various input and output devices.

Bit	Smallest unit of measurement	Single binary digit 0 or 1
Byte	Made up of 8 bits, amount of space required to hold a single character	Value between 0 and 255
Kilobyte (KB)	Equivalent to 1,000 characters	Approximately 1,000 bytes
Megabyte (MB)	Equivalent to 1 million characters	Approximately 1,000 kilobytes
Gigabyte (GB)	Equivalent to 1 billion characters	Approximately 1,000 megabytes
Terabyte (TB)	Equivalent to 1 thousand billion characters	Approximately 1,000 gigabytes

More recently vaster storage capacities have become available to include:

Petabyte	10 ^ 15 1 000 000 000 000 000	Approximately 1,000 terabytes
Exabyte	10 ^ 18 1 000 000 000 000 000 000	Approximately 1,000 petabytes
Zettabyte	10 ^ 21 1 000 000 000 000 000 000000	Approximately 1,000 exabytes
Yottabyte	10 ^ 24 1 000 000 000 000 000 000000 000	Approximately 1,000 zettabytes

TABLE 4.1 *Storage capacities*

FIGURE 4.1 *A floor standing tower case*

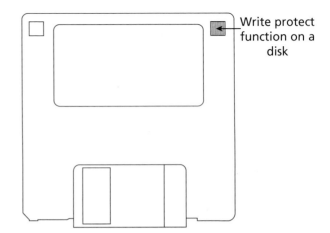

Write protect function on a disk

FIGURE 4.2 *The write-protect function on a disk*

What does it mean?

The motherboard is the main circuit board, that provides the base on which a number of other hardware devices are plugged in. The printed circuits on a motherboard provide the electrical connections between all of the devices that are plugged into it.

Devices that plug into a motherboard include:

* CPU
* BIOS memory
* RAM.

In addition there are a number of slots that can be used for expansion boards and cards to provide the system with extra features. Expansion cards can be used for modems, graphics cards, TV cards, network cards, sound cards and SCSI cards, and so on.

Controllers are devices that transfer data from a computer to a peripheral device and vice versa. For example, VDUs, printers and disk drives all require controllers. Controllers are often single chips that are usually pre-installed in most personal computers. If additional devices are required, these may have to be inserted separately via an expansion board.

To allow communication between different parts of the computer system, a 'bus' system is required. The bus system is made up of a number of communication channels that connect the processor and other components such as memory, input and output devices together. A computer will normally have several buses that are used for specific purposes.

What does it mean?

A bus is a group of parallel wires, along which data can flow.

In addition to these components, other features exist within the main processing unit, one of these being a co-processor. The function of a coprocessor is to speed up certain types of computations – for example, a graphics accelerator card will sometimes have its own built in processor to deal with graphics computations independently of the main motherboard processor.

Disk drive storage

When a PC is switched off, the contents of memory are lost. It is the PC's hard disk that serves as a non-volatile, bulk storage medium for a user's documents, files and applications. By write protecting a file or disk you are ensuring that the contents cannot be modified or deleted. On a floppy disk, you can flick over a tab to write protect the data. Many operating systems include a command to write-protect files.

Data compression enables devices to transmit or store the same amount of data in fewer bits. There are a number of ways to

WINZIP 9.0

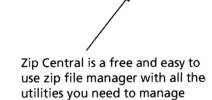

Zip Central is a free and easy to use zip file manager with all the utilities you need to manage your zip files

FIGURE 4.3 *ZIP software examples*

compress data, for example, using a file compression format such as ZIP. Data compression is also used to backup utilities and applications (see Figure 4.3).

There is a range of media available for storing data. These include hard disks, floppy disks, CDs and DVDs, USB pens, MP3 players and so on.

Printers, plotters and VDUs

Printers

There are many different types of printer that can fall into a number of categories depending upon the technology they use. These include the following:

* Line – contains a chain of characters or pins that print an entire line at a time. Line printers are very fast, but produce low-quality print.

* Dot matrix – this creates characters by striking pins against an ink ribbon. Each pin makes a dot, and combinations of dots form characters and illustrations.

* Ink-jet/bubble jet – sprays ink at a sheet of paper. Ink-jet printers produce high-quality text and graphics.

* Laser – produce very high quality text and graphics.

* LCD and LED – use liquid crystals or light-emitting diodes rather than a laser to produce an image on the drum.

When information is sent to a printer from the computer, the data is stored temporarily in a buffer. By buffering the data prior to processing,

the application that has sent the data can be released to carry out other tasks.

Plotters

These fall under the category of 'large format printer'. They are usually used for design work, and can manage poster images easily and professionally. Plotters differ from printers in that they draw lines using a pen. As a result, they can produce continuous lines, whereas printers can only simulate lines by printing a closely spaced series of dots. In general, plotters are considerably more expensive than printers.

VDUs

The visual display unit is a general term that is used to describe the visual output from a computer. On a desk-top computer this term is often used to refer to the screen on monitor.

There are a number of features that can classify a type of monitor:

* The most basic feature is its colour, whether it is monochrome, grey-scale or colour.

* The next feature of a monitor is its size. The screen size of a monitor can be 14 inch, 17 inch or larger. In addition to their size, monitors can be either portrait (height greater than width) or landscape (width greater than height).

* The screen resolution of a monitor indicates how densely packed the pixels are. In general, the more pixels (dots per inch) that a monitor has, the sharper the image is. Most modern monitors can display 1024 by 768 pixels, the SVGA standard.

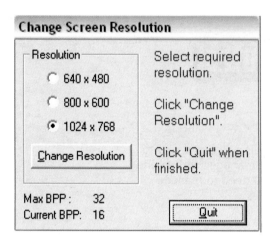

FIGURE 4.4 *Screen resolution*

✳ Another feature of monitors is the type of signal they accept, in terms of analogue or digital. Nearly all modern monitors accept analogue signals. A few monitors are fixed frequency, which means that they accept input at only one frequency. Most monitors, however, are multi-scanning which means that they automatically adjust themselves to the frequency of the signals being sent to it. This means that they can display images at different resolutions, depending on the data being sent to them.

The quality of a monitor can also be measured by its:

✳ Bandwidth – the range of signal frequencies the monitor can handle. This determines how much data it can process, and therefore how fast it can refresh at higher resolutions.

✳ Refresh rate – how many times per second the screen is refreshed. To avoid flickering, the refresh rate should be at least 72 Hz.

✳ Interlaced or non-interlaced – when a screen's contents are refreshed, this involves a scanning process where an image is built up line by line. Within a monitor there are two types of scanning processes: interlaced and non-interlaced. The interlaced scanning approach refreshes the screen in two separate passes, whereas the non-interlaced is refreshed in a single pass. Interlacing enables a monitor to have more resolution. However, it reduces the monitor's reaction speed.

✳ Dot pitch – the amount of space between each pixel. The smaller the dot pitch, the sharper the image.

✳ Convergence – the clarity and sharpness of each pixel.

Connector plugs and sockets

Almost all connectors come as either male or female. There are also speciality connectors that mix the two types into one. A male connector usually has pins that plug into a female connector. The male connectors are often referred to as plugs. The female connectors are often referred to as sockets, or sometimes jacks.

There are a range of connectors, plugs and sockets available in a computer system – a large majority of these are associated with the motherboard. On the motherboard there can be a number of ISA and PCI slots for expansion boards. Other sockets can include ZIF sockets, IDE connectors for connecting hard drives, CD-ROM drives and backup drives such as ZIP drives, power supply connectors and port connectors (see Table 4.2).

Installation, configuration and testing systems components

You will be expected to safely install, configure and test complete systems and individual system components to include:

✳ applications software (word processing, spreadsheet, database, desktop publishing, graphics, communications software, etc.)

✳ disk or optical drives

✳ mouse

✳ expansion cards (video, sound or network)

✳ printer.

There are a number of initial steps and precautions that should be taken when installing hardware. These include the following:

✳ Shutting down and switching off you computer.

✳ Unplugging the power cord from the wall socket or rear of the computer.

✳ Giving yourself sufficient room to move around the computer and desk area.

Computer chips and hardware such as motherboards and hardware cards are sensitive to static electricity. Before handling any hardware or working on the inside of the computer, you should

PLUG, SOCKET OR CONNECTOR	WHAT IT DOES, WHAT IT CONNECTS TO
ISA (Industry Standard Architecture)	Plug and Play ISA enables the operating system to configure expansion boards automatically so that users do not need to fiddle with DIP switches or jumpers.
PCI (Peripheral Component Interconnect)	A local bus standard developed by Intel Corporation. Most modern PCs include a PCI bus in addition to a more general ISA expansion bus.
ZIF (Zero Insertion Force) socket	A chip socket that allows a user to insert and remove a chip without special tools.
IDE (Intelligent Drive Electronics or Integrated Drive Electronics)	An IDE interface is an interface for mass storage devices, in which the controller is integrated into the disk or CD-ROM drive.
BNC (Bayonet Neill Concelman) connector	A type of connector used with coaxial cables. BNC connectors can be male or female and are used to connect cables and some monitors, which increases the accuracy of the signals sent from a video adapter. BNC connectors are used with high frequency or noise sensitive signals.
Coaxial	A type of wire that has a grounded shield of braided wire that minimises electrical and radio frequency interference. Coaxial cabling is the prime type of cabling used by the cable television industry and is also widely used for computer networks such as ethernet.
RJ Series plugs	Plug normally used for single (RJ-11) or multi-line (RJ-12) telephone. The UTP (unshielded twisted pair) plug (RJ-45) can also be used for an ethernet network line.
DB Series	A variety of male and female connectors, also called D-Sub connectors. They normally come in 9, 15, 25, 37 and 50-pins or sockets.

TABLE 4.2 *Plugs, sockets and connector types*

also ensure that you have discharged the static electricity from your body. At the very least you should make sure you unplug your computer from the mains and touch the bare metal case with your hand to discharge any static that may have built up in your body. Ideally you should wear a grounding strap and/or use an anti-static mat to reduce the risk of any components being 'zapped' by static.

Applications software

The majority of computers that are bought today have pre-installed applications software as part of the package. If you need to install additional software, this can be done very easily by inserting the disk, that then launches into the step-by-step visual installation process.

Disk or optical drives

If you are installing a new hard drive you should put it in a closed front bay (one that cannot be accessed from the front of the PC case). If you are installing a new CD or DVD ROM you will need to put it in an open bay, which can be accessed from the front of the PC case. An open front bay is easy to locate because of the removable front panel which can be unclipped once the case is open. There may also be a metal trim which has to be snapped off before inserting the new drive.

Mouse

Installing a mouse used to involve physical connection and then configuration so that the mouse and the computer could communicate with each other. These days, however, especially with a USB mouse, the only real requirement is to connect the mouse physically.

Expansion cards

In terms of installing expansion cards, you would need to identify the type of slot to install your new hardware into. If you don't have a spare slot of the type you need, you will have to remove one of the other cards in your computer in order to use the new one. If you are installing the new hardware into a previously unused slot, you will more than likely have to remove the backing cover from the case before you proceed. This is a metal clip or cover designed to stop dust from getting inside the case. It is normally held in place by a single screw or can be 'snapped' out of the casing using pliers. Remove the retaining screw and/or unclip the backing cover.

Printer

Printer installation and configuration involves a physical connection using a parallel, serial or USB cable. In terms of software, most printers have accompanied printer drivers that can be installed to ensure that the computer and the printer are communicating on the same level. In most modern-day operating systems however, printer configurations can be selected from a list covering the majority of printer makes.

4.2 Software

There are a number of different types of software. Some software is designed to support and enable the user to operate the system (operating system software). Other software provides the programs and tools to design, model, input, manipulate and output data. This type of software includes spreadsheets, word processing, databases, graphics, presentation, communication and desktop publishing. This software is referred to as 'applications software'. Finally, utility software is available to service and manage the system. This category of software is solution based, addressing issues such as security and system protection. Utility software examples include printer drivers, virus checkers and partitioning software, firewalls and disk management software and so on.

For the requirements of this unit you will be expected to know about the minimum software needed to allow a user to communicate with a computer. You will also be required to configure various setting safely and correctly.

ROM-BIOS start-up

What does it mean?

ROM-BIOS is an abbreviation of Read Only Memory Basic Input Output System.

In PCs the BIOS contains all the code required to control the keyboard, monitor/display, disk drives, serial port/s, and a number of other low-level functions – for example, memory timing. The BIOS is typically placed in a ROM chip that comes with the computer. This ensures that the BIOS is always available and cannot be damaged by disk failures.

The PC BIOS is fairly standardised, so all PCs are similar at this level (although there are different BIOS versions). Additional DOS functions are usually added through software modules. This means you can upgrade to a newer version of DOS without changing the BIOS.

A computer's BIOS holds details of the hardware that is installed and the settings for individual components. When the computer starts up, the BIOS starts the 'power-on self test' (POST) routine. This routine checks the motherboard and its components to make sure that they are operating normally and the hardware that is installed is checked to see that it matches the system's BIOS. If an error is identified during this start-up process, the system reports it to the user via an error message or 'beep'.

Parameters that are defined within the ROM-BIOS include being able to select start-up (boot) disk drive, setting a system password, defining a new disk drive or configuring a new card – for example, a video card. The BIOS Set up program should also be run after power on to configure specific settings for any new hardware that you have installed.

During the POST (power on self test) routine there is usually a key which needs to be pressed to start the BIOS Set Up program. Depending on the make of your BIOS this will normally be one of the following keys – F1, F10, Escape, Delete or Insert. Sometimes a message appears on screen to tell you which key to press.

Once the set up program has started, specific settings for any new hardware can be entered.

Graphical user interfaces (GUI)

Graphical user interfaces, such as Microsoft Windows® 95, 98, 2000 and XP can be characterised by a number of features that include the following:

✳ A pointer – a symbol that appears on the screen that allows you to move and select objects or commands. Usually, the pointer appears as a small angled arrow.

✳ Pointing device – such as a mouse or trackball, that enables you to select objects on the screen.

✳ Menus – most graphical user interfaces allow the user to carry out tasks and functions by selecting an option from a menu.

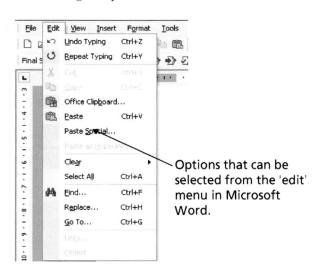

Options that can be selected from the 'edit' menu in Microsoft Word.

FIGURE 4.5 *A menu*

New Open Save E-mail Search Print Print Preview

FIGURE 4.6 *Icons*

✳ Icons – these are miniature pictures that represent commands, files or windows. The pictures represent pictures of the actual commands – for example, a rubbish bin to represent 'rubbish' and a disk to represent 'save'. When the picture is selected the command is executed.

✳ Desktop – this is the area on the display screen where icons are grouped. This is often referred to as the desktop because the icons are intended to represent real objects on a real desktop.

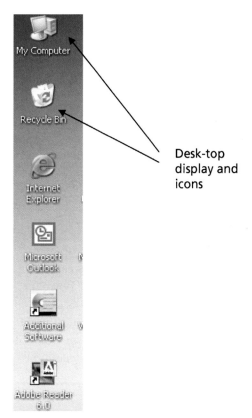

Desk-top display and icons

FIGURE 4.7 *Desktop display*

✳ Windows – these can divide the screen into different areas. In each window, a different program or different file can be displayed.

Operating system software

Computers need operating system software to function. Operating systems perform basic tasks, such as recognising input from the keyboard, sending output to the monitor or display, keeping track of files and directories on the disk, and controlling peripheral devices such as printers and scanners. In large corporate systems the operating system has an even greater responsibility, in that it acts as a mediator to ensure that other programs running simultaneously do not interfere with each other. In addition, the operating system also ensures that users do not interfere with the system by restricting access to certain areas.

Operating systems can be classified into the following types:

* Multi-user: allowing two or more users to run programs at the same time. In an organisation, some operating systems permit hundreds or even thousands of users to run programs simultaneously.
* Multi-processing: allows a program to run on more than one CPU.
* Multi-tasking: allows more than one program to operate at the same time.
* Multi-threading: allows different parts of a single program to run at the same time.
* Real time: responds instantly to an input command.

ICT systems can be configured to start-up and operate in different ways. Much of this can be controlled by the ICT system manager; however some can be configured to suit the needs of the end user. You will be expected to set up different systems to meet the needs of an end user. You will also be expected to use the operating system for settings and diagnostics such as:

* time and date
* printer, mouse and keyboard configuration
* password properties
* multimedia configurations
* scheduled tasks
* GUI desktop and display set-up

* virus protection configuration
* directory (folder) structure and settings
* applications software icons
* checking and setting system properties
* power management.

The majority of configurations can be carried out through the control panel on your operating system, although some, such as the setting of the time and date, can also be done through the ROM-BIOS start-up.

In the image featured on the control panel you can actually see how the majority of settings can be adjusted to suit user needs. These include the time and date, printer, mouse and keyboard configurations, password properties and, in addition, user accounts can also be set up to protect and restrict log-ins to certain applications.

Multimedia configurations such as adjusting the graphics and sound can be addressed through the control panel. Scheduled tasks such as backing up data can be carried out through the operating system. Depending on whether you are using a networked or stand-alone computer, the backup procedure will download your data onto a local hard disk or onto the network, where specific storage areas are designated for individual users. With most graphical operating systems,

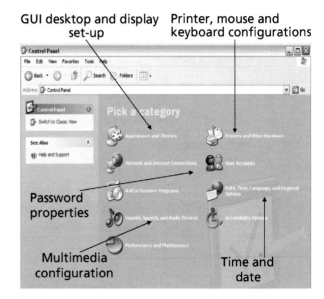

FIGURE 4.8 *GUI desktop and display set-up*

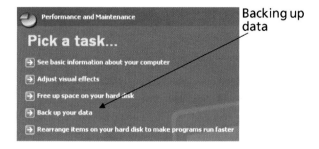

FIGURE 4.9 *Performance and maintenance menu*

FIGURE 4.11 *Applications software – traditional icons*

procedures for carrying out scheduled tasks either involve 'point and click' or 'drag and drop'. On the performance and maintenance menu in the control panel you can also carry out a range of scheduled tasks.

Through the operating system you can change the way your GUI desktop and display set-up looks. This can be done through the 'appearance and themes' setting on the control panel.

Virus protection software can be installed or downloaded from the Internet and configured to start-up every time you boot up your computer. Reminders will also be activated to enable you to check and update the version and level of virus protection at regular intervals.

Access to directories and folders can be gained from the 'start' menu in operating systems such as Windows®, where you can look into 'my computer' or 'my documents' to locate directories and folders. In addition 'folder options' can also be viewed through the control panel.

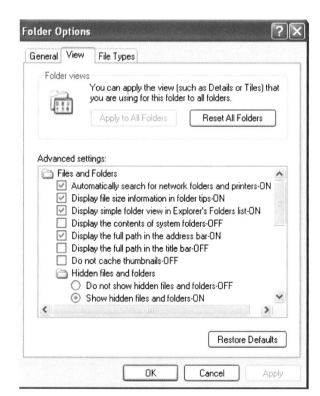

FIGURE 4.10 *Directory (folder) structure and settings*

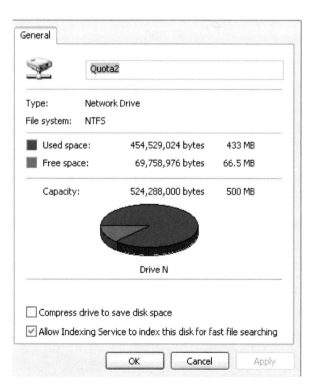

FIGURE 4.12 *Checking how much space is available on your hard disk*

Applications software icons can be changed through the 'properties' function, by right-clicking on the icon. In addition, icons can be downloaded and used as a replacement of the ones that are supplied with the operating system.

Checking and setting system properties, such as running diagnostics, can also be carried out through your desktop and control panel. You can check how much space is available on your hard disk through 'properties' and then free up space on your hard disk.

Power management functions that control your ability to log-off, switch between users and shut down can be accessed through the 'start' menu.

FIGURE 4.13 *Logging off*

Software and data processing activities

Data processing relates directly to the type of processing activity used to convert data into information. There is a range of processing activities. Some of the more common ones include:

* calculating

* merging

* sorting

* selecting and interrogating

* manipulating.

In terms of software applications such as databases, desktop publishing, multimedia, graphics, spreadsheet and word processing, a number of processing activities can be carried out. Some examples are given below.

A	B	C	D	E
1				
2	SMY Computing			
3				
4				
5	Monthly motherboard sales			
6				
7				
8	Month ending March 2003	Total sold	Unit Price £	Total Price £
9				
10	Week 1	83	79.2	=SUM(C10:D10)
11	Week 2	69	79.2	=SUM(C11:D11)
12	Week 3	78	79.2	=SUM(C12:D12)
13	Week 4	113	79.2	=SUM(C13:D13)
14				
15				

TABLE 4.3 *An example of a calculation*

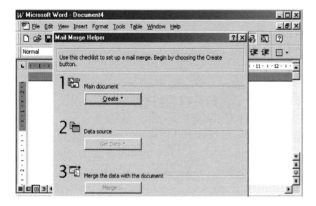

FIGURE 4.14 *A mail merge facility*

Calculating

You can use a spreadsheet to add up two columns of data automatically and present a final value.In this example, columns C and D are being multiplied together to present a final total for each week that is presented in column E (Table 4.3 opposite).

Merging

You can merge two or more pieces of data together – for example, a mail merge, to make a combined document. This is a common function in word processing packages where a standard letter template might be produced to suit a general purpose, and information such as names and addresses is retrieved from another document and merged with the template to create a customised letter.

Sorting

This allows users to sort through information using specific criteria – for example, sorting information alphabetically in ascending or descending order.

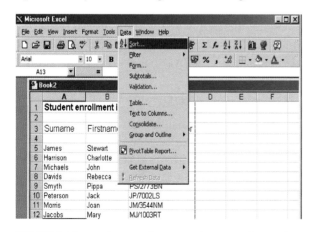

FIGURE 4.15 *Sorting student enrolment information alphabetically by surname*

Selecting and interrogating

These activities focus on fetching and retrieving data and using this data for another purpose. An example of this would be using a query to generate a report in a database, to retrieve information that is stored on a table/tables.

Manipulating

This implies that data is being used, changed or updated in some way. An example of this would be applying a filter to a certain dataset in order to extract specific data types – for example, only customers who lived in Norwich. Individual processing activities will change depending upon the type of software, system or processing requirement.

Configuring applications software

As part of the unit requirements, you will be required to carry out practical activities, such as configuring applications software in different ways. Configuring applications software can involve a variety of tasks depending on the requirements of the end user. Some users will require options such as 'shortcuts' as a preference to enable them to access folders easily without having to search through various pathways and directories. Other preferences might include changing the size of the font, colour or icon to provide easier recognition and use.

Setting up data templates and macros varies depending upon the type of software that you are using. For example, in Microsoft Word® various templates are offered for use and can be saved as a default document for future use. However, in Powerpoint a master slide would need to be set up and used as a standard template.

Saving and backup procedures are standardised across a range of software. Each piece of software will allow you to save work using a drop down menu facility that is usually found on the 'file' menu. Once this menu has been accessed, the options of where to save, the file name and file format are straightforward.

FIGURE 4.16 *Choosing menu items*

Menus, toolbars and buttons can be selected or de-selected from the toolbars. For example, in Microsoft Word® the user can choose which menu items they wish to have on their active window.

Users can also set up their own directory structures by creating new folders to store files. In 'my documents' where you can view all of your

current saved files, you can right click to bring up a menu. By selecting 'new' and 'folder' a new folder can be created and named accordingly.

4.3 Ergonomics

Ergonomics is concerned with designing safe and comfortable machines for humans. In conjunction with the Health and Safety at Work Act (1974), additional European legislation was passed in 1992. This legislation has become known as the 'Six Pack' and it set a minimum standard of provision for health and safety across the European Community. It incorporates maintaining good working practices and having positive and actionable health and safety policies. The ergonomic considerations that relate to the legislation are discussed below.

The workstation

The workstation should be designed to provide sufficient space for the user to change position and vary movements. Users' daily work activities should also involve tasks other than just using the VDU. Taking regular breaks is also essential to people that frequently use a VDU. In terms of the VDU screen, screen images should be stable and flicker-free. The top of the VDU should be just below eye level and filters should be made available to reduce glare and reflection.

Display Screen Equipment (VDU) Regulations 1992

These regulations were set up to protect users of information systems and general ICT. Under these regulations an employer has six main obligations to fulfil.

For each user and operator, the employer must:

∗ assess the risks arising from their use of display screen workstations and take steps to reduce any risks identified to the 'lowest extent reasonably practicable'.

∗ ensure that new workstations (first put into service after 1 January 1993) meet minimum ergonomics standards set out in a schedule to the regulations.

* inform users about the results of the assessments, the actions the employer is taking and the users' entitlements under the regulations.

For each user, whether working for the employer or another employer (but not each operator), the employer must:

* plan display screen work to provide regular breaks or changes of activity.

In addition, for his or her own employees who are users, the employer must:

* offer eye tests before display screen use, and at regular intervals and if they are experiencing visual problems. If the tests show that they are necessary and normal glasses cannot be used, then special glasses must be provided.

* provide appropriate health and safety training for users before display screen use or whenever the workstation is substantially modified.

In terms of other hardware and workstation items, the keyboard should be placed in a position where the user has room to manoeuvre it comfortably and at a height where the forearms, hands and wrists can be in a straight line when typing. Ergonomically designed keyboards are available that can relieve pressure on the wrists, arms, neck and shoulders. Wrist and arm supports are also available to relieve the pressure when typing.

Software

Ergonomic software can be classified as measures and steps that are taken to ensure that an end-user can interact with software effectively as a result of acceptable colours, graphics, font size and other HCI (human computer interface) issues. Ergonomic software can also refer to the range of software that is available to support organisations in terms of 'risk assessment'. Software is available that will look at the health and safety procedures in place and assess how ergonomically orientated your organisation is.

Seating

In terms of furniture and its layout, people generally underestimate the importance of the office chair. The Workplace (Health, Safety and Welfare) Regulations 1992 includes seating as well as workstations. The right office chair used correctly is fundamental to the welfare of the user. It is important to ensure that seating in the workplace is safe, suitable for the task performed and comfortable.

* Employers are required to provide seating that is safe and meets the needs of the individual. It should also be suitable for the tasks involved.

* The work chair should be stable and allow the user freedom of movement and a comfortable position.

Layout

Consideration should also be given to the positioning of wires, filing cabinets, natural lighting and adequate ventilation. The layout of a room can have a profound effect upon an employee, therefore consideration and adequate planning should be undertaken before any workstations are installed so that provisions can be made for cabling, routers, servers and so on. In addition, adequate space needs to be provided so that users not crammed into small office areas and restricted by items such as shelving, filing cabinets and desks.

4.4 The basic principles of software development

The systems life cycle is a stepped approach based on a sequence of activities leading up to the research, analysis, design and implementation of a system. The development of systems involve input from a range of people including:

* the management team
* end users
* systems analysts
* programmers and designers
* software developers.

There are a number of stages in the systems life cycle, and there are a number of different systems life cycles. The systems life cycles that are commonly referred to include:

* the waterfall model
* the spiral model
* RAD (rapid applications development)
* systems analysis and design
* DSDM (dynamic systems design methodologies).

Although there are differences between each of these life cycles, the one thing that they have in common is a defined framework for systems development. The main stages involved in the systems life cycle are outlined below.

Project request

The first stage in the systems life cycle is the project request; this could have arisen from strategic IT planning or from a problem identified by the users of the system. The project request is the first initiation stage for familiarising yourself with the system and the proposed requirements.

Feasibility study

The feasibility study establishes the purpose of the investigation and establishes whether there is the need for a new system. In addition, the terms of reference can be specified, and objectives can be set. The purpose of the feasibility study is to investigate the project to sufficient depth so as to be able to evaluate whether the development of a new system is justified. In other words, this stage of the development cycle is to establish the overall feasibility of the system being considered.

This will involve answering the following questions:

Can it be done?

* Is it technically feasible?
* Is it worth doing?
* Is the investment in the new system commercially and economically sound?
* What is the result of the cost/benefit analysis?

Is it legal?

* Does it breach the legal requirements of the Data Protection Act, Computer Misuse Act or Health and Safety Act?

Can we do it?

* Is it operationally feasible given the current work practices, and the resource capabilities of the system/organisation?
* Is the time frame realistic to develop the schedule and implement the system?

The outcome of the feasibility study will be a feasibility report. This will be presented to the management so the next course of action can be decided. It will contain suggestions and reasoned arguments with regards to the feasibility of the project.

Analysis

Once the feasibility report has been accepted, a more detailed investigation of the current system will take place. It will cover the following:

* The data – it is necessary to obtain a clear and detailed picture of the flow of data and to identify its uses, volumes and characteristics.
* The procedures – what is done, where when and how, and how errors and exceptions are handled.
* The future – development plans and expected growth rates.
* New information requirements, their contents and frequency.
* Problems with the existing system.

Systems design

The objectives of system design are to produce a system that is:

* practical – can it be used by a range of end users.
* efficient – makes the best use of people and equipment. It must also ensure accuracy, timeliness and relevance of information.
* minimum cost – with respect to running new system, without compromising system efficiency and output requirements.
* flexible – the system needs to be able to respond to the needs of the user and be able to evolve and grow. It also needs to be portable to

enable the transfer of data from one computer system to another.

* secure – ensuring hardware reliability and using backup procedures.

Testing and implementation

After the system has been designed it needs to be tested and implemented. Things to consider include how the new/revised system can be physically installed, what testing procedures are going to be used and final considerations such as:

* time scales

* users

* existing data and new data transfer

* compatibility issues

* training in the new system.

The testing of a system also involves software testing to ensure that it is reliable and compatible. Testing is paramount to the development and implementation of software. The stages of software testing will vary depending on which phase is being addressed. For example, during the prototyping phase, testing may be more *ad hoc* as the focus is to identify any features that are missing or define different ways of performing a task or function. During the implementation phase however, testing becomes more structured in order to identify as many faults as possible.

Throughout the software life cycle a testing model can be applied to test the requirements specification (user acceptance test) and the detailed design (unit testing). This model is known as the V-model (Figure 4.17).

Although software may go through a number of testing stages, it may still fail to work or initiate successfully when implemented as part of an IT system. The reasons for this can include:

* incompatibility of coding, programs and data across platforms.

* level and expertise of the end-user.

* problems with the systems hardware; not fast enough, inadequate memory, etc.

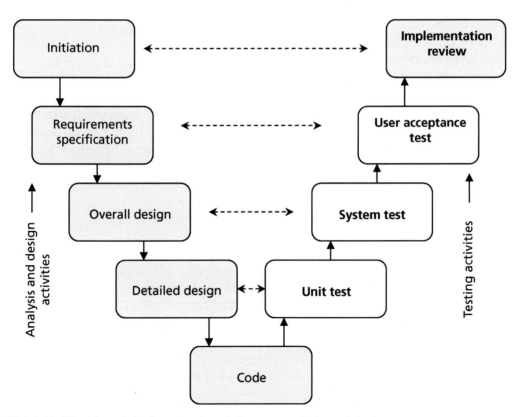

FIGURE 4.17 *The V-model of testing in relation to analysis and design*

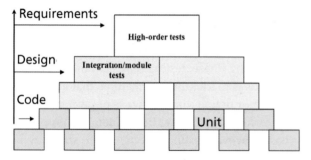

FIGURE 4.18 *Testing hierarchy*

Testing can be broken down into a number of levels and stages, structured in the form of a hierarchy (Figure 4.18).

High-order tests

High-order testing can be broken down into a number of areas. These include:

✳ validation tests (alpha and beta tests)

✳ system tests

✳ other specialised tests (performance, security, etc.)

Alpha and beta tests take place prior to a packaged software release. The purpose of alpha tests is to identify any bugs or major problems that may affect software functionality or usability in the early build phase. This type of testing is usually carried out in-house by staff members or selected customers.

Beta tests occur after the alpha tests to identify any bugs in the software before it is released to customers. An example of beta testing can be seen in the following case study.

CASE STUDY: MICROSOFT RELEASES XP SERVICE PACK 2 FOR TESTING

The company released the advance copy of XP SP2 to give IT professionals a chance to test and give feedback on latest features and configuration changes in SP2. Many of those changes were introduced to make computers running XP less susceptible to viruses and worms, such as the recent Blaster.

Microsoft called the XP SP2 beta version release a 'milestone' in its effort to make XP and its customers more secure. The features released this week are a 'subset' of those that will be included in the final release of SP2. Beta testers' feedback will help Microsoft determine which features to include and omit.

Among the changes in the operating system is an improved version of firewall software that ships with XP. Formerly known as the Internet Connection Firewall, that software is now called the Windows Firewall and is turned on by default, blocking Windows communications ports that are not being used by software applications installed on an XP machine.

Beta testing will ensure the Windows Firewall does not disrupt software applications running on Windows when SP2 ships to customers, Microsoft said.

Microsoft also turned off a controversial administrative tool called Windows Messenger service, which allowed computers on a network to display text messages in pop-up desktop windows. That feature had been discovered by spammers and used to display advertisements and had recently been the subject of a critical security patch from Microsoft.

Other security changes in XP SP2 are more subtle.

Microsoft changed Windows implementation of RPC (Remote Procedure Call) that will make it harder for attackers to exploit that service. Recent worms such as Blaster and Nachi used a security vulnerability in RPC to infect Windows machines.

The company also locked down the Component Object Model (Com) that governs

(continued)

the way software applications run in the Windows environment and exchange information over a computer network. Security holes in a component of Com called the Distributed Component Object Model (DCom) were behind the Blaster and Nachi internet worms earlier this year.

Changes in the software used to compile Windows XPs underlying computer code has also made the operating system less vulnerable to buffer overrun attacks, which are flaws in underlying software code that can allow hackers to crash Windows or take control of vulnerable systems.

On the application front, Microsoft has changed the Internet Explorer web browser, Outlook Express® e-mail client and Windows Messenger instant messaging program, making it harder to use those programs for launching malicious programs disguised as web page downloads or email and IM file attachments.

Windows XP SP2 also contains a host of other enhancements, including improvements to the Automatic Update feature so that updates are easier for users with low-capacity dial-up connections to download and install.

Other improvements include a new version of Windows Media Player, better support for wireless hotspots and wireless devices such as keyboards, wireless printers and PDA using the Bluetooth wireless technology.

Feedback from developers on the beta version of XP SP2 will be used to improve the final version of the product, due in the first half of 2004.

1 **What changes did Microsoft make to this latest release?**
2 **Why were these changes required?**
3 **What is meant by RPC and what have Microsoft done to make this more secure?**

Implementation methods

In terms of implementation, there are a number of things to consider, the most crucial points being:

* timing – when is the best time to implement a new system

* impact – how will the implementation impact on other users and systems

* compatibility – how compatible will the new system implementation be with existing systems

* data management – what will happen to data before, during and after the implementation

* cost – in terms of time taken to implement, loss or processing, etc.

As a result of all of these issues, there are a number of ways that a system can be implemented, the choice being dependent on which one of the points mentioned is considered to be of a higher priority.

* Some organisations will have a new system implementation running alongside an existing system, so the conversion of processing, tasks and data can take place gradually, thus causing minimal disruption at the expense of a longer implementation time and possibly higher costs. This is known as a 'parallel implementation'.

* Direct or 'big bang' implementation occurs when the existing system shuts down and the new system starts up (like switching a light on and off). This is more direct and efficient in terms of timing – however, users may not have time to adjust to the new processing methods and so therefore this could impact negatively on operations in the future.

* A pilot or phased implementation is introduced in stages, over time, so existing systems will convert over to the new system in blocks. This method will allow end users to gradually convert to the new system. However it can be confusing having two or more versions of a system running simultaneously.

Post installation issues

Post installation issues include:

* Who will maintain the new system?

* What day-to-day procedures are in place to ensure the smooth running of the system?

* What maintenance contracts are in place?
* Will the maintenance be on-site?
* What is the cost of the maintenance?
* Is the system a success or failure?

Alternatives to life cycle development

The systems life cycle is appropriate for large transaction processing systems and management information systems where requirements are highly structured and well-defined. However, the prescriptive and rigorous framework of the life cycle makes it both costly, time consuming and inflexible. Smaller, less complex systems could not afford to go down a traditional life cycle pathway, therefore other alternative approaches to system builds have been identified.

Some alternatives to life cycle development include:

* prototyping
* acquisition of application software
* development of bespoke software
* end user development
* outsourcing.

Prototyping

Prototyping provides the opportunity to design an experimental system or part of the actual system design to test whether or not it meets the specified user or system requirements. By building an actual working system, refinements can be made, making it a flexible approach to system design.

Applications or bespoke software

If resources are limited, a viable alternative to a system build is to purchase appropriate software that can improve your existing system features. For example, if a new finance system is required, purchasing either specific accounting software or general spreadsheet software means the system instantly becomes updated and fulfils the requirements of the finance system expectations (providing the hardware is in place to support it).

End user development

This type of systems design has evolved from a culture of 'learning-by-doing', where end users design new systems with the help of modern day tools such as visual and graphical languages. Users can explore the capabilities of applications software that enables them to create input and output screens, customise menus, introduce security measures and stipulate the functions of application software, modelling them into a specific information system.

Outsourcing

As an alternative to designing systems in-house using either traditional life cycle methodologies or drawing upon the skills and knowledge of end users, outsourcing is an attainable option. The use of an external agency provides quality assurances and also a reduction in costs as resources to be used are focused off-site.

Theory into practice

There are a number of different life cycle models. In groups of three or four, carry out research on one of the following life cycle models and present your findings in a poster format to the rest of the group:

* the waterfall model
* the systems development life cycle
* DSDM
* rapid application development.

4.5 Security, backup, user rights, file permissions and management issues

Backup strategies

The consequences of an organisation losing data can be very severe and the disruption to processing activities costly and time consuming. Attempts to retrieve lost data (if retrievable) can prove to be a fruitless exercise putting strain on both manual and financial resources. There are a number of backup options available to an organisation, these include:

* simple backup

* stack backup

* advanced stack backup

* incremental backup

* grandfather, father, son backup.

Simple backup is the elementary backup type. Each time an archive is created the oldest version of the backup file is replaced with the newly created one.

Stack backup consists of the last created backup and previous versions, the previous versions being organised into a stack format.

The advanced backup procedure differs in that it does not permit unchanged or unedited files in the old backup version copies to be stacked.

An incremental backup provides a fast method of backing up data (much faster than a full backup). During an incremental backup only the files that have changed since the last full or incremental backup are included, as a result the time it takes to conduct the backup may be a fraction of the time it takes to perform a full backup.

The grandfather, father, son technique is probably the most common backup method. It uses a rotation set of backup disks or tapes so that three different versions of the same data are held at any one time. An example of this method is shown in Table 4.4.

Security

There are a number of security issues to consider when working with ICT systems. To protect organisations, users and the general public, for whom information about them may be stored, a number of measures and guidelines have been introduced that fall broadly into two categories:

* data security

* data protection.

Although these two issues are closely related, data security examines the area of physical security issues, whereas data protection looks at the measures that have been introduced to protect consumer data.

Keeping data secure can be quite difficult because of the environment in which users work and levels of user and access requirements to the data. With the movement towards a totally networked environment promoting a culture of 'sharing', the issue of data security is even more important and should be addressed at a number of levels, as shown in Figure 4.19.

Security measures need to be integrated at each user level within an organisation. In addition to the security measures outlined below, the issue of physical security also exists, ensuring that hardware and software are kept physically secure under lock and key.

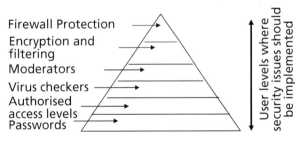

FIGURE 4.19 *Levels of security*

CUSTOMER ORDER DATA					
Monday		Tuesday		Wednesday	
Disk 1	Grandfather	Disk 2	Grandfather	Disk 3	Grandfather
Disk 2	Father	Disk 3	Father	Disk 1	Father
Disk 3	Son	Disk 1	Son	Disk 2	Son

TABLE 4.4 *Grandfather, father, son backup method*

The actual protection of data can be resolved by introducing good practice measures such as backing up all data to a secondary storage device and limiting file access, imposing restrictions to read only, execute only or read/write.

Firewall protection

The primary aim of a firewall is to guard against unauthorised access to an internal network. In effect, a firewall is a gateway with a lock; the gateway only opens for information packets that pass one or more security inspections. There are three basic types of firewalls:

* Application gateways: these are the first gateways, and are sometimes referred to as proxy gateways. They are made up of hosts that run special software to act as a proxy server. Clients behind the firewall must know how to use the proxy, and be configured to do so in order to use Internet services. This software runs at the 'application layer' of the ISO/OSI Reference Model, hence the name. Traditionally application gateways have been the most secure, because they do not allow anything to pass by default, but need to have the programs written and turned on in order to begin passing traffic.

What does it mean?

ISO/OSI Reference Model: the International Organisation for Standardisation was founded in 1946, an international organisation represented by over 75 countries all bound together by 'national standards'. The OSI (open system interconnection) is an ISO standard for worldwide communication based on a networking framework for implementing a format/protocol through seven layers.

---

* Packet filtering: this is a technique whereby routers have 'access control lists' turned on. By default, a router will pass all traffic sent to it, and will do so without any sort of restriction. Access control is performed at a lower ISO/OSI layer (typically the transport or session layer). Due to the fact that packet filtering is done with routers, it is often much faster than application gateways.

* Hybrid systems: these are a mixture between application gateways and packet filtering. In some of these systems, new connections must be authenticated and approved at the application layer. Once this has been done, the remainder of the connection is passed down to the session layer, where packet filters watch the connection to ensure that only packets that are part of an ongoing (already authenticated and approved) conversation are being passed.

Encryption and filtering software

Encryption software scrambles message transmissions. When a message is encrypted, a secret numerical code is applied (an 'encryption key'), and the message can be transmitted or stored in indecipherable characters. The message can only be read after it has been reconstructed through the use of a 'matching key'.

Moderators

Moderators have the responsibility of controlling, filtering and restricting information that gets shared across a network.

Virus checkers

These programs are designed to search for viruses, notify users of their existence and remove them from infected files or disks.

Authorised access levels and passwords

On a networked system, various privilege levels can be set up to restrict users access to shared resources such as files, folders printers and other peripheral devices. A password system can also be implemented to divide levels of entry in accordance to job role and information requirements. For example, a finance assistant may need access to personnel data when generating the monthly payroll. Data about employees however, may be password protected by personnel in the human resources department, so special permission may be required to gain entry to this data.

Audit control software will allow an organisation to monitor and record what it has on its network at a point in time and provides it with an opportunity to check that what it has on its system has been authorised and is legal. Over a period of time a number of factors could impact upon how much software an organisation acquires without their knowledge. These can include:

* illegal copying of software by employees

* downloading of software by employees

* installation of software by employees

* exceeded licence use of software.

These interventions by employees may occur with little or no consideration for the organisation and its responsibility to ensure that software is not misused or abused.

User rights and file permissions

Within certain IT systems, users are given permissions to access some areas of a folder, application or document, but may be restricted from others. By allowing users certain rights within a given system, security of data can be reassured and the span of control can be limited. An example of this can be seen in the case of an IT system in a doctor's surgery. The administration staff may have access to appointments and scheduling, the nurses may have access to patient information, and the GP could have full access and rights to print out prescriptions and authorise medication.

In addition, certain permissions may also be set up to allow certain users partial access to a file. For example, information can be read (read only), but not written, or users may be able to run a program (execute only) but not view it. Users with full read/write permissions would be able to view, update, amend and delete accordingly.

Management issues

Risk analysis examines how liable an rganisation is to security breaches based on its current security provisions. This can identify the elements of an information system, assess the value of each element to the business, identify any threats upon that element and assess the likelihood of that threat occurring. Threats that can occur can be broken down into a number of areas that include:

* physical threats – theft of hardware, software or data

* personnel threats – staff members deleting or overwriting data

* hardware threats – system crashes or processor meltdown

* communication threats – hackers or espionage

* virus or trojan threats – infection and propagation

* natural threats – disasters such as fire, flood, earthquake or lightening

* electrical surge or power loss threat – overloading the system or rendering the system disabled

* erroneous data threats – inaccurate data in the system.

Once potential threats and risks have been identified, policies can be put in place to address them. A corporate ICT security policy can be drawn up to address such threats. Typical content would include:

* access controls – identifying and authenticating users within the system, setting up passwords, building in detection tools, encrypting sensitive data

* administrative controls – setting up procedures with personnel in case of a breach of security; disciplinary actions, defining standards and screening of personnel at the time of hiring

* operations controls – backup procedures and controlling access through smart cards, log-in and log-out procedures and other control tools

* personnel controls – creating a general awareness among employees, providing training and education

* physical controls – secure and lock hardware, have another backup facility off-site, etc.

Contingency plans

Contingency plans can be used to combat potential and actual threats to a system. The majority of organisations will have an adopted security policy that employees are aware of, the plan and policy being open to continuous review and updating. The structure of a contingency plan would be unique to an organisation and its requirements.

Some organisations are more at risk than others depending upon:

* their size

* their location

* their proximity to known natural disasters and threats, flood areas, etc.

* their core business activity.

A strategy based on recovery recognises that no system is infallible. As a result, a number of companies provide 'disaster recovery' services if no internal organisation contingency plan has been drawn up. These companies will maintain copies of important data and files on behalf of an organisation.

A disaster recovery plan can include a provision for backing up facilities in the event of a disaster. These provisions can include:

* subscribing to a disaster recovery service

* an arrangement with a company that runs a compatible computer systems

* a secondary backup site that is distanced geographically from the original

* use of multiple servers.

Knowledge check

1 What security measures can be enforced within an organisation?

2 What is meant by the term 'risk analysis'?

3 Why are some organisations more at risk than others in terms of potential threats to their systems?

4 What measures can a large and a small company take to protect their data?

Some large organisations may have a 'backup site' so that data processing can be switched to a secondary site immediately in the case of an emergency. Smaller organisations might employ other measures such as RAID or data warehousing facilities.

4.6 Evaluation

Evaluation is an essential part of any project. Being able to reflect on the work that has been carried out and provide a justified statement outlining what went well, or not so well can add value to any investigation or research that you have undertaken. There are two areas that need to be addressed under the term 'evaluation'. The first is an evaluation of the solution, and the second is an evaluation of your own performance.

There are a number of ways that can be used to evaluate a document, solution, a piece of evidence, presentation, performance or a self-evaluation. An evaluation should be based on the following criteria:

* what have you done/produced?

* how have you done it?

* what did you use in terms of resources and know-how?

* what have you learned?

* what issues or problems have you had to address and overcome?

* what went well?

* what would you change and why?

An evaluation can be based on qualitative or quantitative criteria and information. Qualitative criteria may be generated from any feedback that you have received about your evidence/solution. This feedback may include written comments and observations, and completed fact-finding documents such as interview notes or questionnaires. Quantitative criteria may be generated from numerical or statistical data – for example, data relating to any testing that has taken place.

The feedback you receive from other people, in conjunction with any actual results that you have, should all form part of evaluating your own performance. Throughout the evaluation you must remain objective, and justify any decisions or comments made from evidence collected throughout the period of data collection, analysis, design and testing. By evaluating your own performance, you should be able to identify any strengths and weaknesses that have developed during the project. For example, a strength may be the fact that you have developed new skills and acquired new knowledge that has helped in the final solution.

By evaluating your own performance you can set out recommendations that could be used to help with work that you might produce in future projects.

The ability to remain objective in the evaluation stage is sometimes very difficult, especially if you have strong personal views as to why the project did or did not meet expectations. By identifying the strengths and weaknesses of the project, you will be able to view the project more objectively.

UNIT 5

Fundamentals of programming

Introduction

This unit looks at developing computer programs. This is a highly complex topic, and this unit will only be introducing the basics. Some people find understanding programming more difficult than others, but all ICT professionals should have a reasonable grasp of the process involved, even if they are not going to work as programmers. We will be looking at the whole development process including designing, writing, testing and documenting programs.

What you need to learn

* To identify problems that may be solved and tasks that may be completed by programming
* To explore the use of a programming language to create customised software
* To apply the principles of program design
* To design, implement and test a program to meet a given specification
* How to produce technical and user documentation
* Know about good practice in use of ICT

Resource toolkit

To complete this unit, you need these essential resources:

* access to a computer with the Sun Java development toolkit installed.

How you will be assessed

This unit is assessed through a portfolio of work that is set and marked by your teacher. Your portfolio will need to include:

* a design for the program you will produce, based on a specification which your teacher will provide

* evidence of the program you wrote, such as the program code and screen prints of the program working

* evidence of the testing you did to ensure your program works correctly (including a test plan and evidence of the results)

* technical documentation for your program describing how the program works, from a technical rather than a user point of view

* an evaluation of your work and your own performance in completing the unit

* evidence that you have used standard ways of working, and considered health and safety and ergonomics.

You must use appropriate written communication, with correct grammar and spelling throughout your portfolio.

> ### *How high can you aim?*

You will need to make sure your program makes use of the full range of facilities (such as data types and operators) listed in the specification, but to achieve higher marks you will also need to explain and justify their use in the technical documentation.

You will also need to ensure that, when designing and implementing the program's user interface, you fully consider issues such as ease of use, ergonomics and health and safety. You will also need to describe in detail the legal implications of developing and using software in relation to the Data Protection Act, the Computer Misuse Act and copyright legislation.

Your technical documentation will need to be comprehensive, with clear explanations of your program and annotations to your program listing. Your testing will also need to be detailed and you will need to explain what changes you made to the program as a result of your testing.

To gain the higher marks your evaluation of the program you produced and your own performance in developing the program will need to be detailed, comprehensive and written in a style which suits the complex technical nature of the subject. You should evaluate how well your program matches the user's requirements and the process you went through to develop the program. You will also need to show evidence of time management by producing a project plan which shows targets and timescales. You should monitor your progress against this plan and modify it if necessary.

5.1 Program design

Computer programs can be written to carry out a wide range of tasks, from writing letters to guiding a space rocket. Programs are particularly good at repetitive tasks, since they can work very fast and do not get bored or tired. However, computer programs do not have any in-built intelligence and are not capable of independent thinking – they can only follow the instructions the program has written into them.

Writing all but the simplest of programs is a complex process that requires planning. Just as when building a house, the first step is for an architect to produce a detailed design, so when creating software, the first step also involves producing a design. A program is a set of instructions that tells the computer what to do. Whatever function you want a computer to perform, all you have to do is write the program.

Programming languages

A program is like a recipe for cooking a meal. A recipe lists, in detail, the steps you must follow to make the meal. Recipes are written to be understood by humans and assume a level of common sense from the cook. Computers, on the other hand, do not have common sense, and require a very precise set of instructions. The microprocessor or chip at the heart of a computer can only understand instructions in the form of

LANGUAGE	FEATURES
C++	Low-level technical programming
Cobol	Traditionally used for business applications (stands for COmmon Business Orientated Language)
Fortran	Traditionally used for complex scientific programming (stands for FORmula TRANslation
Java	Popular modern language, designed for object orientated programming, supports a wide variety of hardware platforms
Pascal	Often used for teaching programming
Visual Basic	Easy-to-use Windows programming language, developed by Microsoft®

TABLE 5.1 *Different programming languages*

binary codes (made up of 1s and 0s), but as binary codes are very difficult for humans to understand, all modern programming is done using symbolic languages with English-like statements, known as high-level programming languages. Over the years, many different high-level programming languages have been developed, each with its own set of features: some of the best known are listed in Table 5.1.

The choice of which program language to use is often a complex one. Some programming languages are more suited to particular types of applications. In a commercial programming environment, the programmers that work for a particular company may already be skilled in using a particular language, so that may be the natural choice for a new project. Another issue that needs to be considered when planning a new programming project is the hardware and software requirements. Some programming languages only work with particular hardware and software. The Microsoft Visual Basic programming language, for example, will only work on PC hardware, running the Windows operating system. Other programming languages, such as Java, are hardware and software platform independent.

The programming language we will use in this unit is Java. Java is a very popular modern programming language, which is widely used both in the computer industry and in schools and colleges. It has many advantages, including the fact that it is platform independent, so Java programs can run in a wide range of hardware and software environments. Java is not just used for writing programs for personal computers; it is also used for writing games and other programs for mobile phones and other hand held devices. Another major advantage of Java is that it is available free of charge. You can download the latest version of Java from the Sun Microsystems website. It includes a simple Java compiler that you can run from the command line.

Splitting the program into manageable procedures

As well as deciding which language to use and what hardware will be required, another important design decision that needs to be made early on is how to split the program into manageable procedures. Although when writing a simple program it might be acceptable to write it from start to finish as one long linear program, with more complex programs this approach would produce a very long program that would be difficult to read and understand. It would also involve a great deal of duplicated code, as most programs need to do the same or similar things on many different occasions, such as validating user input. To avoid these problems, all but the simplest of programs are split into various different modules.

There are a number of simple techniques which can be used to help you decide how to break down a solution into suitable modules. Top-down design has been used for many years and involves breaking the solution down from the top (i.e. the complete problem) into smaller and smaller sections. With Java this means breaking the problem down into what are called 'classes', then splitting these classes into functions or what Java calls 'methods', then within the methods the program code can be broken into sections which use different program structures.

Many modern systems are designed and built using the object-orientated concept.

In a library system, the objects might include books, members and loans.

In a mail order system, the objects might include customers, orders and products.

Classes (and the objects created from them) consist of:

* functions, which are the things a class can do, are called methods

* data, which is the information that relates to the class, are called attributes.

Imagine a library system. We have already mentioned that an object in a library system might be a book. The attributes a book might have would include its title, author, ISBN number and so on. The methods of the book class might include 'add' (for adding a new book to the library), 'go on loan' and 'return from loan'.

The design of a class is represented using a class diagram, which shows the name of the class at the top, the class attributes underneath and the methods at the bottom. An example class diagram is shown in Figure 5.1.

How can a real system that needs computerising be broken down into appropriate

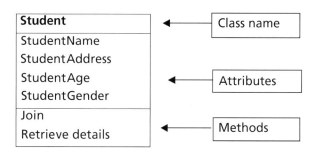

FIGURE 5.1 *A class diagram*

classes? This is a complex question, and a clear understanding of the existing system is needed before this is possible. As a general rule you can identify most of the classes (and the methods of those classes) from a description of the application.

We can therefore identify two classes: students and courses. The methods of the student class are join and retrieve, the methods of the course class are enrol and list. This is shown as class diagrams in Figure 5.2.

Course
CourseCode
Course Name
EnrollStudents
List students

FIGURE 5.2   *Class diagram for the course class*

When a program requests that a method carry out whatever functions it is designed to do, it often needs some input data to carry out its functions. This data is sent to the method by the requesting program and are known as a parameter. Once the method has carried out the function, it usually returns some data (perhaps the results of a calculation) and this is known as the return value.

Processing required

Having decided on the classes and the methods, the next step is to decide how the processing within the methods themselves will be designed. One method that can be used to do this is to divide up the processing based on the different ways the instructions in sections of code will be executed. There are three basic ways that the processing in sections of code can be carried out: sequence, selection and repetition.

＊ Sequence is when the program statements are followed one after the other. An example might be doing a calculation or accepting some input from the user.

＊ Selection is where a choice is made as to which set of instructions to carry out next. The choice is made based on a criterion such as an option the user has selected. In most programming languages, selection is done using the 'if' keyword. Generally, selection constructs take the form:

```
If (condition) then
  (
  statements to be executed if
  the condition is true
  )
else
  (
  statements to be executed if
  the condition is false
  )
end of selection construct
```

＊ Repetition is where instructions are repeated either a certain number of times or until some criterion is met. An iteration construct is sometimes called a loop, or iteration.

What does it mean?

A loop is a part of a program that is repeated. For example, if you wanted a program that printed out a times table from 1 to 12, the most efficient way to write the program would be with a section of code that repeats (loops) 12 times.

Iteration is the name given to each cycle around a loop.

These program structures have real life analogies in the way we complete tasks and solve problems. We often make selections in our life, such as 'if it is raining I will stay in and watch TV, otherwise I will go to the cinema'. Sending out Christmas cards is an example of a repetitive task; write the card, put the address on the envelope, stick down envelope and put stamp on, for each person you are sending cards to.

A structure diagram is a simple way of defining the different control structures that need to be included in a program or module.

CASE STUDY: COLLEGE SYSTEM

As an example, we will draw a structure diagram for the retrieve student details method. We shall imagine that the specification for this system requires that the method returns a student's details when passed the student's surname as a parameter. The structure diagram for this method is shown in Figure 5.3.

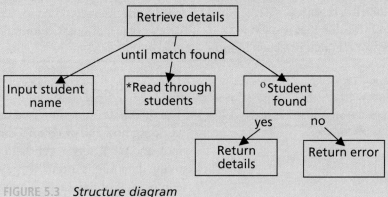

FIGURE 5.3   *Structure diagram*

The diagram consists of boxes that describe the main processing steps and include a indicator of the type of processing ('*' for selection or 'o' for iteration; there is no indicator for sequence).

As you can see, the name of the module is placed in a box at the top of the diagram. Then underneath the processing steps are also drawn in boxes, with the order of processing running from left to right, with lines linking them to the box at the top. Those processing steps which involve iteration have an asterisk in the box and a brief description of the criterion which brings the iteration to an end, which in this case is when a match is found. Those step which involve selection have an 'o' in the corner of the box and the criterion on which the selection is based is also written above the box.

A structure diagram takes us one step further in the design process, but in many cases a design with more detail that is a bit closer to the actual code that will be written is needed. Structured English (sometimes called pseudo-code) is a design technique that uses English-like statements to list in detail the processing steps contained within each of the boxes of the structure diagram. Structured English is a kind of 'halfway house' between the actual programming instructions and normal written English. The benefit of structured English is that it allows the programmer to concentrate on the detailed processing steps (or algorithms) without worrying too much about the exact syntax of the programming language.

What does it mean?

Syntax is the spelling and grammar of a programming language. All programming languages have strict syntax which defines how instructions are written.

Algorithms are formulae or a set of steps for solving a particular problem.

The problem with structured English is that you really need an appreciation of how to write programs and the instructions used in order to write it. An example of the structured English that describes the processing involved in the read through students process box from the structure diagram is shown below. This is a repetition structure so a loop is required.

Loop through every student
```
    if studentName = inputName
```

```
      (
      studentFound = true
      stop loop
      )
   next loop
```

InputName is the name of the student input by the user whose details are required.
StudentFound is an indicator that is used to identify whether or not a match has been found.

Data and variables

The next step in designing a system is to consider what data is required and how that data will be stored in program variables.

What does it mean?

Variables are areas of the computer's memory that are reserved for storing data while the program is running.

Variables are given a name by the program writer, so they can be referred to within the program, and they also have a data type, which defines the type of data that can be stored in them. There are two basic data types – text and numbers – but there are different variations on these (for example, to store whole numbers and real numbers, with a decimal part). We shall look at the different data types that can be used with the Java language and how to declare variables a little later. For now we need to decide what data (or attributes to use the proper object orientated terminology) each of our classes will need.

Input and validation

The final part of the program design involves deciding how the program's input forms will look and what sort of validation will be applied to the data that is input. The layout and ergonomics of the screen is important; it forms the main user interface.

What does it mean?

Ergonomics is the study of the design and arrangement of equipment so that people will interact with the equipment in a healthy, comfortable, and efficient manner.

If the screens are not labelled correctly or clearly or are inconsistent or illogical in the order of the fields, users may find the program confusing and difficult to use. If the screen layout is messy, and contains spelling errors, users may perceive the software to be of poor quality. Screen designs consist of three main parts:

CASE STUDY: COLLEGE SYSTEM

What data will be required by our student class? The attributes of the class have already been named in the class diagram shown in Figure 5.1 – we now need to identify the data types for these attributes. We also need to look at the structured English for the methods and see if we can identify any data variables that will be used internally within the method (known as private variables). A completed table showing the attributes (variables) for the student class and their data types is shown in Table 5.2.

NAME	DATA TYPE
StudentName	Text
StudentAddress	Text
StudentAge	Number
StudentGender	Text

TABLE 5.2 *Data for the student class*

* the screen layout showing the position of the various controls such as labels, input boxes and buttons

* the input data table, showing what data is input to each input box and how it is validated

* a table showing the error messages to be displayed if the validation of input data is unsuccessful.

The screen layout can be hand-sketched or drawn using a graphics program. Screen layouts must be clearly labelled, with the various controls placed in a neat and consistent way, with proper horizontal spacing and vertical alignment. The controls should be in a logical order, that is they should be in the order the user is most likely to use them, from the top of the screen to the bottom.

Theory into practice

Create a screen design for a program that will allow student details to be entered into the college system we have been considering.

Validation of data is important. You must make sure that only correct data is accepted because incorrect data may cause problems when you try to process it (a text value, for example, when a numeric one is expected may cause the program to crash), and incorrect data such as a wrong post code or invalid date of birth is useless. Two main types of validation check can be done:

* a range check checks that numeric data are within a valid range of values. Date checking is an example of this. Month numbers must be in the range 1 to 12. Any value outside the range is invalid and should be rejected.

* a type check tests input to ensure it is the correct data type. A person's surname, for example, must contain only alphabetic characters, while a quantity of items purchased must be numeric.

Remember also that certain combinations of input data may be invalid. For example, imagine a program that allows users to order a new car

on-line. If the user selects the convertible (open top) version of the car, then they should not be allowed to choose a sunroof as one of the optional extras.

In order to validate use inputs, selection constructs are commonly used, such as (in structured English):

```
If month < 12 or < 1
(
    Display "month not valid"
)
```

Theory into practice

Take the table of data items required for the student class, shown in Table 5.2 and add a column to the table showing the validation techniques that could be used for each data item.

Pre-written and standard libraries

All programming languages come with a number of standard libraries which carry out common mathematical functions and other tasks such as text manipulation. These libraries save the programmer a great deal of time and effort as they avoid the need to create these functions themselves. Some of the libraries and the functions contained in them are described in this chapter, but there are many more described in the documentation that comes with the Java development toolkit and on-line at the Sun Java website.

The layout and structure of a program

The Sun Java development toolkit which we will be using does not include an IDE, so our programs will be written in the traditional way using a text editor, for example, Windows Notepad, and then compiled using a separate compiler.

What does it mean?

IDE stands for integrated development environment that is, an editor, compiler, and so on built into one program.

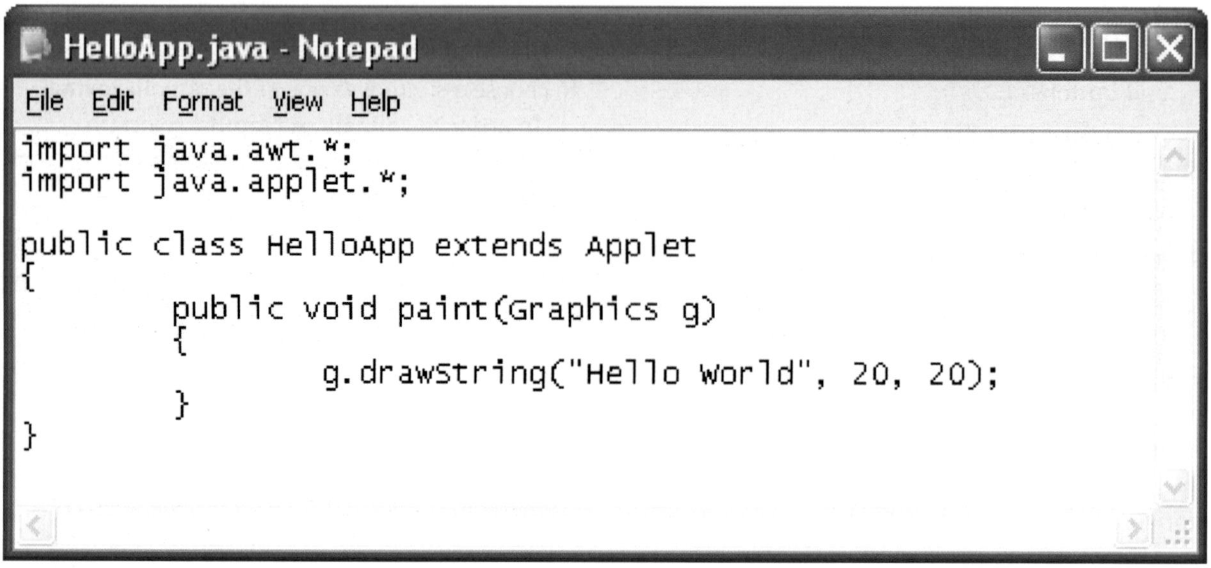


```
import java.awt.*;
import java.applet.*;

public class HelloApp extends Applet
{
        public void paint(Graphics g)
        {
                g.drawString("Hello World", 20, 20);
        }
}
```

FIGURE 5.4 *The helloApp program*

Before you can compile and run any of the examples in this book, you must install the Sun Java development toolkit (SDK). There are also commercial Java IDEs available, such as Microsoft J++ and Borland Jbuilder. Java programs can be written which work in a number of different environments, the simplest of which is text-based MS-DOS programs. Windows-based Java programs can also be written, which work as standalone applications or as applets that work within an Internet browser. Most of the programs we will write will be applets, because they are relatively simple to write and understand. Creating a Java applet is a process that has a number of stages:

* First you must write the applet code using a text editor such as Windows® Notepad.
* The applet code must then be compiled into a type of machine code (code the computer can understand) using the command line compiler, javac.
* An html web page must be created which contains a reference to the applet.
* The web page needs to be viewed either using an Internet browser such as Internet Explorer or using the appletviewer program that comes with the Java SDK.

What does it mean?

Applet is short for application and describes a very short program – a piece of code – written for use on the WWW.

Tradition dictates that the first program students write in any language is the 'Hello World' program. This simply displays the message 'Hello World'. Figure 5.4 shows the code for what we have called the helloApp program, written using the Notepad program.

Note that Java is case-sensitive. You must use upper case (capitals) exactly as shown in the example (except within the quotation marks), so String and string are two different things – only one of which is correct! Instructions in the wrong case will cause compiler errors.

The indentation shown in the program code is good practice but is not essential. Pressing the **Tab** key will indent the line for you. You should get into the habit of indenting the program at each open bracket, and then reducing the indent at each ending bracket. Java programs are broken up into sections using brackets. The programs we will write later on contain a number of sections, so it can be difficult to keep track of the brackets and indenting the code makes this task easier.

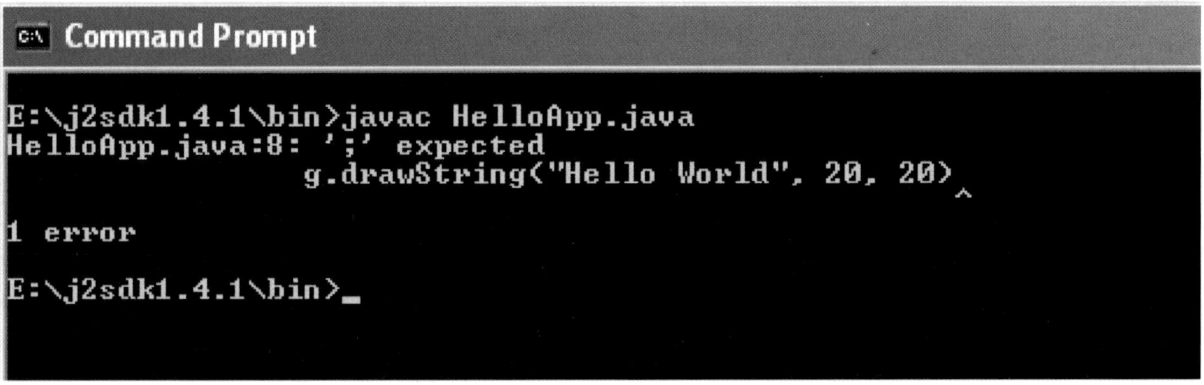

FIGURE 5.5 *Compiler error*

At this stage you should concentrate on understanding how to use the Java development environment, so no explanation of the program code is given here – that will come later.

Having typed the program code using Notepad, the program must be saved. Call it HelloApp.java in the C:/j2sdk1.4.1/bin folder (or whichever drive you have the Java software installed on). This file is known as the source file. Having saved the file, open a MS-DOS command prompt window and change the prompt to the \j2sdk1.4.1\bin folder as noted above. Now type:

```
Javac HelloApp.java
```

Javac is the name of the Java compiler. If you have typed the program correctly, you will just be returned to the command prompt, which means that the program compiled without errors. The compiler will produce a binary file from the source file (called a bytecode or class file) with the name HelloApp.class. This is the file that will be loaded into the Internet browser. However, before moving to the next step, the problem of compiler errors needs to be addressed.

Java, like all programming languages, has strict rules about how instructions are written (the rules are called the language syntax). The fact that typing instructions in the wrong case will cause compiler errors has already been mentioned, and many other typing errors will cause compiler errors. If you do make a mistake – for example, if you omitted the semicolon (;) at the end of the line g.drawString("Hello World", 20, 20) – then you will see an error message as shown in Figure 5.5.

If this happens, go back to Notepad and correct the error. Re-save the file, then return to the command prompt and try again. You can leave the file open in Notepad while you do this, but you must remember to save it each time you modify it.

Before the HelloApp program can be run, an HTML file must be created which will load the HelloApp.class file into an Internet browser. HTML is the language in which simple web pages are created. Writing HTML code is a subject in itself, so only a very simple HTML file will be created here which simply contains a reference to the applet class file. The HTML file can be typed in Notepad in much the same way as the Java source file was, and saved with the '.html' file extension. It must be saved in the same C:\J2sdk1.4.1\bin folder as the Java files. The HTML code is:

```
<html>
<body>
<applet code="HelloApp.class"
width=150 height=100>
</applet>
</body>
</html>
```

This line refers to the applet <applet code="HelloApp.class" width=150 height=100> and it simply tells the browser to load the HelloApp.class file into a window that is 150 pixels in width and 100 pixels in height. There are two ways in which you can now run the applet. The simplest method is to use the appletviewer program that comes with the Sun Java toolkit. At the command prompt (in the C:\j2sdk1.4.1\bin folder), type:

```
appletviewer hello.html
```

Press **Enter** and the applet will run in its own window, as shown in Figure 5.6.

FIGURE 5.6 *The helloApp running using the appletviewer*

An alternative method is to load the HTML file into an Internet browser. In Internet Explorer, you can simply use the **Open menu** command under the File menu, and browse to the HelloApp.html file.

Now let us have a look at the program code in detail and explain what it does:

1 The first two lines:
```
import java.awt.*;
import java.applet.*;
```
tell the compiler to import code that is part of the Java software that provides the tools and components needed to create Windows programming and for producing applets. The Java AWT (Abstract Windows Toolkit) provides lots of classes and methods that are used in Windows programming, some of which will be introduced in this unit.

2 The next line:
```
public class HelloApp extends Applet
```
defines the class name (HelloApp) and tells the compiler that this program 'extends' (adds to) the Java applet class. This is required when writing a Java applet.

3 The next line:
```
public void paint(Graphics g)
```
defines the one and only method (module) in this program. It might seem strange to split the program into only one method, but this is a special method called 'paint' which is an applet method that is called when the applet is loaded. It can be used to draw various types of graphics, as well as simple text, in the applet window. The paint method is sent an object of the graphics class, which we have simply called 'g'. Some of this might sound a little complex at this stage, but as you see other methods being created you will get used to the format.

4 Then the main body of the program:
```
{
g.drawString("Hello World", 20, 20);
}
```
uses the drawString method (which is part of the AWT) to draw the text "Hello World" at the co-ordinates 20, 20 (horizontal position first, then vertical).

5 Finally the program ends with another closing bracket which makes sure the opening and closing brackets match.

Theory into practice

Modify this program so it prints out the message "This is my first Java program", below the existing message.

Java data types

A variety of data types can be used in Java programs. Those used most often are:

* int – which is used for storing integers (whole numbers such as 4, 8, 245)

* double – which is used for storing real numbers (i.e. with a decimal part, such as 1.5 and 27.543)

* char – which is used for storing characters (such as 'y' and 'a')

* Boolean – which is used for storing a value of true or false

* string – which is used for storing multiple characters (such as 'cat' or 'Mr Jones').

The name and data type are set when a variable is declared in a Java program. The value in the variable can be assigned within the program, or it may come from user input. A variable used to store the score in a computer game might be declared like this:

```
int score;
```

Here, score is the name of the variable and int (integer) is the data type. To assign a value to this variable, the equals sign (known as the assignment operator) is used:

```
score = 0;
```

The following example program shows each of these data types in use:

```
import java.awt.*;
import java.applet.*;

public class dataApp extends Applet
{
  public void paint(Graphics g)
  {
    int myInt = 5;
    double myDouble = 2800.124;
    char myChar = 'a';
    String myString = "Data type
    examples";
    g.drawString(myString, 20, 20);
    g.drawString("Integer = " +
    myInt, 20, 40);
    g.drawString("Double = " +
    myDouble, 20, 60);
    g.drawString("Character = " +
    myChar, 20, 80);
  }
}
```

This program is similar in structure to the first one we wrote. Note that the '+' operator can be used to joins two values together, so the instruction:

```
g.drawString( "Integer="+myInt, 20,
40);
```

joins the String "Integer = " and the value in the myInt variable together, as can be seen when the program runs, shown in Figure 5.7.

The class definition for this program gives it the name dataApp. Therefore the program must be saved as dataApp.java and the capitalisation must be the same. Since it is an applet, and an HTML file must also be created for it, you can use

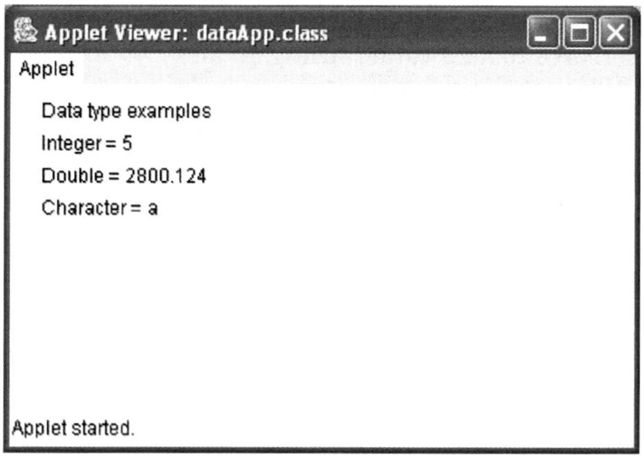

FIGURE 5.7   *The dataApp running*

a copy of the file created for the first program, but you must change the name of the class, as shown below (modified line is highlighted):

```
<html>
<body>
<applet code="dataApp.class"
width=400 height=200>
</applet>
</body>
</html>
```

When you run the program, using the appletviewer, it should look like Figure 5.7.

Boolean variables can only have one of two values true or false. To declare a Boolean variable called myBool and set its state to false you would use the following statement:

```
Boolean myBool = false;
```

The state of a Boolean variable can be set using an assignment statement such as:

```
myBool = true;
```

Boolean variables are often processed using selection structures, which are explained on page 152.

Data structures

So far variables have been used to store a single value each. However, there are situations when it

> ### What does it mean?
>
> An array is a type of variable that can hold multiple values (all of the same data type). The different values held in the array are accessed by their index number.

is useful to have a variable that can store a whole series of related values, using an array.

For example, suppose a program is required that will calculate the average age among a group of six students. The ages of the students could be stored in six integer variables such as:

```
int age1;
int age2;
int age3;
    . . .
```

However, a better solution would be to declare a six-element array, which is done like this:

```
int age[] = new age[6];
```

This creates a six-element array, age[0] through to age[5]. The simple program shown below would calculate the average age:

```
import java.awt.*;
import java.applet.*;
public class arrayApp extends Applet
{
public void paint(Graphics g)
{
  int age[] = new int[6];
  int totalAge;
  double averageAge;
  age[0] = 18;
  age[1] = 19;
  age[2] = 17;
  age[3] = 18;
  age[4] = 16;
  age[5] = 17;
  totalAge = age[0] + age[1] +
  age[2] + age [3] +age[4] + age[5];
  averageAge = totalAge / 6;
  g.drawString("Average age is" +
  averageAge, 20, 20);
}
}
```

The real benefit of arrays is the index number. This identifies the individual elements of the array, and it can be a variable, rather than the fixed numbers used in the example above. However, to process an array using a variable as an index number, you really need a repetition structure (see page 154).

Operators

As well as assigning values to variables, you can also use variables on the right-hand side of an

Theory into practice

Write a program that uses an array to store the predicted daily maximum temperatures over the next five days (you can find these on the BBC weather website through the link at www.heinemann.co.uk/hotlinks). The program should print out each day's predicted temperature and the average over the five day period.

expression. In this case, the value contained in the variable is used. As an example, consider this simple Java program:

```
import java.awt.*;
import java.applet.*;
public class multiplyApp extends Applet
{
  public void paint(Graphics g)
  {
    int x;
    int y;
    x = 2;
    y = x * 4;
    g.drawString(x + "multiplied by
    4 is" + y, 20, 20);
  }
}
```

The asterisk (*) is the Java arithmetical operator for multiplication, so the expression $y = x * 4$ takes the value in x (previously the value of 2 was assigned to x), multiplies it by 2, and places the result in the variable y.

What does it mean?

An expression is a way of writing a mathematical calculation, a type of mathematical shorthand. So an expression such as:

$$y = x * 4$$

means 'take whatever value is contained in the variable x, multiply it by 4, and place the resulting value in the variable y'.

Theory into practice

Modify this program so that as well as multiplying 4 by 2 it also add 10 to the result and prints that out separately.

Java operators

Java, in common with most programming languages, has a full range of arithmetic operators, and parentheses (brackets) can be used to modify the order of mathematical precedence. In Java programs, lines that are comments are preceded by a double slash (//) so that the compiler ignores them.

What does it mean?

Mathematical precedence is the order in which arithmetic operators are evaluated (that is, calculations done). So for example, the formula 4 + 5 * 2, is not completed in left to right order (to give a result of 18), but the multiplication is done first so the result is 14. Multiplication and division are done first, then addition and subtraction next. However, if you include any part of the formula in brackets – such as (4+5)*2 – then whatever is in the brackets is done first. The full set of arithmetic operators are shown in Table 5.3.

JAVA OPERATOR	MEANING
+	addition
-	subtraction
*	multiplication
/	division
%	remainder (modulus)
++	increment
- -	decrement

TABLE 5.3 *Arithmetic operators*

The example program below demonstrates the use of arithmetic operators:

```
import java.awt.*;
import java.applet.*;
public class operatorsApp extends Applet
{
  public void paint(Graphics g)
  {
    int num1 = 10;
    int num2 = 6;
```

```
    int result = 0;
    // Add operator
    result = num1 + num2;
    g.drawString(num1 + "plus" +
    num2 + "is" + result, 20, 20);
    // Subtract operator
    result = num1 - num2;
    g.drawString(num1 + "minus" +
    num2 + "is" + result, 20, 40);
    // Multiply operator
    result = num1 * num2;
    g.drawString(num1 + "times" +
    num2 + "is" + result, 20, 60);
    // Divide operator
    result = num1 / num2;
    g.drawString(num1 + "divided by"
    + num2 + "is" + result, 20, 80);
    // modulus operator
    result = num1 % num2;
    g.drawString(num1 + "modulus" +
    num2 + "is" + result, 20, 100);
    // increment operator
    num1++;
    g.drawString("10 incremented
    is" + num1, 20, 120);
    // decrement operator
    num22 2;
    g.drawString("6 decremented is"
    + num2, 20, 140);
  }
}
```

The output from this program is shown in Figure 5.8.

Most arithmetic operators are self-explanatory. However the modulus and the increment and decrement operators may need some explanation. The modulus (%) operator provides the remainder after division, so:

  10 / 6

gives 1, while

  10 % 6

gives 4.

The increment (++) and decrement (– –) operators allow 1 to be added or subtracted from a variable.

Constants

There are situations when a value that does not change is required within a program. Examples are

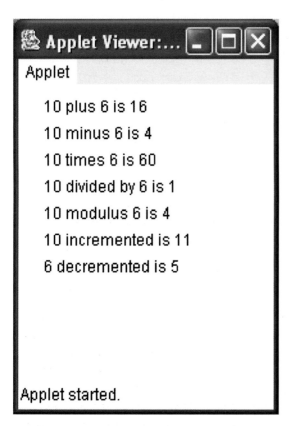

FIGURE 5.8 *Output from the arithmetic operators program*

the mathematical value of pi (about 3.14176) or a conversion between feet and metres. These types of value should be named and declared as constants rather than as variables. Constants are declared in a similar way to variables, except that the keyword final precedes the declaration, like this:

```
final double PI = 3.14176
```

It is a convention in Java that constants are given names in upper-case letters (hence PI). Constants are rather like variables, with one important difference. The value in a constant is set when it is declared and it cannot change. In fact, if you attempt to change the value in a constant you will get an error message when you compile the program.

Dates

There is no data type in Java for dates and times. Instead there is a Date class, which is more complex to use than a simple data type. The date class allows the creation of an object that represents the current date and time. The following statement will create a date object called 'today':

```
Date today = new Date();
```

However, the date is represented as the number of milliseconds since 1 January 1970, so the DateFormat class needs to be used to produce a meaningful date. The getDateInstance method of the DateFormat class is passed two parameters; the format of date required (FULL, LONG, MEDIUM or SHORT), and the locale, which specifies the country specific formatting of the date. For example:

```
DateFormat myFormat =
DateFormat.getDateInstance
(DateFormat.FULL, Locale.UK);
```

This statement will produce a format object, called myFormat, which will provide a full date in UK format. This object is then used to format the date as required, producing a string containing the date:

```
String todayFormatted =
myFormat.format(today);
```

To use the date classes, a number of packages need to be imported. The following program demonstrates how to create, format and display today's date:

```
import java.awt.*;
import java.applet.*;
import java.util.Date;
import java.util.Locale;
import java.text.DateFormat;

public class dateApp extends Applet
{
  public void paint(Graphics g)
  {
    Date today = new Date();

    DateFormat myFormat =
    DateFormat.getDateInstance
    (DateFormat.FULL, Locale.UK);

    String todayFormatted =
    myFormat.format(today);

    g.drawString("Today's date is"
    + todayFormatted, 20, 20);
  }
}
```

The output from this Applet is shown in Figure 5.9.

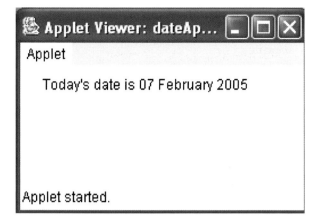

FIGURE 5.9   *The dateApp*

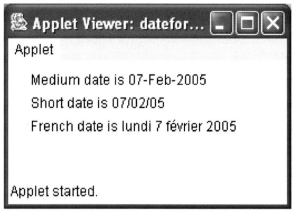

FIGURE 5.10   *The dateformatApp running*

Different date formats and locales can be specified if required, as the example program below demonstrates:

```
import java.awt.*;
import java.applet.*;
import java.util.Date;
import java.util.Locale;
import java.text.DateFormat;

public class dateformatsApp extends
Applet
{
  public void paint(Graphics g)
  {
    Date today = new Date();
    DateFormat myFormat;
    my Format =
    DateFormat.getDateInstance
    (DateFormat.MEDIUM, Locale.UK);
    g.drawString("Medium date is" +
    myFormat.format(today), 20, 20);
    myFormat =
    DateFormat.getDateInstance
    (DateFormat.SHORT, Locale.UK);
    g.drawString(" Short date is" +
    myFormat.format(today), 20, 40);
    myFormat =
    DateFormat.getDateInstance
    (DateFormat.FULL, Locale.FRANCE);
    g.drawString("French date is" +
    myFormat.format(today), 20, 60);
  }
}
```

The output of this program is show in Figure 5.10.

Event handling

The applets we have written so far have been able to output information, but they have not been able to respond to events caused by the user, such as buttons being clicked, keys being pressed or the mouse cursor moving over an object. In Java, events are dealt with by attaching a special class, called ActionListener to the object (such as a button) that will trigger the event. The ActionListener waits for the event (such as the button being clicked) and if it occurs a special method of the class called ActionPerformed is called. The code to deal with the event is placed in the ActionPerformed method. The following applet demonstrates how this works. It introduces an number of new things. Window objects such as buttons are created and then, using a special method called init, () are added to the applet window. Objects that are going to respond to events must have an ActionListener added and have code written to deal with the event in an ActionPerformed method.

```
import java.awt.*;
import java.applet.*;
import java.awt.event.*;

public class eventApp extends
Applet implements ActionListener
{
  private Button clickButton = new
  Button(" Click me");
  String Message = "Waiting for
  event";
  public void init()
```

```
{
this.add(clickButton);
clickButton.addActionListener
(this);
 }

public void paint(Graphics g)
{
g.drawString(Message, 20, 20);
}

public void
ActionPerformed(ActionEvent e)
{
   Message = "Event has happened!";
   repaint();
}
}
}
```

This program now has three methods, which is rather more than the programs we have written so far. Both the init() method and the paint() method are called when the program first runs. Windows components such as buttons must be added to the window in which the applet is displayed using the init() method, while, as we have seen before, the paint method can be used to add text. The ActionPerformed method is only called if the button is clicked, and in this program it simply changes the text of the message and uses the repaint() method to call the Paint method again, so the new message is displayed.

Keyboard events

As well as responding to mouse click events, Java programs can also respond to keys on the keyboard being pressed. The technique for doing this is similar to the one described above for the mouse click events. However, it is slightly more complex since Java requires that three event handlers are provided rather that the one required for mouse clicks. They are:

* keyTyped – this handler deals with any of the character or numeric keys being pressed

* keyPressed – this handler deals with function and other non character keys

* keyReleased – this handler is called when the user releases the key.

The following simple program demonstrates how these handlers can be used:

```
import java.awt.*;
import java.applet.*;
import java.awt.event.*;

public class keyApp extends Applet
implements KeyListener
{
   String Message = "Waiting for event";
   private TextField myText = new
   TextField(10);

   public void init()
   {
     this.add(myText);
     myText.addKeyListener(this);
   }

   public void paint(Graphics g)
   {
   g.drawString(Message, 20, 20);
   }

   public void keyTyped(KeyEvent e)
   {
     Message = "Key pressed was" +
     e.getKeyChar();
     repaint();
   }
   public void keyPressed(KeyEvent e)
   {
     Message = "Function key pressed!";
     repaint();
   }
   public void keyReleased(KeyEvent e)
   {}
}
```

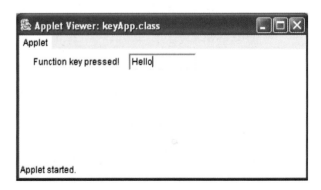

FIGURE 5.11   *The keyApp running*

When this program is run, and you press a character key, the message will tell you what key has been pressed, as shown in Figure 5.11.

Mouse event

Just as keyboard events can trigger program events, so can mouse events. As you might imagine, there is a mouse listener interface which can be programmed in a similar way to the keyboard and event listeners. This is called the MouseMotionListener and it has two methods:

* mouseMoved – this event occurs when the mouse is moved

* mouseDragged – this event occurs when the mouse is moved with the left button pressed (dragged).

The simple program shown below displays the x and y co-ordinates of the mouse pointer while it is in the applet window. It uses the getX() and getY() methods to find the co-ordinates of the pointer.

```
public class mouseApp extends Applet
implements MouseMotionListener
{
   String Message1 = "Mouse not
   inside applet window";
   String Message2 = " " ;
   String Message3 = " " ;

   public void init()
   {
     addMouseMotionListener(this);
   }

   public void paint(Graphics g)
   {
     g.drawString(Message1, 20, 20);
     g.drawString(Message2, 20, 35);
     g.drawString(Message3, 20, 50);
   }

    public void mouseMoved(MouseEvent e)
   {
     Message1 = "Mouse X position
     is" + e.getX();
     Message2 = "Mouse Y position
     is" + e.getY();
     Message3 = "Mouse Moved" ;
```

```
     repaint();
   }
   public void mouseDragged(MouseEvent e)
   {
     Message1 = "Mouse X position
     is" + e.getX();
     Message2 = "Mouse Y position
     is" + e.getY();
     Message3 = "Mouse Dragged";
     repaint();
   }
}
```

Knowing where the mouse pointer is within the applet window is useful in a number of situations. In many games, for example, the player has to click on a particular area of the screen to make things happen.

Windows® components (objects)

A number of Windows® objects have already be introduced, such as buttons and text boxes, but there are a number of other useful objects. Many Windows® programs use dialogue boxes to display messages and collect input from the user. A dialogue box is a type of window that pops up on the screen and must be dismissed (often by pressing an OK or Cancel button on the dialogue) before the program continues. However, you cannot use dialogue boxes with a Java applet, so we shall use one of the many add on components included with the Java language to write a Java application, which unlike an applet, does not run within a web page. The add on component we will use is called the 'Swing' component and we will just use one class of that component which is called the JoptionPane. This class has a number of methods which display various types of dialogue boxes.

We will write a very simple program that will display an input dialogue box into which the user will type their name, and then when they press the OK button on the dialogue box, another message (output only) dialogue box will be displayed which will says "Hello" and then the name that was entered. The code for this program is shown below:

```
import javax.swing.JOptionPane;
class myDialog
```

```
{
  public static void main (String[]
  args)
  {
  String myReply;
  myReply =
  JOptionPane.showInputDialog("Ente
  r your name");
  JOptionPane.showMessageDialog
  (null, "Hello" + myReply);
  System.exit(0);
  }
}
```

Note that the structure of this application is a little different from an applet. The class definition:

class myDialog

is much simpler, it does not start with the keyword 'public' and the 'extends Applet' is also omitted. Rather than paint() and init() methods, applications have a main() method. This program is compiled in the same way as the Java applets we have previously written, using the DOS based Javac compiler. However, since it is a Java application, not an applet, no HTML file is need to display the program. Simply type, at the Command Prompt:

java myDialog

and the input dialog box will appear on your screen, as shown in Figure 5.12.

FIGURE 5.12   *The myDialog program running*

As you can see, the Swing components are quite powerful in that they do a lot of work for you. You do not need to create text boxes or buttons for example, they are all created as part of the showInputDialog method, and you do not need to add an action listener to process the button clicks. If you type your name into the text box and click OK, the message dialogue appears, as shown in Figure 5.13.

FIGURE 5.13   *The message dialog*

Control structures

The Java programming instructions we have looked at so far are executed in sequence one after another. As mentioned earlier, sections of a program which are executed like this are known as sequence structures. The way the selection and repetition control structures are created is now explained.

Selection

Selection structures are needed when programs need to make choices and take different courses of action. For example, many computer games allow the player to choose different levels of difficulty. Based on the user's choice of level, the program then selects a different speed to run at, or introduces more obstacles, or whatever, depending on the type of game. In Java (as in many programming languages), selection is achieved using the if instruction. The instruction takes this form:

```
if (condition)
{
instructions to be followed if
condition is true
}
```

The condition is some kind of test which can have a true or false outcome (known as a Boolean condition). So, for example, in the computer game mentioned above, if the user's choice of level was held in an integer variable called level, then the 'if' instruction might look like this:

```
if (level == 1)
{
instructions to be followed if
condition is true
}
```

The instructions within the curly braces are executed only if the condition is true. If the condition is false, then the instructions within the braces are not executed and the next instruction to be executed is the next one after the ending curly brace.-

Note that the Java operator meaning 'equal to' is two equals signs (==). This is because a single equals sign works as an assignment operator, so 'level = 1' would set the value in the variable level to 1, rather than comparing the value in the variable with 1. The instruction:

```
if (level = 1)
```

will result in a compiler error.

The following simple program demonstrates the use of the 'if' statement. It simulates the tossing of a coin using a random number:

```
import javax.swing.JOptionPane;
class heads
{
public static void main(String args[])
  {
  int coin;
  coin = (int)(2 * Math.random());
  if (coin == 1)
    {
    JOptionPane.showMessageDialog
    (null, "Heads!" );
    }
  if (coin == 0)
    {
    JOptionPane.showMessageDialog
    (null, "Tails!" );
    }
  System.exit(0);
  }
}
```

Random numbers are produced using the random method of the Maths class. This is a built-in (library) class that comes as part of the Java language. The random method produces a random number greater than or equal to 0 and less than 1. Multiplying it by 2 produces a number less than 2. Placing (int) in front of the expression rounds this value to an integer with a value of 0 or 1. The 'if' statement tests the value and if it is a 1 it displays "Heads!", if it is a 0 it displays "Tails!".

In the way the 'if' instruction has been used so far, there is no specific action taken if the condition is false. In contrast, the 'if ... else' instruction is used when some action is required, also if the condition is false. Such an instruction is preceded by the 'else' instruction, as follows:

```
if (condition)
{
instructions to be followed if
condition is true
}
else
{
instructions to be followed if
condition is false
}
```

The next example program demonstrates the use of the 'if . . . else' instruction. This program is similar to the previous one in that it uses the random method. This time it simulates rolling two dice. Since dice are numbered 1 to 6, the value produced by the random method is multiplied by 6 (giving a value between 0 and less than 6). It then has 1 added to it and is converted to an integer, to give a value between 1 and 6.

```
import javax.swing.JOptionPane;
class dice
{
public static void main(String
args[])
  {
  int dice1;
  int dice2;
  String doubles;
  dice1 = 1 + (int)(6 * Math.random());
  dice2 = 1 + (int)(6 * Math.random());
  if (dice1 == dice2)
    {
    doubles = "You rolled a double";
    }
  else
    {
    doubles = "No doubles";
    }
  JOptionPane.showMessageDialog
  (null, "Dice 1 rolled" + dice1 +
  "\n" + "Dice 2 rolled" + dice2 +
  "\n" + doubles);
```

```
    System.exit(0);
    }
}
```

An 'if' statement is used to identify if a double is thrown, in which case a suitable message is displayed. In all other situations (covered by the 'else' statement) the 'no doubles' message is displayed. The message has "\n" included in it to start a new line. You may have to run the program quite a few times before you get doubles.

Write a simple program that will ask a user to enter their gender (M for male or F for female). Use a selection structure to validate their entry and display an error message if they enter anything other than M or F.

Repetition

Often, when writing programs, a block of instructions needs to be repeated a certain number of times or until some condition is met. All programming languages have a number of loop instructions that are used to repeat a block of instructions, and Java is no exception. The first one to investigate is the 'for' loop. A 'for' loop is used to repeat a block of code a certain number of times.

Consider a program that would display the six-times table (that is, 1 * 6 = 6, 2 * 6 = 12 and so on up to 12 * 6 = 72). Such a program could be written using individual instructions, like this:

```
    answer = 6 * 1;
  g.drawString("6 times 1 is" +
  answer, 20, 10);   answer = 6 * 2;
  g.drawString("6 times 1 is" +
  answer, 20, 20);


    . . .

g.drawString("6 times 12 is"+answer,
20, 120);
```

However, it would be much more efficient and require less code to use a 'for' loop. A 'for' loop has a counter, which is an integer variable that keeps track of how many times the loop has been executed.

At the start of the 'for' loop, the counter is used in three conditions, like this:

```
    for (start_condition;
    while_condition; action
    condition)
```

The start condition sets the initial value of the counter, usually 0 or 1. The while condition is used to control when the loop ends, since the loop continues only while this condition is true. The action condition controls how the counter is changed each time around the loop (normally by having 1 added to it). So, for the times-table program, the for instruction would look like this:

```
    for (i = 1; i <= 12, i ++)
```

The loop counter used here is an integer variable called i, which traditionally is the name given to 'for' loop counters. The action condition 'i++' is Java shorthand for 'i = i + 1'. The complete program is:

```
    import javax.swing.JOptionPane;
      class times
{
  public static void main(String args[])
    {
    int i;
    int answer;
    String message;
    message = "6 times table \n" ;
    for (i=1; i <=12; i++)
    {
      answer = i * 6;
      message = message + "6 times"
      + i + "is" + answer + "\n" ;
    }
    JOptionPane.showMessageDialog
    (null, message);
     System.exit(0);
    }
}
```

Note that the loop counter variable can be used within the code of the loop, although the value of the loop counter must not be changed.

The 'while' loop

In some situations, a loop is required which, rather than looping for a fixed number of times (as the 'for' loop does), continues until some condition is met. In these situations, a 'while' loop is used – the loop continues while some condition is true.

The example program below uses a 'while' loop to calculate the sum of the integers of a number that the user enters. For example, if the user enters 6, the sum of the integers is 1+2+3+4+5+6 = 21

```
    import javax.swing.JOptionPane;
class whileExample
{
  public static void main (String[]
  args)
  {
  String myReply;
  int value;
  int i = 1;
  int sum = 0;
  myReply =
  JOptionPane.showInputDialog
  ("Enter a number and click OK");
  value = Integer.parseInt(myReply);
  while (i <= value)
  {
    sum = sum + i;
    i++;
  }
  JOptionPane.showMessageDialog
  (null, "Sum of the integers is"
  + sum);
  System.exit(0);
  }
}
```

This program contains an instruction we have not seen before:

```
    value = Integer.parseInt(myReply);
```

The entries users make into input boxes (and text boxes used in applets) are String values. However in order to calculate the sum of the integers, this must be converted into a integer value. The parseInt method of the Integer class carries out this conversion and places the result in an integer variable called 'value'.

The 'do...while' loop

The third type of loop, the do...while loop, is similar in many ways to the 'while' loop. However, one important difference is that the loop condition is tested at the end of the loop rather than at the beginning. This means that the loop is always executed at least once.

The previous program can easily be modified to use a 'do…while' loop, which would look like this:

```
  do
  {
    sum = sum + i;
    i++;
  } while (i <= value);
```

Note that with a 'do...while' loop a semicolon follows the loop condition, unlike in the while loop.

More GUI components

There are many other GUI components: check boxes and options buttons, for example, can be used for user input with the choices the user makes processed using 'if...else' control structures. You can write Java applications which use the swing components and have action listeners to process the results of clicking buttons. However, they are rather more complicated to write; action listeners are easier to implement in applets. You must therefore remember to create HTML files to display these applets and use the web browser to run the applets.

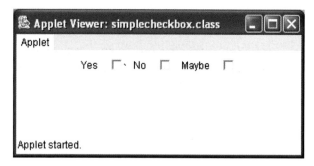
FIGURE 5.14 *The checkbox applet*

Check boxes

Check boxes allow a user to select various options. Clicking the check box with the mouse places a tick in the box, indicating that the option has been selected. The first program to demonstrate how check boxes can be used simply places a series of check boxes in the applet window. The processing of the user's selection will be explained later. The code of the program, which creates three check boxes, labelled 'Yes', 'No' and 'Maybe' – is:

```
    import java.awt.*;
import java.applet.*;
public class checkbox extends Applet
{
 private Label LabelYes = new
 Label("Yes" );
 private Checkbox CheckYes = new
 Checkbox ();
 private Label LabelNo = new
 Label("No");
 private Checkbox CheckNo = new
 Checkbox ();
 private Label LabelMaybe = new
 Label("Maybe");
 private Checkbox CheckMaybe = new
 Checkbox ();
 public void init()
 {
 this.add(LabelYes);
 this.add(CheckYes);
 this.add(LabelNo);
 this.add(CheckNo);
 this.add(LabelMaybe);
 this.add(CheckMaybe);
 }
}
```

Check box objects are created and added to the applet window in the same way as the other components looked at so far. With a similar HTML file to that used previously, this applet will appear as shown in Figure 5.14 when it is run.

Radio buttons

You will find that, if you try clicking the check boxes, you can select any combination of the boxes. This may suit some applications, but others may require that only one of the check boxes can be selected at a time. These types of check box are sometimes called radio buttons. To create radio buttons, they must be assigned to a group. The example program, modified to create radio buttons, is shown and explained below, with the modified lines highlighted:

```
    import java.awt.*;
 import java.applet.*;
 public class checkbox extends
 Applet
 {
 private Label LabelYes = new
 Label("Yes");
 private Checkbox CheckYes = new
 Checkbox ();
 private Label LabelNo = new
 Label("No");
 private Checkbox CheckNo = new
 Checkbox ();
 private Label LabelMaybe = new
 Label("Maybe");
 private Checkbox CheckMaybe = new
 Checkbox ();
 private CheckboxGroup decision =
 new CheckboxGroup();
```

```
public void init()
{
CheckYes.setCheckboxGroup(decision);
CheckNo.setCheckboxGroup(decision);
CheckMaybe.setCheckboxGroup(decision);
this.add(LabelYes);
this.add(CheckYes);
this.add(LabelNo);
this.add(CheckNo);
this.add(LabelMaybe);
this.add(CheckMaybe);

   }
}
```

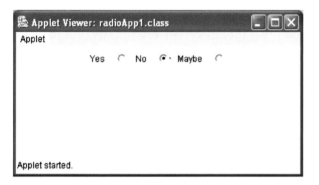

FIGURE 5.15   *The modified checkbox applet*

The applet is shown running in Figure 5.15. Note that the shape of the check boxes is different (circular rather that square) when they are part of a group.

Processing the user's check box selection is done using an ActionListener, as previously explained.

What does it mean?

An ActionListener is a section of code that deals with an event such as the program user clicking a button, or in this case making a selection from a check box.

The code for the modified program is shown below. A text box has been added to show the choice made, and a button to trigger the event. The lines that have been added are shown inbold:

```
import java.awt.*;
 import java.applet.*;
```

```
import java.awt.event.*;
public class checkbox extends
Applet implements ActionListener
{
private Label theLabel = new
Label("You choose");
private TextField choice = new
TextField(5);
private Label LabelYes = new
Label(" Yes");
private Checkbox CheckYes = new
Checkbox ();
private Label LabelNo = new
Label("No");
private Checkbox CheckNo = new
Checkbox ();
private Label LabelMaybe = new
Label("Maybe");
private Checkbox CheckMaybe = new
Checkbox ();
private CheckboxGroup decision =
new CheckboxGroup();
private Button okButton = new
Button ("OK" );

public void init()
{
CheckYes.setCheckboxGroup(decision);
CheckNo.setCheckboxGroup (decision);
CheckMaybe.setCheckboxGroup
(decision);
this.add(theLabel);
this.add(choice);
this.add(LabelYes);
this.add(CheckYes);
this.add(LabelNo);
this.add(CheckNo);
this.add(LabelMaybe);
this.add(CheckMaybe);
this.add(okButton);
okButton.addActionListener(this);
}

 public void ActionPerformed
 (ActionEvent makeChoice)
{
if (CheckYes.getState() == true)
  {
  choice.setText("Yes");
```

```
            }
        else if(CheckNo.getState() == true)
            {
            choice.setText("No");
            }
        else if(CheckMaybe.getState() ==
        true)
            {
            choice.setText("Maybe");
            }
        }
    }
```

The check boxes are tested using the getstate() method. This will return a value of 'true' if the check box has been selected, or 'false' if not selected. The applet is shown running in Figure 5.16. The user must first click one of the check boxes and then click the **OK** button, which will then display the option chosen in the text box.

The getstate() method is one of the methods of the check box class. It returns a value of 'true' if the check box has been clicked by the user, and 'false' if it has not. It can therefore be used within an 'if...else' construct in the ActionListener section of the program to identify which check box has been clicked.

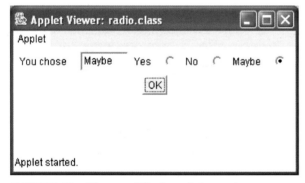

FIGURE 5.16 *The modified applet running*

Software development

Developing a new piece of software from scratch is a complex and time-consuming process. Once your initial design is complete you will start work on writing the code for the various classes in the programs you are developing. It will probably take you several attempts to get each class to compile without errors, and of course, just because the program compiles successfully does not mean it will work correctly. It is likely that you will need to modify and recompile the program several times before you are happy with the result. You may also find that your original design was not correct and you need to go back and modify it if your system ends up working a different way.

Program development can therefore be a frustrating task and you may need help from your teacher or other students. You may find it easier to develop your programs in an incremental way. That is, start off with a simple version of the program you have in mind, get that working correctly, and then add more and more functionality, getting each new feature or group of features to work before moving on to the next. It is wise to keep separate versions of your program as you develop them; that way, if things go wrong or you want to try a different approach to a problem you can always return to a previous version. The best way to do this is to include version numbers in the names of your programs, so if your program is called 'myProg', you should save the first version in a file called myProgV1.java then subsequent versions in myProgV2.java, and so on. Remember that the name given in the class definition at the start of the program must match the filename you save the file in. You must also create backup copies of your programs on floppy disk or other removable media to protect your work in case of system failure. However, your programs must be located in the c:\j2sdk1.4.1 folder or a sub-folder to compile and run them.

We will look at two programs which bring together the techniques described in the previous sections.

CASE STUDY: FOREIGN CURRENCY CONVERTER

The first program is an example of how a reusable class can be created and used. It was mentioned earlier that Java did not have a data type for currency. What if we wanted to write a program which displayed numbers as currency with two digits after the decimal point? One way to deal with this problem would be to write a class that would format numbers in this way. The class we will write is reusable because we can use it in any program that needs to display numbers that always have two digits after the decimal.

First we will write a Java applet that demonstrates the problem of not having a currency data type. This program is a foreign currency converter. For simplicity it only converts from pounds sterling to US dollars or Euros. The applet is shown in Figure 5.17.

FIGURE 5.17 *The foreign currency conversion applet*

The code for the applet is shown below:

```
import java.awt.*;
import java.applet.*;
import java.awt.event.*;
public class convertApp
```

```
extends Applet implements
ActionListener
{
 private Label title = new
 Label("Currency Converter -
 Enter £");
 private TextField moneyIn =
 new TextField(6);
 private Button
 convertButton = new
 Button("Convert");
 private Label euroLabel =
 new Label("Euros");
 private Checkbox checkEuro
 = new Checkbox();
 private Label dollarLabel =
 new Label("US dollars");
 private Checkbox checkUS =
 new Checkbox();
 private CheckboxGroup
 choice = new
 CheckboxGroup();
 String Message = "Enter
 amount and click button";

 public void init()
 {
 this.add(title);
 this.add(moneyIn);
 checkEuro.setCheckboxGroup(
 choice);
 checkUS.setCheckboxGroup
 (choice);
 this.add(euroLabel);
 this.add(checkEuro);
 this.add(dollarLabel);
 this.add(checkUS);
 this.add(convertButton);
 convertButton.addAction
 Listener (this);
 }

 public void paint(Graphics g)
 {
  g.drawString(Message, 20,
  80);
 }
```

(continued)

```
public void
ActionPerformed(ActionEvent e)
  {
    double currencyIn;
    double converted;
    double rate = 0;
    char symbol = '$';
    if (checkUS.getState() ==
    true)
    {
      rate = 1.8;
    }
    if (checkEuro.getState() ==
    true)
    {
      rate = 1.43;
      symbol = '€';
      }
    currencyIn =
    Double.parseDouble(moneyIn.
    getText());
    converted = currencyIn * rate;
    Message = "That is" +
    symbol + converted;

    repaint();
  }
}
```

FIGURE 5.18 *Result with many digits after the decimal point*

This program will work correctly, but because the converted foreign currency amount is held in a variable called 'converted' which has a data type of double, when displayed you get a variable amount of digits after the decimal point, which looks rather odd (Figure 5.18)

To resolve this problem we will write a separate class that has a single method that will format currency amounts for us. The

code to do this could of course be added to the applet we have just written, but then the code would not be reusable. Everywhere we needed to format currency values we would need to add the same code. Duplicating code in this way is problem once in the class, and the five programs would not need to be changed.

How will this currency format class work? We need to develop a design for the class, as the task it will do is actually quite complex. The class needs to search through the number from the leftmost digit looking for the decimal point. When it finds the decimal point the class then needs to either insert the next two digits to the right of the decimal point, or if there is only one digit to the right of the decimal point it needs to insert this and add a zero. This is shown in Figure 5.19.

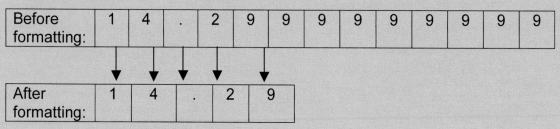

FIGURE 5.19 *Formatting the number*

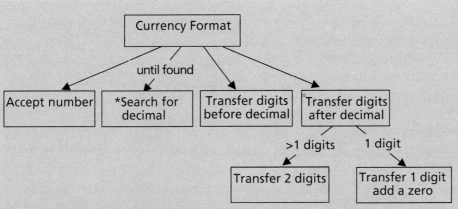

FIGURE 5.20 *Structure chart*

This can also be represented using a structure diagram. A repetition structure is needed to search through the number for the decimal point, then a selection structure to add the digits after the decimal point. A double value will always have one digit after the decimal point, even if it is a zero. In the situation where there is only one digit after the decimal point, another zero needs to be added, since the currency format always has two digits after the decimal. The structure chart is shown in Figure 5.20.

A more detailed design can now be created for the required structures using structured English. The structured English for the 'find decimal point' process is as follows:

```
Number is the unformatted
double value passed to the
program
For(i=0, i=number(length))
(
  if(number.digit(i) = "."
  (
  end loop
  )
)
```

The structured English for the transfer digits before and after the decimal point processes is:

```
fnumber is the formatted
number that is returned
  number is the unformatted
  double value passed to the
  program
```

```
fnumber = number(up to the
decimal point)
If (number(length) > i+2)
(
  fnumber = fnumber + number(2
  digits after the decimal)
)
else
(
  fnumber = fnumber + number(1
  digit after the decimal)
  fnumber = fnumber + 0
)
```

Having completed the design we are now ready to write the code. The class we will write will be passed the number to be formatted as a value with the data type double. The easiest way to inspect and manipulate the individual digits of a number is to convert it to a string. This is because the string class comes with a lot of built in methods as part of the Java language. The two methods of the string class that we will be using are:

* length() – this returns the length of the string. We need to know the length of the string which contains the number to be formatted so the loop which searches for the decimal point will loop the correct number of times.

(continued)

substring(int, int) – this selects a portion of the string (a substring). This method is passed two integers which indicate the starting point of the substring and the character after the ending point. For example, to extract the substring 'gram' from the string 'programming' you would use substring(3, 6). Note that the characters of the string are counted from zero. We need the substring method to allow us to inspect and manipulate the individual digits of the number.

The completed code of the class (currencyFormat) and its single method (doFormat) is shown below:

```
    class currencyFormat
{

  public String doFormat(double
  theValue)
  {
  String uString = "" + theValue;
  String fString;
  String partString;
  // find the decimal point
  int i;
  for (i = 0; i 
uString.length(); i++)
  {
    partString =
uString.substring(i, i+1);
    if (partString.equals("." ))
    {
      // decimal point found
      break;
    }
  }
  // copy digits left of decimal
point
  fString = uString.substring(0, i);
```

```
if (uString.length() > i + 2)
{
  fString = fString +
  uString.substring(i, i + 3);
}
if (uString.length() == i + 2)
{
  fString = fString +
  uString.substring(i, i + 2);
  fString = fString + "0";
}
return fString;
}
```

Although this class is quite complex, most of the concepts included in it have already been introduced. The break instruction, however, has not. It allows a 'for' loop to be prematurely ended if some condition is met, in this case that condition is the decimal point has been found. When the 'for' loop ends the loop counter tells us how many times the loop has been repeated, which in turn tells us the character position of the decimal point.

Having written our reusable class to format values as currency, we can now modify the foreign currency converter program so it uses the class. The modified code is shown below, with the changes highlighted in bold:

```
import java.awt.*;
import java.applet.*;
import java.awt.event.*;
public class convertApp2
extends Applet implements
ActionListener
  {
private Label title = new
Label("Currency Converter -
Enter £");
private TextField moneyIn =
new TextField(6);
```

```
private Button convertButton = new
Button("Convert");

    private Label euroLabel = new
    Label("Euros");
    private Checkbox checkEuro =
    new Checkbox();
    private Label dollarLabel = new
    Label("US dollars");
    private Checkbox checkUS = new
    Checkbox();
    private CheckboxGroup choice =
    new CheckboxGroup();
    String Message = "Enter amount
    and click button";
    currencyFormat myFormat = new
    currencyFormat();

    public void init()
    {
    this.add(title);
    this.add(moneyIn);

    checkEuro.setCheckboxGroup
    (choice);
checkUS.setCheckboxGroup(choice);
    this.add(euroLabel);
    this.add(checkEuro);
    this.add(dollarLabel);
    this.add(checkUS);
    this.add(convertButton);
convertButton.addActionListener(this);
    }
    public void paint(Graphics g)
    {
       g.drawString(Message, 20, 80);
    }

    public void
ActionPerformed(ActionEvent e)
    {
       double currencyIn;
       double converted;
       double rate = 0;
       char symbol = '$';
       String displayValue;
```

```
       if (checkUS.getState() == true)
       {
          rate = 1.8;
       }
       if (checkEuro.getState() ==
       true)
       {
          rate = 1.43;
          symbol = '†';
       }
       currencyIn =
       Double.parseDouble(moneyIn.
       getText());
       converted = currencyIn * rate;
       displayValue =
       myFormat.doFormat (converted);
       Message = "That is" +
       symbol + displayValue;
    repaint();
    }
}
```

This new version of the program will now display the foreign currency amounts correctly formatted, as shown in Figure 5.21.

FIGURE 5.21   *The modified program working*

CASE STUDY: COLLEGE SYSTEM

This second example program is an implementation of part of the College system described in the section on design. In that section a class called student was identified, which had two methods, add and retrieve. For simplicity only the student's name, age and gender will be recorded by the system. It is also worth mentioning that in a real college system these details would need saving in a database file. However, this is beyond the scope of this unit so the details are only held temporarily in the computer's memory, using an array, and are therefore lost when the program terminates.

The class diagram, showing both the attributes and the methods is shown in Figure 5.22. A ten-element array is used to store the student details, which limits our college to only ten students. We could of course use a much larger array, but in this simple example program, ten will be more than adequate.

This class diagram is slightly more detailed than the ones we have drawn before. The data type of each attribute is shown, and for each method, the data type of the parameters which must be passed to the method are shown in brackets after the method name, and the return value data type is shown after that. You should also refer back to structure diagram shown in Figure 5.1 and the pseudo code. As well as the two methods, the class includes a constructor that simply sets the number of students in the college to zero.

Student
StudentName : String[10] Age : int[10] Gender : String[10] NoOfStudents : int
enrol(String, int, String) :int retrieve(String) :String

FIGURE 5.22 *Class diagram for the student class*

What does it mean?

A constructor is a special method of a class which caries out initialisation tasks when an object is created. A class does not have to have a constructor; the currency format class created previously did not have one as no initialisation tasks were needed.

The code for the complete class is shown below:

```
    class Student
{
  // the attributes
  private String studentName[] =
  new String[10];
  private int age[] = new int[10];
  private String gender[] = new
  String[10];
  private int noOfStudents;
  // the constructor
  public Student()
  {
    noOfStudents = 0;
  }

  // enroll method
  public int enroll(String
  nameIn, int ageIn, String
  genderIn)
  {
    noOfStudents ++;
    if (noOfStudents < 11)
    {
      studentName[noOfStudents]
      = nameIn;
      age[noOfStudents] = ageIn;
```

```
        gender[noOfStudents] = genderIn;
    }
    return noOfStudents;
}
//retrieve method
public String retrieve(String
nameIn)
{
    int i;
    boolean found = false;
    String rString;
    for (i=1; i<=noOfStudents; i++)
    {
    if (studentName[i].equals
    (nameIn))
    {
    found = true;
    break;
    }
    }
    if (found)
      {
      rString = "ID no:";
      rString = rString + i;
      rString = rString + "Age:";
      rString = rString + age[i];
      rString = rString + Gender:";
      rString = rString + gender[i];
      }
    else
        {
        rString = "Not found";
        }
    return rString;
}

}
```

As with the previous example program, this class is not a stand alone program – its methods are available to provide services to other programs, but it does nothing on its own. The benefit of writing program this way only becomes evident when writing a much larger software system, when the modular functions (methods) provided by this class can be reused whenever required by the other modules in the system.

To demonstrate that this class and its methods work, we therefore need to write a program which will test them out. The example shown below does just that. For simplicity this program uses the JoptionPane class to provide input and output. This gives the program a rather basic user interface, a much neater one could be provided by creating an applet, but this would require a rather more complex program:

```
    import javax.swing.
    JOptionPane;
  class StudentTester
  {
    public static void main
    (String[] args)
    {
    String sName;
    String sGender;
    int sAge = 21;
    int IDnumber;
    String sDetails;
    String reply;
    Student myCollege = new Student();
    do
    {
      reply = JOptionPane.show
      InputDialog("Enter A to add
      or F to find");
      if (reply.equals("A"))
      {
      // add student
      sName = JOptionPane.show
      InputDialog("Enter student
      name");
      sGender = JOptionPane.show
      InputDialog("Enter gender"
      );
      sAge = Integer.parseInt
      (JOptionPane.showInput
      Dialog("Enter age" ));
      IDnumber = myCollege.enroll
      (sName, sAge, sGender);
JOptionPane.showMessageDialog(nul
l, "ID no is" + IDnumber); (continued)
```

```
        }
        if (reply.equals("F"))
        {
        // find student
        sName = JOptionPane.showInput
        Dialog("Enter student name");
        sDetails = myCollege.retrieve
        (sName);
        JOptionPane.showMessage
        Dialog(null, "Details are:
        \n" + sDetails);
        }
        reply = JOptionPane.showInput
        Dialog("Enter C to continue");
    }
    while (reply.equals("C"));
    System.exit(0);
    }
}
```

This program uses a 'while' loop to continue running unless the user chooses to exit. It offers the user two options, add or find a student. If add is chosen the program requests the student details, then uses the enrol method to add the student, and responds with the student ID number. If find is chosen the user enters the student name and the retrieve method is used to attempt to find a match.

This program has a number of limitations; for example, it does not test to see if too many students have been enrolled (remember the class only caters for ten students). However, code has been kept to a minimum for simplicity and further features could be easily added.

Theory into practice

Students in this college can only be aged 16 to 25. Add the validation required to reject students who are older or younger than this. You could also include the code you created earlier to validate the gender.

5.2 Documentation

Technical documentation describes the purpose of the program you have written, and how it works. It is not created for the users of the program – its purpose is to assist those who will need to maintain and update it. Once a program is in use, problems may occur with it that were not identified when it was tested, or it may need to be updated or improved perhaps by adding additional features. Whether it is the program's original writer or someone else who will make these changes, they will need to refer to the program's technical documentation to understand how it was written.

If the programs are written well in the first place, using meaningful variable names and detailed comments for example, certain aspects will be self-documenting. Also, if the programs follow the design closely, then the design documents can be used to understand the working of the program. It is considered good practice to include comments in the actual code which explain what it does.

The sections included in the technical documentation for each program within a complete system should include:

* details of what the program should do – this should come form the original design specification

* a description of the program structure – this should also come from the design and should include the class diagrams and pseudo-code or other design diagrams

* a list of all variables and constants used, their names, data types and purpose

* a listing of the program – this should include comments that explain what each part of the

program does, and it should be indented to aid readability. The comments and indents should, of course, be added when the program is written.

* testing documentation – this is described in the next section

* notes – these should include details of any unusual or complex features the program has, what operating system and version it has been written for and what version of the software development environment it has been developed using.

It is important to remember that the documentation should not just simply be a collection of papers and documents. It needs to be made into a single coherent document, with a table of contents, page numbers, a glossary and preferably an index. It should be properly presented with a document structure that includes consistent formatting of headings, titles and subtitles. It should also be spell checked and proof read.

> **Think it over...**
>
> How would user documentation differ from technical documentation?

5.3 Testing programs

Testing is an important, if often unpopular part of the software development process. The users of the software would not be very impressed if the program produced the wrong answers, nor would they be happy if the program kept crashing while they were using it. Testing is the process of checking that all the functions of the program work as they should and give the correct results. The definition of terms like 'work as they should' and 'correct results' needs to come from the original program specification that was agreed by the users and the developers before the program was written.

It is worth mentioning that the person who wrote the program is probably not the best person to test the program. The programmer tends to be too 'gentle' or 'forgiving' with his or her creation!

It is much better to get someone else to test the program, as they are likely to do a more thorough job.

As well as checking that the program works correctly when used correctly, the software developer also needs to check that the program is robust and can withstand being used incorrectly without crashing. The reason why this is important is because the users of the program are unlikely to be computer experts, they may misunderstand how the program is supposed to be used. They may also make mistakes when using the program, pressing keys or clicking buttons in error or making inappropriate entries in a text box (a text entry, for example, rather than numeric). Making sure a program works properly may sound like a fairly simple task, but software testing, except for the very simplest of programs, is a complex and involved task which requires planning.

Testing a program is often split into data testing and event testing. Data testing involves checking that the program can deal correctly with the data that is input by the user and produces the correct output. Event testing involves checking that all the different options, such as buttons and menu options produce the expected results.

> **Think it over...**
>
> Why do so many commercial programs have errors or bugs in them? Is it just that they haven't been tested properly?

Data testing

The first step in data testing is to produce some test data. This involves choosing some input values and then manually working out what output the program should produce with these chosen inputs (the expected outputs). The program is then run using these input values and the expected outputs are compared with the actual ones the program produces. If there is a difference between the expected outputs and the actual outputs then the program has failed the test and will need to be modified so that the actual and expected values match.

Date:		System:		Type of tests:	
Tested by:		Version:			

TEST NO:	INPUT FIELD	DATA INPUT	EXPECTED RESULT	ACTUAL RESULT

TABLE 5.4 *Example test log*

The choice of input values is important. A range of values needs to be chosen in each of the following categories:

* Normal values – what would normally be expected as an input value.

* Extreme values – unusually large or small values. The specification should state the maximum and minimum acceptable values in a numeric input filed. In the case of a text value they might be a very large number of characters or very small. For example, in a text box where someone's name is to be entered, two extreme values might be 'Ng' and 'Fotherington-Thomas'.

* Abnormal values – incorrect entries. For example, 32/10/02 for a date, 205 for someone's age or a text value where a numeric one is expected.

The results of testing a program are normally recorded using a document called a test log. This is created before the testing begins and lists the test data that will be input and the results that are expected. An example text log is shown in Table 5.4.

Once the test log has been created and the test data listed, it is used as input to test the program. The results of each test are recorded on the test log. If the expected outcome and the actual outcome match then the program has passed the test, but if they differ then the program has not passed the test and an error log should be completed. An error log is a report which describes all of the situations where the program did not pass the test. This is passed back to the programmer to investigate and correct the problems. Once this has been done the program should be tested again. You might imagine that when the program has been corrected and is to be retested only those tests that failed need to be done again. However, it is possible that the programmer, in correcting the faults identified in the first set of tests has inadvertently introduced other faults. Therefore, to be sure the program works properly, the complete set of tests should be done again.

Event testing

Event testing involves testing that the program responds correctly to events such as mouse clicks on buttons and the selection of menu options. These can simply be tested by making a list of all the events that the program is supposed to respond to, and describing what the correct responses to those events are. Once the list is made, each event on the list can be tried on the program and the actual results compared with

CASE STUDY: TESTING THE CURRENCY CONVERTER.

To illustrate the process of testing a program we shall develop a test plan for the currency converter program created earlier.

TEST LOG

Date:	8/2/05	System:	Currency Converter	Type of tests:	Event
Tested by:	Alan Jarvis	Version:	1		

TEST NO:	EVENT	EXPECTED RESULT	ACTUAL RESULT
Normal tests			
1	Click Euro box, enter £ value and click Convert button	Converts amount to Euro	same
2	Click Dollar box, enter £ value and click Convert button	Converts amount to Dollars	same
Abnormal tests			
3	Neither the Euro or the Dollar box are clicked. Enter £ value and click the Convert button	Displays error message	Shows result as $0.00

TABLE 5.5 *Event test plan*

what is supposed to happen. As with data testing this list should be written up into a test plan, with columns for the expected and actual outcomes. Event tests should fall into two categories:

* Normal tests – valid selections or combinations of actions.
* Abnormal tests – invalid selection of actions which should be rejected.

The process of testing using an event testing test plan is the same as with data testing. In some cases, especially if the program is a fairly simple one, the process of data and event testing may be combined into one, with input data and user events shown on the same form.

Event testing this program is fairly simple since there are only three events it can respond to:

* Click the Euro button
* Click the Dollar button
* Click the convert button.

The various combinations provide two normal tests and one abnormal, as shown in the test plan in Table 5.5.

It can be seen from the results of these tests that the abnormal test, which involved selecting neither the Euro nor the Dollar button, produced a result which did not match the expected result. Instead of displaying an error message telling the user they needed to select one of the options, the program displayed a result of $0.00. This is an example of where the programmer has failed to add an input validation code which would check that at least one of the buttons is selected.

Data testing for the program is a little more complex, as we need to select data in each of the three categories, normal, extreme and abnormal. Table 5.6 shows an example data test plan.

The conversion rates of 1.43 for the Euro and 1.8 for the dollar are used to manually calculate the expected outcomes, and then the inputs are used with the actual program. You might wonder how the input values for each type of test are chosen. For the normal tests, the inputs are just typical values chosen at random. For the extreme values an assumption has been made that the original specification for the program stated that acceptable input for the sterling (British £) amount is in the range £0 to £500,000.

The test plan shows some differences between expected and actual outcomes.

* All the tests in the abnormal section have expected and actual outcomes that do not match. Once again this shows that the program does not validate inputs correctly, and does not produce user-friendly error messages.

* The first test in the normal section also shows a difference, with the expected outcome worked out on a calculator to be 7.15, but the program producing 7.14. This is something of a surprise since the other results are correct. This highlights a problem with way the format currency class works. When it converts a number with a variable number of digits after the decimal point to a value with only two digits after the decimal point, it simply truncates (cuts off) the extra digits. What it should do is round them, so if the third digit after the decimal is 5 or higher, it should increase the second digit by one.

5.4 Evaluation

Having completed your assignment(s) for this unit you will need to evaluate the program(s) you have created (the finished product) and the development process that you went through.

When evaluating the development process you need to consider the following:

* How accurately did you plan the development process? You should have drawn up a project plan with identified deadlines for all the major steps in the development process. Were your timescales realistic? Did you keep to your deadlines, and if not, why?

* How closely does the finished product match the original design? If you needed to change your design, why was this?

* Did you have access to the resources (such as hardware and software) you needed?

* How much assistance did you need to get your program working? What areas caused particular problems and how did you overcome them?

* If you need to complete a similar development process again, what would you do differently?

When evaluating the program you have produced, you need to consider:

* How well does the program you have produced match the stated client needs?

* How thoroughly has the program been tested and how confident are you that it is free from any bugs?

* Has the program been evaluated or tested by anyone other than yourself? Getting other people to evaluate or test your program is a excellent way to evaluate your program.

* What are the strengths and weaknesses of the finished product? How would you improve it if you had more time? How does it compare with commercial products?

You will need to:

* create a complete design for the system. This should include appropriate designs for the processing required (for example, structure diagrams and structured English), designs for the data, including validation, and screen designs.

* produce a working program

* test the program, with appropriate test plans for event and data tests. Correct any problems that your testing identifies

TEST LOG

Date:	8/2/05	System:	Currency Converter	Type of tests:	Data
Tested by:	Alan Jarvis	Version:	1		

TEST NO:	INPUT FIELD	DATA INPUT	EXPECTED RESULT	ACTUAL RESULT
Normal tests				
1	Enter £	5, € selected	€7.15	€7.14
2	Enter £	25, € selected	€35.75	€35.75
3	Enter £	83, € selected	€118.69	€118.69
4	Enter £	4, $ selected	$7.20	$7.20
5	Enter £	17, $ selected	$30.60	$30.60
6	Enter £	128, $ selected	$230.40	$230.40
Extreme tests				
7	Enter £	0, € selected	€0.00	€0.00
8	Enter £	0, € selected	$0.00	$0.00
9	Enter £	500000, € selected	€715000.00	€715000.00
10	Enter £	500000, $ selected	$900000.00	$900000.00
Abnormal tests				
11	Enter £	ten,€ selected	Error message	No response, error code shown in command window
12	Enter £	five, $ selected	Error message	No response, error code shown in command window
13	Enter £	-5, € selected	Error message	€-7.14
14	Enter £	-13, $ selected	Error message	$-23.40
15	Enter £	null, € selected	Error message	No response, error code shown in command window
16	Enter £	null, $ selected	Error message	No response, error code shown in command window

TABLE 5.6 *Data test plan*

* write technical documentation for the program that you have developed

* write an evaluation of the development process and the program you have produced.

You will also need to demonstrate that you have followed standard ways of working and that you have considered the implications of ergonomics and health and safety in the design of the user interface. You must also write a statement considering the legal implications of using software in relation to copyright law, the Data Protection Act and the Computer Misuse Act.

5.5 Quality of written communication

When completing your assignment for this unit, there may be a temptation to just hand in a lot of program print outs, screen shots, test plans etc. However, you will need to bring all the evidence of the tasks you have performed as part of this unit together in a single coherent document. The document should explain what you have done and what the evidence you have collected shows. This needs to be written to a professional standard and structured properly with sections, headings and sub headings, page numbers and a table of contents. You may find it easier to include some of your evidence (such as program print outs and test plans) as appendices at the back of your document, which are referred to within the main text. Remember that your document must be written properly using appropriate language, with correct grammar and spelling.

UNIT 6

Computer artwork

Introduction

Computer artwork can be created using ICT, and work done by designers, illustrators, newspaper artists and draughtspeople often involves skilled use of vector-based and bit map painting software. This unit will help you to learn and develop these skills – and to create and edit artwork using ICT tools. It will also help you to improve your skills in manipulating computer-based images.

This unit focuses on the need to understand the commercial requirements of a client whose requirements are to be met. It looks, in particular, into how you might research a client brief, plan a response and produce a quality solution.

What you need to learn

By the time you have completed this unit, you should have achieved these learning outcomes:

* Be able to use vector-based drawing software.
* Be able to use bitmap painting software.
* Understand the hardware and software requirements for creating computer artwork.
* Be able to develop and edit images using ICT tools.
* Be able to create printed output.
* Know how to develop and edit images.

Resource toolkit

To complete this unit, you need these essential resources:

* access to appropriate computer hardware and software, including graphics software
* access to the Internet
* wide range of information sources, such as books, IT trade journals and newspapers
* contacts working within the graphics industry: designers, illustrators, newspaper artists and draughtspersons.

How you will be assessed

This unit is internally assessed and externally moderated. There are four assessment objectives:

AO1   Practical capability in applying ICT

AO2   Knowledge and understanding of ICT systems and their roles in organisations and society

AO3   Apply knowledge and understanding to produce solutions to ICT problems

AO4   Evaluate ICT solutions and your own performance.

To demonstrate your coverage of these assessment objectives, you will produce a portfolio of evidence, showing what you have learnt and that you can:

* produce a range of samples that show your ability to create both vector and bitmap images using a variety of software packages
* produce a design according to a brief given to you by a client
* include final copies of the artwork as well as evidence of the development of the artwork
* provide evidence to show that you gave due consideration to your client's needs, that initial ideas were presented to the client and feedback was gathered
* evaluate your finished artwork and your own performance. This will offer you the

opportunity to demonstrate that you have used a style of writing which is appropriate for the portfolio produced, and will provide evidence of the quality of your written evidence. (See page 209 for more details of the requirement to show evidence of quality of written communication.)

You are also expected to adopt standard ways of working so as to manage your work effectively, and show evidence of this. Standard ways of working is covered separately in the preliminary pages of this book.

How high can you aim?

The presentation of your portfolio is important. You should aim to present your work in a format that would be acceptable in industry.

For this particular unit, how you present your artwork, and show the development process will determine the maximum number of marks that you earn (Table 6.1).

You need to show that you have knowledge and understanding of ICT systems and their roles in organisations and society. In particular, you must ensure that you have followed your client's brief (Table 6.2).

In line with your client's brief, you will apply knowledge and understanding to produce solutions to ICT problems, and you will produce outline sketches and ideas for approval (Table 6.3).

Having produced your artworks, you will evaluate them and your own performance in producing the solution for your client (Table 6.4).

So, in working thorough this unit, remember that the maximum number of marks that you can earn – and hence your grade – will depend on how well you match your client's brief, how you develop your solution and how you communicate your ideas to your client.

	1–5 MARKS	6–10 MARKS	11–15 MARKS	16–21 MARKS
Produces a series of draft artwork using appropriate software	Yes	Yes; annotated, showing consistency of style	Imaginative range of annotated ideas	Uses a variety of appropriate software
Methods of capturing and developing images			Yes, a variety of methods used	Yes, a variety of methods used
Presentation of ideas to be shown to the client	Limited	Creative presentation	Creative ideas, justified	Creative ideas, justified and fully documented
Final designs using artistic effects	Limited	Includes a variety of different effects	Artwork enhanced by a variety of different effects	Artwork enhanced by a variety of different effects
Meets client's needs	Partially	Yes	Yes	Fully
Uses of a range of file formats when saving computer artwork		Yes	Most appropriate selected to meet memory available	Most appropriate selected to meet memory available; and explained and justified
Standard ways of working	Shows an awareness	Attempted	Demonstrated	Close adherence at all times

TABLE 6.1 *How to present your artwork*

	1–4 MARKS	5–9 MARKS	10–14 MARKS
Background information of the organisation	Attempted	Described	Fully described
Notes following a briefing from the client	Yes		
A description of the task, in context, for which the artwork is to be produced		Yes	Full description
Understanding client needs	Partial	Most described	Described clearly
Software and hardware used to produce the artwork to meet the clients needs	Stated	Justified	Fully justified

TABLE 6.2 *How you have followed your client's brief*

	1–5 MARKS	6–10 MARKS	11–15 MARKS	16–21 MARKS
Design ideas	Outline sketches of the initial design ideas	Annotated designs and sketches	Detailed and annotated	Produced to accurate scale
Agreement with the client		Yes		Justified to client
Planning	Attempted	In detail	Yes, in detail	
Documentation of ideas		In detail		
Changes to be made to the finished artwork to meet client needs	Identified	Annotated	Described	Justified editing
Placement of material in portfolio			Planned	Planned, described and justified

TABLE 6.3 *How you produced solutions to ICT problems*

	1–4 MARKS	5–9 MARKS	10–14 MARKS
Describes actions taken to solve the problem	Briefly	Yes	Yes
Identifies strengths and weaknesses and areas for improvement		Yes	Yes, and makes appropriate changes as a result
Time management or planning	Limited evidence	Some	Strong evidence
Monitors progress		Partially	Fully
Meet deadlines		Some	Yes, reasons explained for any missed deadlines
Evaluation criteria for the solution produced	Some	Yes, some	Yes, appropriate to client needs
Testing carried out	Some	Yes, some	Yes, taking full account of evaluation criteria

TABLE 6.4 *How you evaluated your work*

Ready to start?

In this unit, you will learn and develop the skills and techniques used in the creation and editing of artwork using ICT tools.

You will have an opportunity to improve your skills in manipulating computer-based images. You are expected to understand commercial requirements by working alongside a client whose needs you must meet. You will research a client brief, plan a response, and produce a quality solution.

This unit may be useful if you want to use your artistic skills along with your ICT skills in your career.

This unit should take you about 60 hours to complete. Why not keep a log of your time?

6.1 Vector-based drawing software

In computer artwork, there are two types of images – vector and bitmap – and the two types of software used to create them: drawing and painting.

This chapter considers both drawing software for vector graphics (in this section) and painting software for bitmaps in section 6.2 (page 185).

Your end-product will be an original image to suit your client's needs, but you will need to practise using many drawing software tools before you are ready to create 'final' images for your portfolio.

There are several graphics software packages that you might use, but you may also create images within other software, for example, the drawing tools provided within Word® or Microsoft Draw® embedded within Office® – or use photo manipulation software to edit your bitmap images.

CASE STUDY: GERRY BAPTIST

Gerry is an artist. He draws and paints, using a variety of media: water colour, oil, pen and ink. He uses his computer (an Apple Macintosh with a 21-inch screen) to hold copies of his material and to promote his work through his website. Sometimes he uses his computer and Adobe Illustrator® and Photoshop® to create his art.

Gerry may start with a concept that he wants to express, or he may be working for a commission, for example, to produce something to suit a client. He is skilled in various artistic techniques, such as drawing, and he uses his talents through drawing or painting. He uses colour to create mood, shape and form and pattern to establish an effect. There are three ways that Gerry creates images using his computer.

* He may scan in a sketch from one of his many sketch pads. He places the image in one layer, and freehand draws in another layer. This technique is the modern equivalent of camera obscura – a way of creating an image on a wall using photographic ideas before cameras were invented. The scanned image is effectively a backdrop for a drawing that Gerry creates by tracing edges on screen.

* He may scan in a photo, trace the edges and then print this out to use as a template for an oil painting. The photo captures the detail–for example, the shape, form and perspective of a landscape.

* He may draw directly onscreen and then experiment with colour to create the effect he wants.

Often, Gerry uses a combination of techniques, and his portfolio of work shows a wide range of art: sketches, water colours, oil paintings.

The computer is just a tool, like any other. It helps you to experiment, for example with colour, very quickly. But a computer cannot produce art. The artist has vision and brings to life the line he or she draws. A line created by the computer is flat and dead, so while you may use techniques to help to create an effect, some tools such as edge-finder will kill a painting.

1 Follow the links from www.heinemann.co.ukhotlinks and visit Gerry's website. Compare the abstracts, portrait and figures. Which do you think were based on photos? Which on sketches?
2 Research the Internet to find out more about the technique of camera obscura. How was it used by painters such as 17th century Vermeer?
3 Find out how artists – like Michaelangelo – planned huge painting such as the Sistine chapel before computers were invented. How might a modern day artist use a computer to plan a mural?

Components of a vector image

This section focuses on using drawing software to create vectors graphics; images that are defined by shape and position. Vector images comprise lines, shapes and text.

So, for example, a circle can be defined by the position of the centre, and the length of the radius. A line segment can be defined by its starting point and ending points, or by the starting point, an angle (with some fixed direction) and its length.

Lines

A line can be drawn of a particular style and thickness. There are a variety of pens, pencils and brush tools that you can use to draw the line and, for example, in Adobe Illustrator®, there are four brush types: calligraphic, scatter, art and pattern.

A line is anchored according to where you start drawing, and then you drag the mouse (or other pointing device) to draw the line and create additional anchor points. As you draw, the resulting line is called a path. The path could be a simple straight line, or it could form a closed shape. The line can curve to form an arc, and you can make complex shapes such as a spiral. The path can be reshaped using a variety of tools, and you might erase part of the path. The ends of a line can styled with arrowheads or other shapes.

Shapes

A variety of shapes are available: rectangles, ellipses, polygons, stars, and so on.

The lines that form the shape can be styled as for any line. You can also control the inside of the shape, filling it, or making it see-through.

Text

Text can be used to label an image, and you can control the type (or typeface), and attributes (bold, italic, etc.) of that text. It is also possible to distort the orientation of the characters on a path. This creates an effect similar to that of WordArt (Figure 6.1).

FIGURE 6.1 *WordArt*

Image enhancement

Having drawn an object, you could paint the outline (called its stroke) in a particular colour. You might paint the inside of the shape (called its fill) with a pattern or a gradient. To create the illusion of 3D, you can apply shading, rendering and lighting to vector images. So, a simple shape like a cube can be given a 3D perspective by shading part or all of one side (Figure 6.2).

For more complex 3D shapes, such as a car, rendering involves colouring in an outline sketch to produce a detailed image of a solid object. A single colour would give a very flat effect.

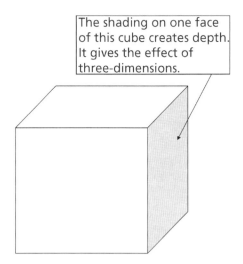

The shading on one face of this cube creates depth. It gives the effect of three-dimensions.

FIGURE 6.2 *Shading to create a 3D effect*

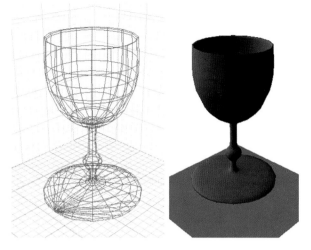

FIGURE 6.3 *Shading to create a realistic image*

There are various methods of determining what colours should be used to fill a shape, to create the 3D effect. One particular type of shading, used in animation and 3D graphics, is called phong shading. This relies on how lighting is reflected from surfaces. Another type of shading is called Gourand shading; this measures the colours and brightness at the vertices of the polygons that make up an object and mix these to determine colour values within the polygons (Figure 6.3).

Within Adobe Illustrator®, there are a number of ways of creating a 3D object:

* A 2D object can be given depth along the third axis by extruding the object (Figure 6.4a).

* A 2D object can be revolved around one axis through 360° to create a 3D object (Figure 6.4b).

You may also need to include a border so that the image is clearly separated from surrounding text.

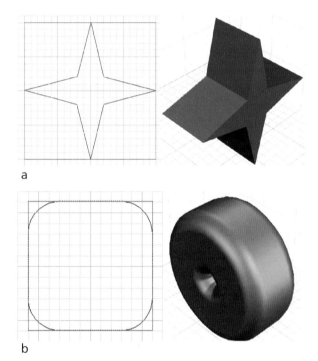

a

b

FIGURE 6.4 *3D objects created from 2D shapes*

Drawing accurately and to scale

Plans to be used to construct something, be it a conservatory or a section of an oil pipe, need to be drawn to scale and accurately. If your drawing needs to be to scale, a number of tools can be used to help you. In Adobe Illustrator®, the default unit of measurement is the point. You can change this to inches or centimetres or millimetres, or to picas.

This unit of measure is then used for rules, measuring the distance between two points, setting grids and guide spacing and creating shapes.

What does it mean?

A point is equal to 0.3528 mm. A pica equals 12 points (or 4.2333 mm)

✱ A control grid appears as lines or dots behind your artwork; it does not appear on the printed output. It therefore acts as a guide, helping you to lay out objects or elements of your drawing symmetrically. Adobe Illustrator® offers two styles of grid (dots or lines) as well as a choice of colours, and of spacing between the major gridlines and subdividing gridlines (Figure 6.5).

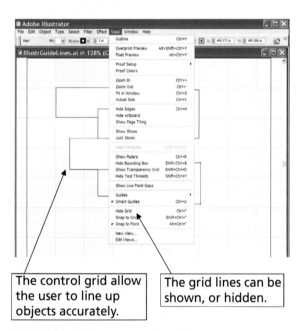

The control grid allow the user to line up objects accurately.

The grid lines can be shown, or hidden.

FIGURE 6.5 *Using a control grid*

✱ A guide is similar to a grid in that it appears on the screen as a help to you. Adobe Illustrator® offers two types of guides. A ruler guide is a straight line created with the ruler which appears horizontally or vertically on screen, and thus helps you to set alignment lines across the length or width of your work area (Figure 6.6). A guide object is created from an object such as a rectangle or any other artwork, and is used to

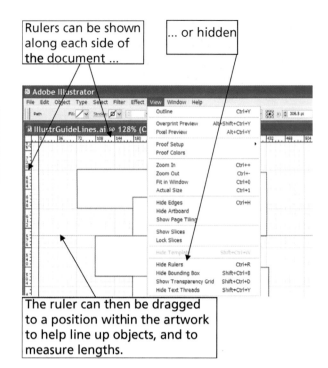

Rulers can be shown along each side of the document ...

... or hidden

The ruler can then be dragged to a position within the artwork to help line up objects, and to measure lengths.

FIGURE 6.6 *Using a guide*

help you to place and create your artwork around one or more objects.

✱ A ruler or some measuring tool allows you to measure the distance between two points on your drawing. Notice that the Info palette (Figure 6.7) displays the horizontal and vertical distances from the x and y axes, the absolute horizontal and vertical distances, the total distances and the angle measured.

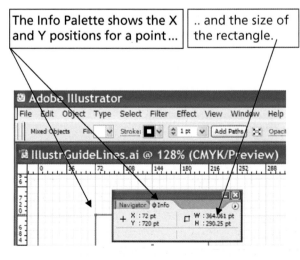

The Info Palette shows the X and Y positions for a point...

.. and the size of the rectangle.

FIGURE 6.7 *The Info palette in Adobe Illustrator®*

✱ When dragging objects into position, the snap and lock tool helps you to align your cursor with anchor points and guide in the document window (Figure 6.8).

A path has a number of anchor points.

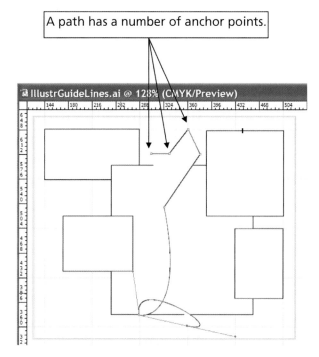

FIGURE 6.8 *Anchor points*

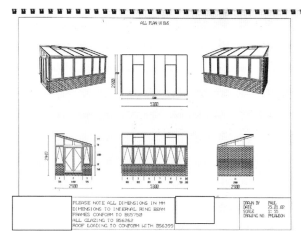

FIGURE 6.9 *Scaling and dimensions*

Theory into practice

1 Create a scale drawing of an everyday household object.

2 Label your image to show what scale and dimensions you have used.

Theory into practice

1 Using drawing software, experiment with setting up grids and guides and using a ruler to create vector images.

2 Change the unit of measurement from the default setting to centimetres and then to millimetres.

Deciding on an appropriate scaling (Figure 6.9) involves measuring the 'real' object, measuring the size of the paper on which the plan is to be printed, and working out what scale will work. Scaling is specified as a ratio such as 1:25. The '1' relates to a length on the plan; the '25' relates to the 'real' object. The dimensions should also be clear. It is important that the reader of a plan know whether the dimensions are in millimetres or centimetres (or whatever), and that you are consistent in your labelling.

Images in 3D

Some drawing software will offer perspective and orthographic projection to show your objects in 3D.

✱ Perspective is an illusion of 3D drawn on a 2D surface caused by the use of a focal point and lines leading to or from that point (Figure 6.10).

✱ Orthographic projection (Figure 6.11) involves looking at a 3D object from three different view points – and these view points are at right angles to each other. In the plans for a house or other buildings, the three views are called plan view (looking from vertically above the object), side view and front view.

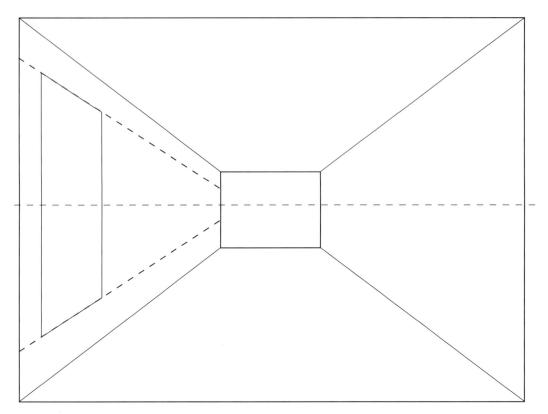

FIGURE 6.10 *Perspective*

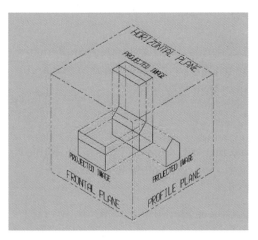

PLAN VIEW	SIDE VIEW	FRONT VIEW

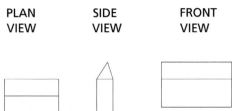

FIGURE 6.11 *Orthographic projections*

Complex shapes

More complex shapes can be formed using Bezier curves and polygons.

* A Bezier curve is a curve defined by four points (called knots): the two end points and two other control points that define a polygon within which the curve lies. A Bezier curve

provides a way of defining a smooth path for a curve as well as the direction of the line at the end points, and all points along the path. Increasing the number of control points effectively blends together curves and, from this, increasingly complex curves can be drawn.

✳ A polygon (see Figure 6.12) is a closed shape with a certain number of sides.

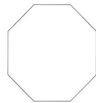

FIGURE 6.12 *Polygons*

✳ You may import images that someone else has already created – or one that you created earlier.

✳ You may utilise object libraries, including clip art, symbols, flow/organisation charts (Figure 6.13).

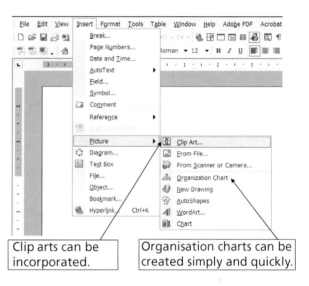

FIGURE 6.13 *Importing images*

Notice that both Bezier curves and polygons involve a finite number of points and then some rule for the path between the points. They can therefore be enlarged and reduced without loss of clarity of the path.

Theory into practice

1 Create an image including at least one Bezier curve and two different polygons.

2 Label your images to show how you created the shapes.

Combining images

In creating an image, you do not need to generate all components of the image from scratch.

Theory into practice

1 Create an image which involves two or three clip arts.

2 Incorporate symbols into a flow chart or organisation chart.

You may also need to rearrange the objects in some way.

✳ If an image comprises lots of separate components, you may need to be able to ungroup them (Figure 6.14) to isolate part of the image and then to regroup objects. The group of object can then be treated as a single object, for example, to reposition on the screen.

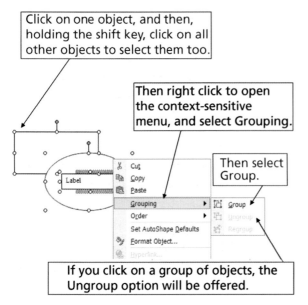

Click on one object, and then, holding the shift key, click on all other objects to select them too.

Then right click to open the context-sensitive menu, and select Grouping.

Then select Group.

If you click on a group of objects, the Ungroup option will be offered.

FIGURE 6.14 *Ungrouping objects and controlling grouped objects*

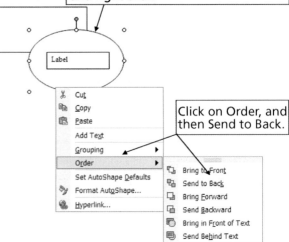

To make one component of an image (e.g. the oval) appear behind another (e.g. the rectangle), select the oval and right click.

Click on Order, and then Send to Back.

FIGURE 6.15 *Reordering objects*

* You may need to bring some objects to front of others (Figure 6.15) or to push objects to back of others, so that you can see what you want to be able to see. This involves controlling the order of objects.

* You may decide to use object overlays. This creates a single image from two disparate images.

Theory into practice

1 Create an image that incorporates a variety of objects showing how positioning of these objects can be controlled by grouping and ordering.

2 Label your image to show the tools that you used.

CASE STUDY

Simon works for a kitchen design company. He creates drawings that are used to order the fittings for a new kitchen, and from which the kitchen fitters will work. At the showroom, a computer aided drawing package is used to create the drawings (Figure 6.16). Simon selects equipment – like a cooker or a base unit – and these are placed on the drawing in the position preferred by the client.

1 **Why might a client be shown many different views of the kitchen plan?**

2 **For your client, produce a vector image using drawing software.**

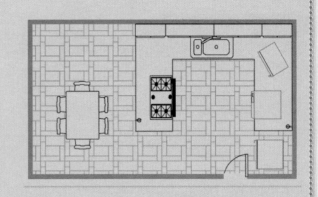

FIGURE 6.16 *Plans for a new kitchen*

1 Explain these terms: vector, bit, bitmap, pixel.

2 Give examples of each of the components of a vector image: line, shape and text.

3 Explain these terms: anchor point, path, arc, spiral.

4 Distinguish between these terms: stroke, fill and render.

5 Explain the effect of extruding and revolving a 2D object.

6 What are points and picas?

7 Explain how you might use a control grid and a ruler guide.

8 What is a snap and lock tool?

9 Explain the different views in an orthographic projection.

10 What is a Bezier curve?

6.2 Bitmap painting software

Bitmap images, sometimes called raster images, are based on pixels. They can be imported from a digital camera, scanned in, or drawn using painting software. Painting software includes packages such as Paint® and Painter®. Paint can used to create simple or elaborate drawings. These drawings can be either black-and-white or colour, and can be saved as bitmap files.

This section looks at the painting tools you need to be able to use to create screen-based images. Like any artist, these include pens or brushes with varying nibs, and a palette of colours.

Image quality

The quality of an image depends on its resolution.

✱ Sourced resolution depends on the resolution used on a camera (see page 197), the resolution used when scanning (see pages 201–202) and the resolution that you set when saving the image.

✱ Resolution is measured in ppi and dpi. When taking a digital photo, or scanning an image, the ppi setting will determine the amount of raw data collected for the image. When viewing or printing images, the resolution is expressed in ppi. If there are too few dots per inch, the gaps between the dots will become visible and the image will look grainy.

What does it mean?

ppi stands for pixels per inch. dpi stands for dots per inch.

✱ The greater the resolution, the better the clarity of the image and the more successfully the image can be enlarged without loss of clarity. However, the greater the resolution, the greater the storage required for the image.

The amount of storage space required for a bitmapped image also depends on the size of the image, and the colour depth.

✱ The size of an image (its dimensions) are its height and width. This can be measured in pixels or as a length, for example, in millimetres.

✱ The colour depth of an image is determined by the number of bits allocated to each pixel.

Colour depth and hence image contrast is determined by the number of tonal values (Figure 6.17) available for each pixel.

✱ If each pixel is allocated one bit, then the pixel can be set to 0 (black) or 1 (white). Your picture would have only two tone levels, and look rather flat.

✱ If each pixel is allocated 8 bits, that is, one Byte, then the light energy on a pixel can be converted into a number in the range 0–255, where 0 represent black (no light) and 255 represents the brightest value. There are then

255 tone levels, and your image will have a more continuous look to it.

✱ If 2 bytes (or 3 bytes) are allocated to each pixel, this will provide even better image quality.

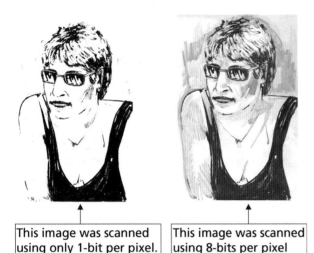

| This image was scanned using only 1-bit per pixel. There is very little detail. | This image was scanned using 8-bits per pixel on a grey scale. |

FIGURE 6.17 *Tonal levels*

Theory into practice

1 Check on the file size of an image. Change the image to greyscale and check the change in file size.

2 Change the dimensions of an image and see the effect that has on the file size.

Image style

A **bitmap** image can be created using text, brush effects and colour fill.

Text

Text is keyed into a text frame (Figure 6.18). You can control the text font (Arial, Times Roman, etc.), the point size (10pt, 12pt, up to 72pt) and attributes such as bold, italic and underline – all under the Text toolbar within Paint.

The colour of the text within a text box is defined by its foreground colour. The background can be set as opaque, and then it is

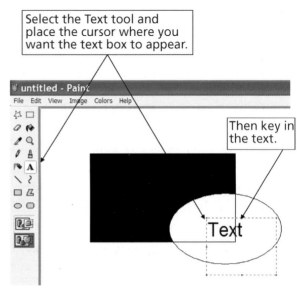

FIGURE 6.18 *Entering text into a text frame within Paint*

defined as the background colour. Alternatively, the background can be transparent. Having clicked away from the text box, the text is converted to a bitmap image, and you cannot then edit it as if it were text. However, you can use the eraser to rub it out!

Brush

In the same way that an artist uses a variety of pencils or pens or brushes, with painting software, the toolbox includes a variety of pens and brushes, and a range of widths and effects (Figure 6.19).

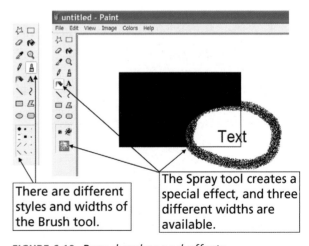

| There are different styles and widths of the Brush tool. | The Spray tool creates a special effect, and three different widths are available. |

FIGURE 6.19 *Pens, brushes and effects*

Fill

If you draw a closed shape, you may want to fill it with colour. If the shape is not closed, beware or the whole image may be flooded with colour. Use the undo option to clear the colour, and check that there are no gaps in the shape's outline.

Image manipulation tools

A bit mapped image can be developed and manipulated, pixel by pixel.

Cut/Copy/Move/Paste

In Paint, there are two tools that allow you to 'cut' a region of an image (Figure 6.20). One creates a rectangular patch; the other allows you to trace a freeform mask for cutting. The pixels that are 'cut' are placed on the clipboard and can then be pasted (copied or moved) to another position on the canvas.

The free form tool lets you trace around a part of your image.

Using the Rectangular cut tool, you can select a rectangular part of an image.

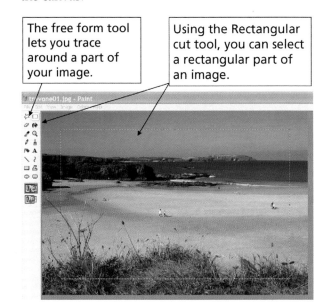

FIGURE 6.20 *Cut, copy and move in Paint*

Crop

Cropping an image involves cutting away slices from any side of the image until you are left with the part of the image that you want to retain.

Figure 6.21 shows a photo taken at Saville Gardens, before and after it has been cropped.

(a)

The cropped version loses the buds which detract from the main bloom – and fixes the less-then-perfect composition of the original photograph.

(b)

A small amount has also been cropped from the left-hand edge to place the image more centrally within the frame.

FIGURE 6.21 *Saville Gardens (a) before the crop (b) after the crop*

Mask

Setting a mask allows you to work on a section of an image, while leaving other parts as they are. The mask is created in one layer and then this is laid across the original image, and will cover it with varying levels of opacity.

What you paint in black will obscure the original image; what is left white will allow the original image to show through. Shades between white and black (the grey shades) will show in various levels of transparency.

You might also use a mask to remove an object, for example from a photo, by drawing a selection around the object. There are a number of tools that will help you to do this, depending on the shape of the object, and the complexity of the outline (Figure 6.22).

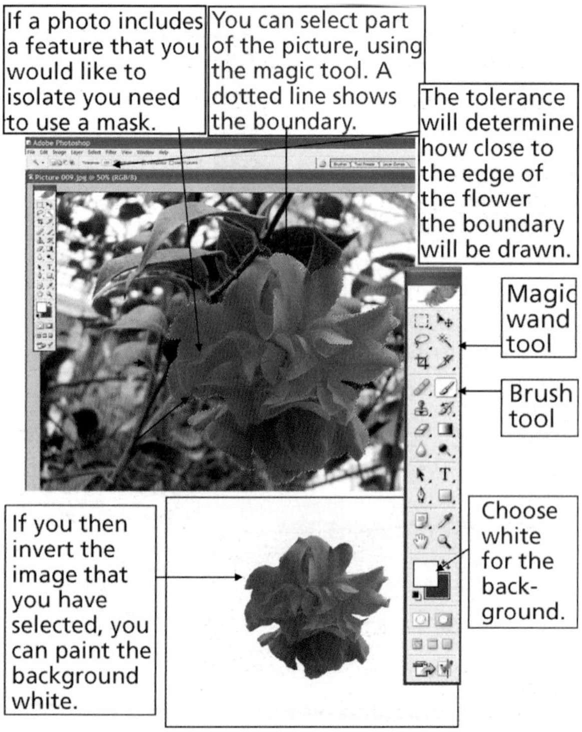

Theory into practice

1 Experiment with the masking tools in your bitmapped painting software.

2 Use a mask to remove unwanted detail from an image.

Drawing lines and shapes

Like drawing software, painting software such as Paint can be used to draw lines and shapes such as polygons. However, the image is saved as a bit mapped file, not as a vector graphic. So, if you were to enlarge an image of a shape created using Paint, its clarity would deteriorate.

Using colour

What is colour? Light is an energy source, comprising rays of different frequencies. In your eye, you have colour sensitive receptors, one sensitive to blue, another to green and another to red. Your brain interprets combinations of these to create any colour in the spectrum (Figure 6.23).

If a photo includes a feature that you would like to isolate you need to use a mask.

You can select part of the picture, using the magic tool. A dotted line shows the boundary.

The tolerance will determine how close to the edge of the flower the boundary will be drawn.

Magic wand tool

Brush tool

Choose white for the background.

If you then invert the image that you have selected, you can paint the background white.

FIGURE 6.22 *Using selection tools to create a mask and isolate part of an image*

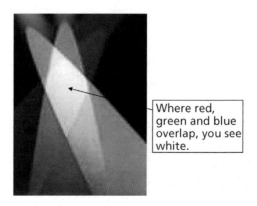

Where red, green and blue overlap, you see white.

FIGURE 6.23 *Combining colours*

The RGB method of adding colours is just one way of interpreting colour: the additive method. This method is used to produce colour on a VDU screen, there are three colour rays and the combination creates the colours you see.

A second method, CMYK (called the subtractive method) uses filters to cut out colours (Figure 6.24). This method is used for printing colour onto paper, the layers are overprinted to create the full colour effect.

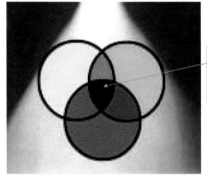

FIGURE 6.24 *Using filters to create colour*

Where the filters overlap, you see black (no light)

The terms hue, tint and saturation are also used to describe colour.

Interesting effects can be created using colour inversion (Figure 6.25). Each colour is replaced by its colour complement. For example, red becomes cyan, and blue becomes yellow.

Making patterns

Having created an image, you could repeat the image to create a pattern, similar to the patterns used for household wallpaper, or curtains. These tessellations may involve a full drop or a half drop of the image. A pattern could be created by tiling a section of an image, and inverting alternate tiles (Figure 6.25).

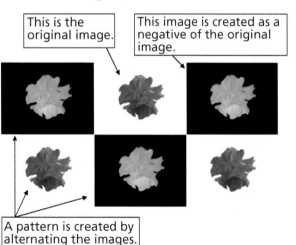

This is the original image.

This image is created as a negative of the original image.

A pattern is created by alternating the images.

FIGURE 6.25 *Colour inversion pattern*

Technical terms

You need to understand some technical terms and know how to apply the techniques they describe appropriately: washing, dithering, pixelation, posterisation, edge-finding and distortion.

Packages such as Paint do not address these techniques so you need more sophisticated software such as PaintshopPro®, Photoshop® or Adobe Illustrator®.

Washing

In the same way that an artist might apply a colour wash to a canvas before starting to add the detail of the picture, graphic software lets you apply a colour wash to an image, before or after you have drawn the rest of the image.

Dithering

Full-colour photos may contain an almost infinite range of colour values. Dithering is a way of reducing the colour range of images down to the 256 colours seen in 8-bit GIF images. Dithering places pixels of different colours or grey levels next to each other to simulate missing colours or greys, those that are not available in the colour display system of a computer. Within PaintshopPro®, three algorithms for the dithering pattern are available: Floyd-Steinberg; Burkes; or Stucki. In Corel Painter®, the Dither Colors option applies a stippled effect to the colours chosen, generating a more accurate, less banded effect. However, it can reduce the effectiveness of the GIF file compression.

Dithering does reduce the overall sharpness of an image, and it can introduce a grainy effect. When displaying images on a web site, using colours outside the browser-safe palette may result in amateur looking images; this is because the browser will automatically dither colours that are not found in the web-safe palette. So, for navigation buttons and other important images, it is best to use browser-safe colours. The browser-safe palette of colours is the selection of colours that Mosaic, Netscape and Internet Explorer use within their browsers. It contains only 216 out of a possible 256 colours, because the remaining 40 colours vary on Macs and PCs. By eliminating the 40 variable colours, this palette is optimised for cross-platform use.

Pixelation

Pixelation describes how a printed image is turned into a digitized image file. As the image is captured, it is processed into a vectorised or rasterised file that comprises many pixels (picture elements). Too low a resolution causes pixelation, or large pixels that produce coarse output (Figure 6.26).

Pixellation distorts the image. This top right section of the image has been mildly pixellated. With larger blocks, it can be used to make someone unrecognisable, e.g. the children of Posh and Becks.

FIGURE 6.26 *Pixelation*

Posterisation

Posterisation involves reducing the colour palette of an image to create an effect. This may be necessary to restrict the all the colours in an image to the 216-colour browser-safe palette. An area of smooth colour transition is rendered as an abrupt colour change; the resultant visual effect is of an abrupt 'step' in the image.

Edge-finding

Within any given image, there are gradients of colour between adjacent pixels. When this gradient is steep (that is, there is a big change in the colours) this would indicate an edge. Painting software offers a tool to find these edges, and to reduce the image to produce an outline of the edges found (Figure 6.27).

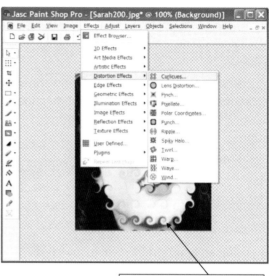

Distortion can create some interesting effects.

FIGURE 6.28 *Distortion effects*

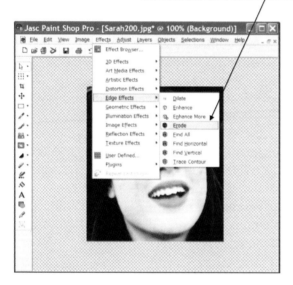

Eroding the edges has the effect of softening a photo.

FIGURE 6.27 *Edge-finding*

The edge created is quite 'flat'; see the case study comments on page 177. However, if this is the effect you are trying to create, this tool can prove useful.

Distortion

You can apply a variety of distortion effects to an image as illustrated in (Figure 6.28).

✱ Painter® offers a Glass Distortion dynamic layer and a Liquid Lens. It also has effects such as Marbling, Blobs and Blur.

✱ PaintshopPro® offers distortion effects such as Punch, Ripple, Wave and Wind.

Theory into practice

1 Experiment with dithering options available for your software. Compare your results with others. Which effect do you prefer?

2 Experiment with distortion effects to create some interesting images, for example, for a calendar.

Knowledge check

1 What is a raster image?

2 Explain these terms: resolution, ppi, dpi.

3 What effect does changing the number of tonal values have?

4 Explain these terms: foreground, background, opaque and transparent.

5 Explain the mechanics and uses of the two colouring systems: RGB and CMYK.

6 Explain these terms: hue, tint, saturation, colour inversion.

7 Explain these terms: washing, dithering, pixilation, posterisation, edge-finding, distortion.

6.3 Software and hardware features

This section focuses on the hardware and software implications of computer artwork, and then looks at the special requirements for some forms of output:

* using different background styles to create an effect
* creating scientific drawings
* producing hand-drawn cartoons
* choosing an appropriate style to match the needs of the audience.

Hardware and software

There are two basic platforms that designers work from: Microsoft or Macintosh. These refer to the operating systems that are installed on the computers, but they also tend to determine the hardware that is purchased.

Processor type and speed

Whichever platform the designer is using, the type and speed of the processor can have an impact – favourable or otherwise – on the work rate. Designers need processors that are as fast as possible, due to the heavy work load imposed by processing images. They also need as much RAM (random access memory) as they can afford.

> **What does it mean?**
>
> RAM stands for random access memory and ROM stands for read only memory

To display graphics on screen takes a lot of processing power. Building a 3D digital image as a wire-frame, and then transforming that into a set of patterns that will display on a 2D screen, rendering it to cover it with surfaces, lighting it from various sources and so on as seen in Figure 6.3 on page 179, requires a lot of mathematical calculations. Most designers will have installed a special graphics

card to take care of much of this processing, leaving the main processor to cope with ordinary tasks like printing out images, or saving and retrieving files from the hard disc drive.

Output devices and drivers

Designers may work on screen but, invariably, will need to print out their work to show to clients. 'Normal' office printers such as an inkjet or laser printer may be fine for printing drafts of some design drawings. Some designers, though, need high-colour and high-resolution printouts requiring either a high-quality colour laser printer or a plotter. A plotter is also necessary when the size of the drawing goes beyond the standard dimensions of A4 or A3 paper, or when producing printed output onto specialist materials, for example, to produce banners or signs.

In most printers, the paper travels through the printer, guided by rollers and past a print area where print heads sweep across the paper, leaving marks on page. With a plotter, the paper may stay still and the pens (there may be several of different colours) draw the image on the page (see Figure 6.29). Commands that drive the pen include PENUP, PENDOWN, turning commands (like RT 90) and drawing commands (like DRAW 500). The paper may lie flat (as in a flatbed plotter) or be wrapped around a drum (in a drum plotter).

FIGURE 6.29 *Plotter*

Storage media devices

Designers generate files of work of their ideas, illustrations and plans. These image files can take up a lot of storage space. Initially, a file may be retained on the hard disc, but to send it to a client, the designer may transfer the file to a portable storage medium like a CD. Image files may also be sent as attachments to emails.

Input devices

To input ideas, designers can choose from a variety of devices, depending on the type of work they are doing.

* To enter commands and make selections within the software, the designer is likely still to use the keyboard and mouse – the 'normal' input devices.

* To capture images that are on paper, a scanner may be used.

* A digital camera may be used to take still photos, and a video camera to take moving pictures with or without an audio track.

Designers who hand draw tend to use a graphics tablet (Figure 6.30) as a way of inputting their ideas.

Applications software

Designers, regardless of the platform (Apple Mac or Windows PCs) can choose from a wide range of software for drawing and painting. Most software manufactures support both platforms, so apart from being careful when choosing which version to download, the designer has a free choice.

FIGURE 6.30 *Graphics tablet*

Special effects

Part of the challenge for a designer is to create an image that looks like a real-life representation of the object. To help the designer, the software offers special effects. This section now looks at some of these special effects and considers how you might recreate them.

Background styles

If a designer is preparing material to appear in a text book, the design brief may require the use of a special background effect.

CASE STUDY

Pauline works as an illustrator. She uses notepads and sketch books for her initial ideas, but then works on her Apple MacIntosh computer to develop her ideas into animations for her clients. To draw, Pauline uses a Wacom tablet as well as a scanner to import drawings that she has already produced on paper. Her printer is an Epson, a colour inkjet printer, and she has a 17 inch screen.

Pauline uses three software applications (Adobe Illustrator®, Photoshop® and Flash®)–often all three on a particular project.

1 What are the benefits of using a tablet as an input device, instead of a mouse, for drawing?
2 What are the benefits of having a 17 inch screen?

* Graphs may need to appear on what looks like graph paper.

* Charts may need to look as if they are written in a book.

* A newspaper article may need to look like it is printed on newspaper.

* A shopping list may need to look handwritten, on a spiral notepad.

Scientific diagrams

Mathematics and science books call for particular levels of accuracy. Not only do the diagrams need to be accurately drawn, the labelling may include special symbols, and the angles and other features marked in an appropriate way.

Cartoons

Cartoons (Figure 6.31) or hand-drawn sketches require artistic talent, plus the appropriate choice of pen, to illustrate a point well.

Matching style to an audience

As with any writing, the designer has to meet the needs of an audience. Material written to appeal to 5-year-olds will (probably!) be very different to that expected to appeal to 50-year-olds. Images, and their presentation, must be chosen to meet the needs of the client (as per the brief), and be targeted at the expected audience as closely as possible.

LIFE GOES ON — by Gerry Baptist

FEW PEOPLE KNOW THAT EARLY ATTEMPTS AT CREATING A RULE BOOK FAILED

FIGURE 6.31 *A cartoon (Source: Gerry Baptist)*

6.4 Working to a commission

Designers, illustrators, newspaper artists and draughtspersons rely on commissions: instructions from a client to produce computer artwork, by a set time and for a set price.

There are some basic steps that a designer will follow, for any particular commission:

* the first step is to negotiate a brief with the client

* having obtained all the details from the client, the designer then needs to check that he or she has all the ICT tools they may need to complete the commission

* from a range of options and ideas, the designer then chooses a suitable solution to meet the needs of the client

* the solution is presented as a portfolio of ideas to the client

* finally, the designer obtains product approval from your client.

It is unlikely that, during your course, you will be commissioned to complete some work for a client. However, in producing your portfolio of work, you will simulate these working conditions.

What tips might a professional designer give to a newcomer to this work? Well, here are some suggestions from the designers who appear in the case studies of this chapter.

* Make sure you find out what the client expects of you before you agree to a price and a deadline.

* Meet the deadline; work that arrives late is of no use to a client.

CASE STUDY: RED EYE

Steve Austin is a designer, working at Red Eye. Red Eye offers a complete print-design-copy service so clients often ask Red Eye to design and print commercial stationery. For example, they were commissioned by The Global Property group to design a logo and layout for a business card, a compliments slip and business letterhead. Global supplied basic information: the full company name, main contact information (full postal address, telephone numbers, website address), names of employees for whom business cards were needed and their individual phone numbers.

Designing logos is a competitive market, so Steve has a minimal budget to produce something that will appeal to the client and win the order for printing the stationery. Time is of the essence.

At college, you learn how to use features of graphics software, but the important skill of speed cannot be taught. You need to be 100 per cent familiar with all the features of the package (and use only the professional packages like Adobe®) and then practise until you can work very quickly. Only then will you be of value to a design company such as Red Eye.

The first step for Steve was to think of an image to match the name of the client, or the products or services that the client provides. One obvious choice would be a globe, showing the land masses of the UK and nearby continents. However, Steve sketched five different ideas to give his client a choice.

Steve then used Adobe illustrator® to draw these images accurately. He chose Illustrator® because the logo will need to be resized for the various formats and clarity will be essential, therefore vector graphics were his best option.

He then developed a panel to fit down the side of a sheet of A4 paper to act as a watermark for the letterheads. Using PhotoShop®, Steve put a copy of the globe logo in a number of layers, each containing the globe image in slightly different sizes and vertical positions, and of different transparencies, to create a busy effect – like bubbles percolating up the side of the page. He worked to size because, with PhotoShop®, the image is stored as a bitmap, and if the size if changed, clarity may be lost. He combined all the layers to create a single image to fit exactly the space required.

Having created his images (the logo and the panel) Steve started to work in Quark®. Quark® is designed for layout to fit precisely sized pages, and for the entry of text. Images should first be created in the appropriate software and then be inserted. Steve can match the colours very precisely so that, for example, the text on a business card is the same colour as the sea on the globe image.

1 For a particular client, create a logo that can be used on business cards and letterheads.
2 Create a watermark, based on a logo, for a letter head, using at least three layers.
3 Create a design for a business card, a compliments slip and a letter head, using prepared artworks and text that you obtain from your client.
4 Annotate your work to show what software you have used, and what tools were used to create any special effects.

* Present alternative ideas. You have more chance that one of your pieces of work will be accepted, and to receive repeat commissions.

* Keep a record of everything you prepare, even the early sketches. You own the copyright and need to keep copies of all your own work.

* Make time to look at other designers' work. Learn from it.

* Keep abreast with technological developments, both in IT and using 'real' materials.

* Keep a positive attitude, especially when presenting your work.

Think it over...

Discuss, with others in your group, ideas for meeting a deadline.

Knowledge check

1 What is a commission?

2 What terms need to be agreed between a client and a designer?

3 What information would a client need to supply to a designer who has been commissioned to design a range of business stationery?

4 Why is it necessary to have deadlines?

6.5 Developing and editing images

Images may be created, as described in sections 6.1 and 6.2, or taken from existing sources. This section looks at how you might capture an image using digital cameras, video cameras and players, scanners and on-line information systems. You then need the skills to develop these images.

Digital cameras

Figure 6.32 shows the general process of taking a digital photo.

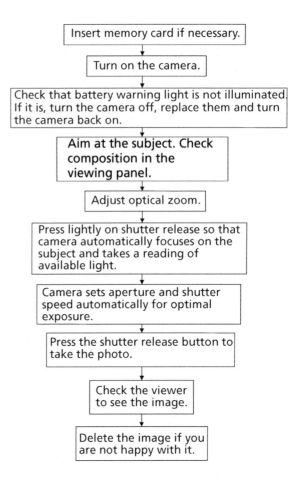

FIGURE 6.32 *The process of taking a digital photograph*

You can make use of the automatic shooting features of a digital camera, or make partial use of them, or decide the settings manually. If you want to use automatic settings, you must select the appropriate mode, and give the camera as much information about your subject as possible.

* You may be offered choices such as portrait, landscape, sorts (for freezing motion in rapidly moving subjects) or night-time.

* You may be offered specific scenarios such as party-time; beach/snow, sunset, dusk/dawn, museum, fireworks, and so on.

Each choice made will result in the automatic settings, for example, for the aperture and shutter speed. These settings are called the default settings.

Selecting flash settings

What time of day is it? What light is available? If there is insufficient light, you may need to use a flash, and your camera may offer a number of flash modes:

✳ the automatic setting will operate the flash whenever there is poor light

✳ an automatic setting may also offer a red-eye correction. This involves a pre-flash, and if there is still evidence of red-eye in the photo, this may be automatically corrected before the shot is stored.

✳ you can set the flash off. You would need this if you want to take the photo in dimly lit conditions to create a particular effect.

✳ you may set the flash on, regardless of the light. This will light up what would have been shadowy areas. Objects that are back-lit will also show clearly.

✳ there may be the option to synchronise the flash with a slow shutter speed. This would result in the detail of shadow areas being visible, as well as lights such as street cars or car lights. This type of shot is best taken with a tripod. Otherwise, any movement of the camera would result in a blur.

Selecting image quality

Sensitivity is a measure of how sensitive the camera is to light. It is given by an ISO number.

✳ With lower ISO, the slower the film, the smaller the grain and the sharper the image, i.e. the softer the contrast. This works particularly well when taking portraits because it is kinder on the face.

✳ An ISO of 400 is fast enough to cope with most light situations. More important perhaps for the beginner, it is also fast enough to reduce the effect of camera shake.

✳ For action shots, you might choose a higher ISO number, for example, 1600, although this may give a more grainy effect.

Image quality settings determine the level of compression prior to storing an image:

✳ Fine image quality will be good for enlargements or high quality prints. The file will be reduced to about 25 per cent of its original size.

✳ Normal image quality if the default setting and is suited to most applications. The file size is about one-eighth of its original size.

✳ Basic image quality is suitable for pictures that will be distributed by e-mail or for use on the Internet. The file size if about one-sixteenth of the original size.

Transferring images from a camera to your computer

There are a number of different ways of transferring the images from your camera to your computer (Figure 6.33).

* You may have a card reader, which has a cable that you can attach to a port on your computer. This is most probably a USB port.

What does it mean?

USB stands for universal serial bus. USB is a higher speed serial connection standard that supports low speed devices such as mice, keyboards and scanners as well as high speed devices such as cameras.

* You may have the option to transfer images using wireless i.e. infrared, technology. For this, your computer needs an infrared port, and you need to set up a link so that it will recognise the material when it arrives.

* You may have a direct cabling link between your camera and the computer.

* You may transfer your images straight from your camera to a printer. However, it will be important that both camera and printer support this method of transfer; one such standard for transfer between a camera and a printer is called PictBridge.

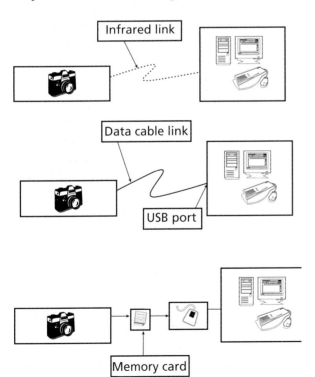

FIGURE 6.33 *Methods of image transfer*

Theory into practice

1 Check out how images are transferred from your camera to your computer.

2 Compare this with different methods used by others in your group.

Video cameras and players

A video camera is similar to a digital camera. However, instead of just taking still shots, a video camera takes moving pictures too, and there is the option to record a sound track as well.

The moving picture is not actually moving, it just looks that way when you view it. Actually, frames are taken every 1/30th of a second, so there are 30 frames per second. Played back to the human eye, this looks continuous.

The operation of a video camera is very similar to a digital camera: point and click the start button, using the LCD screen to see what is being captured. As with taking digital stills, you need to take into account the composition of the images, keeping the subject within frame. However, you also need to allow talking/walking room. If the video is of someone talking, they may look directly at the camera but if they are looking to one side then the frame should allow space where a speech bubble might appear to show what they are saying. Similarly, in an action shot, there must be room in the frame to show where the subject is going.

Choosing suitable lighting is also essential. If you move the video camera slowly the image will not be blurred. Avoid quick movements or you may make the viewer giddy, unless of course that is your intention, for example, if you were showing a bird's eye view of a helter-skelter ride.

There are various ways to move the video camera:

* panning involves moving the video camera in the horizontal place: from left to right or right to left

* tilting involves moving the video camera in the vertical plane – up and down – for example,

focusing on the trunk of a tree and then tilting the camera so you can see the whole tree.

* Zooming, as with a digital camera, appears to bring you closer to the subject. Reverse zoom is when you appear to move away from the subject.

You can also keep the video camera still and zoom in or out, focusing on a particular subject. Or, combine a zoom with a pan. To create an interesting video sequence, you need to vary the type of shots that you take.

* A *close up* is used to home in on the subject, perhaps to show the emotion on the face, or so allow the viewer to study the face.

* A *wide shot* (also called an establishing shot or long shot) shows the whole scene. This might be used to establish the location or the people involved in the film.

* A *medium shot* shows less of the scene, but more than the close up. It acts as an intermediate image, because to jump from a wide shot to a close up would be jarring on the viewer. You may also use this when there are two or three people to include in the shot.

How long you shoot for will depend on the subject matter. If there is lots of action, you may record for up to 20 seconds. However, since your ultimate aim is to produce a film that holds the attention of the audience, unless it is gripping stuff, you might need to present it interspersed with cutaway ('over the shoulder') shots. These are short clips of the presenter or interviewer looking very interested; nodding or shaking the head, smiling or frowning according to what the interviewee is saying. It is called 'over the shoulder' because the cameraman has to be positioned on the shoulder of the interviewee, looking towards the interviewer. You also need to consider using stationary shots (with no movement of the camera) to start and end a sequence, and to use transitions between types of shots.

If you are recording a sound track as well, remember to switch the microphone on. There are several types of microphone:

Theory into practice

1 Watch a video, for example, of a news broadcast. The presenter may be facing the camera, but the viewer's interest may be maintained by shots being taken from more than one camera. Make notes on what types of shots are used: wide, medium and close-up.

2 Look carefully at the shots that are used during an interview. Working with others, create a storyboard to show the sequence of shots used during a two-minute sequence of video.

* The microphone might be built into the video camera, in which case it is closer to you than it is to the subject. So, you need to avoid giving instructions to the subject, otherwise that's what will be recorded.

* A very small portable microphone, powered by a battery pack that can be hidden, might be attached to the clothing of the person who is to speak. This 'lavaliere microphone' is often used by television presenters and their guests.

* Hand-held microphones may be attached to the camera by a long cable, giving flexibility of movement and good quality of sound recording. A hand-held microphone may also be wireless, powered by a battery pack.

* The previous three types of microphone may be omni-directional, meaning that sound is picked up from all directions. Shotgun microphones, by contrast, are designed to pick up sound from a greater distance, and from a limited range so you have to point it at the subject. This type of microphone might be used to record what the referee is saying to a player when he sends him off.

The images may be stored on a video tape (a serial medium) or directly onto a DVD (a direct access medium). The format of the tape is important: it may be 8mm or VHS (240 lines of resolution), SVHS or Hi-8 (400 lines) or Beta (500 lines). The greater the number of lines, the better quality film, but it has to be compatible with the video camera, so having chosen the camera you may be limited as to which type of tape can be used. Video taped images may be viewed on a video player, but not all types of tape can be viewed on all video players; compatibility is an issue here too. DVDs can be viewed on a DVD player, or on your PC.

In the same way that you can edit images taken on your digital camera, the video can be edited. In fact, it is almost essential to edit the video. It is unlikely that the raw footage is exactly what you planned, or that it will be entertaining enough for the intended audience. However, you can delete frames (the outtakes) and reorder the sequence of frames, and splice parts of the video together to create a film sequence in the order you want to show it.

If you recorded onto tape, you will need another tape (a blank one) to copy the frames onto, in the sequence you want them to be shown. You will need a log of what is on the raw tape: a description of the shots and how long they are. From this you can work out the order in which to copy sequences on to the new tape. The editing equipment is attached to two VCRs: one to see the raw footage, the other to see what you have recorded on to the new tape. Then for each tape, you need to mark where you want to start copying, the In (insertion) point, and on the new footage tape where you want to stop the copying, the Out point. When you press 'Edit' the copying process will start, and you continue doing this for each sequence on the raw footage that is to end up on your final film. The bits you don't use are called outtakes.

Digital editing is somewhat simpler. The software provided with the digital video camera allows you to re-sequence the frames and delete frames, so that the final sequence is what you want to show the audience. You can also build a film from a number of sequences by splicing them together.

Theory into practice

1 Experiment with using a video camera to record an event. What features does it have, extra to your digital camera?

2 Shoot a video including sound to introduce one of your friends to the audience. Edit the video and the sound track. Compare your video to others prepared in your group.

Scanners

A scanner can be used to scan documents of text, black and white line drawings, colour photos, slides or transparencies (Figure 6.34).

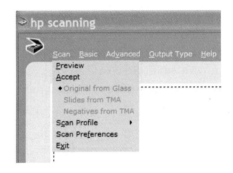

FIGURE 6.34 *Scanning mode*

You will need to attach a scanner (or a combined printer/scanner) to your computer and install any drivers that are supplied with the hardware. You may also be provided with software that will handle the scanning process (Figure 6.35) and may also set preferences as to how the scan is done, balancing quality against the speed of the scan.

FIGURE 6.35 *Software supplied with a printer/scanner*

The hardcopy image is placed face down on the glass window of the scanner. There will be markers on the frame of the window to indicate where to position the hardcopy, possibly with arrows pointing to where the top-left corner of the image should be.

To start the scanning process, you may have several options.

✱ There may be a Scan button on your scanner. This may automatically open the scanning software, or you might open the software manually and click on the Scan option.

✳ You might activate a scanning process through some other software, such as PaintshopPro® or Adobe Photoshop® (Figure 6.36).

FIGURE 6.36 *Photoshop® Quick Guide*

Using scanning preview

The scanning process is time-consuming and it is important to scan only that part of the scan window that interests you. For this reason, there is a Preview option (Figure 6.37).

Notice the narrow areas along the top, left and bottom edges of this photo, shown as white. This is due to careless placement of the photo on the scanner window. You can either reposition the photo and take another preview, or select the scanning area as explained next.

Selecting the scanning area

The scanner scans the whole scan window. It then estimates the border of your image by the areas where there is most colour. In the preview mode, you can reduce the scan area so that the scan, when done for real, only captures the part of the

> If you are happy with the Preview, click on Accept to start the Scan/Save action.

FIGURE 6.37 *Previewing a scanned image*

original hard copy that you want (Figure 6.38). This provides an opportunity to improve the composition (see page 183) of the image, if need be.

> The top (and bottom) may be cropped to tidy up the edges.

> The right-hand edge could be cropped, if you think this improves the balance of the image.

FIGURE 6.38 *Selecting the scanning area*

Selecting the scanning resolution

The resolution chosen (Figure 6.39) determines the number of pixels; the higher the resolution, the greater the number of pixels. This directly affects the storage needs for the image, and ultimately the time it takes to scan the image, how long it will take to upload/download to/from a website and so on.

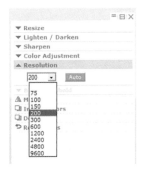

The same image, scanned with resolution settings of 12, 75 and 200.

FIGURE 6.39 *Setting the scan resolution*

Table 6.5 lists the files sizes for various dpi for a given photo size.

EFFECT OF RESOLUTION ON FILE SIZE	
Resolution (dpi)	**File size**
75	342 KB
100	608 KB
150	1.37 MB
200	2.44 MB
300	5.48 MB
600	21.98 MB
1200	87.66 MB
2400	350.66 MB
4800	1.40 GB
9600	5.61 GB

TABLE 6.5 *Effect of resolution on file size*

Theory into practice

1 Preview a scanned image and experiment with different resolutions to see what file size would be needed.

2 Scan one image using three different resolutions, such as 75 dpi, 200 dpi and 300 dpi. Time how log it takes to scan each one.

3 Give your three scanned images different names so you know which is which resolution. View them on screen. Print them out. Can you tell the difference?

Selecting filter options

Your scanning software may offer a variety of features prior to scanning the image. Figure 6.40 shows an option to enhance the colour of an image. Changing the colour to 0 would turn the photo into a greyscale image (shades of grey ranging from white to black).

FIGURE 6.40 *Filter options*

After you have scanned the image, there may be even more options to alter the image before you save it, (Figure 6.41) although you may decide to wait and develop the image within your image editing software.

The scanning software offers tools to improve the image before you save it.

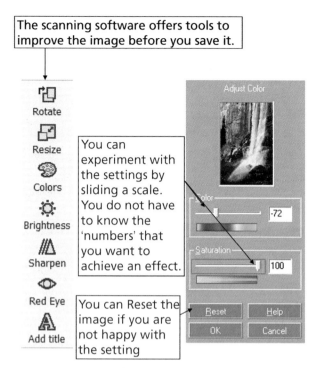

You can experiment with the settings by sliding a scale. You do not have to know the 'numbers' that you want to achieve an effect.

You can Reset the image if you are not happy with the setting

FIGURE 6.41 *Adjusting colour, brightness*

Saving images in an appropriate format

There are lots of different file formats that you might choose to save your scanned image (Figure 6.42).

There are many different file formats to choose from.

FIGURE 6.42 *Choosing a suitable aving in a suitable file format*

Having scanned the photo, if you decide on a JPEG format, you need to select the extent of compression, balancing quality against file size (Figure 6.43).

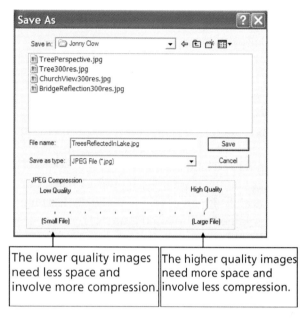

The lower quality images need less space and involve more compression.

The higher quality images need more space and involve less compression.

FIGURE 6.43 *Selecting the JPEG resolution*

On-line information systems

You may consider obtaining images from the Internet. If you do, there are two issues to consider: quality and copyright.

✳ Images that appear on the Internet are rarely free of charge, so you cannot just copy and paste them into your own artwork. However, if you ask, you may be given permission to use an image, and may or may not have to pay a fee.

✱ Images that appear in the Internet will have been sized to fit the available space and compressed to minimise download time. Because of this, the quality may be quite low, and certainly unlikely to withstand any further manipulation. However, if you ask to use an image, the source may offer you a better quality image.

Image development

You need to demonstrate the editing of digital images to modify their appearance. For this, you will need access to software that offers digital editing tools. There are many such software packages on the market. Each product may offer you tutorials or online help to make the learning process smoother for you (Figure 6.44).

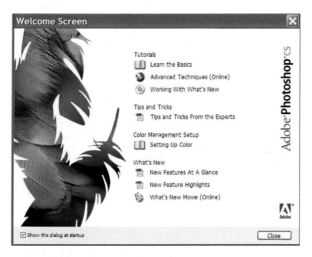

FIGURE 6.44 *Online help available with digital editing tools*

An image exists in a layer. Some editing involves removing some pixels altogether (cropping, see below) and changing the boundaries of the layer. Some editing affects the RGB values of individual pixels. If all pixels are to change in the same way (all become redder or less bright), this may involve creating a second layer, and combining the two layers. You need not worry about the particular RBG values; whatever changes you decide to make, you will be offered a 'before' and 'after' picture, and can therefore experiment with values until you achieve your desired effect.

Sharpening

Sharpen and blur are used to create an effect on the edges in an image. Sharpening improves the clarity of the edges in an image. Blurring has the opposite effect. Figure 6.45 shows examples of images before and after sharpening and Figure 6.46 shows how different types of blurring filter can be used to create an effect.

Blurring can also be created by moving the camera or keeping the camera still while the object moves.

This is the original photo ...

... and this is after a sharpen filter has been applied ...

... and this is after even more sharpening has been applied. Notice the grainy effect and how the background is more evident.

FIGURE 6.45 *Sharpening an image*

This is the original image, and the three other images shown here were created from it.

This is what Adobe Photoshop® calls a Smart blur.

This is what Adobe Photoshop® calls a Radial blur.

This is what Adobe Photoshop® calls a Zoom blur.

FIGURE 6.46 *Using blurring*

Removing scratches and blemishes

If you have an old photo, or one that has been folded or scratched, you could scan it in, and then renovate it by cloning. This technique is also used for removing unwanted content (see page 206).

Your image editing software may offer other techniques and you should explore all options. Image editing software recognizes red eye as a common problem and provides the tools to correct it. Within Adobe Photoshop®, for example, there is a Color Replacement tool (within the Toolbox). You will need to zoom in on an eye so that you can work carefully and accurately. You will also have to choose a brush tip that is small enough, smaller than the width of any area you need to recolour.

Darkening/lightening shadows (dodge/burn)

Within an image, the shadows are the darker areas. Dodge and burn are distortion effects that focus on the shadows and leave the rest of the image unchanged.

✴ Burn makes the darker areas even darker, so they look burnt.

✴ Dodge lightens the darker areas, and brings light to them.

Colour correction (loading)

The human eye sees white as white, regardless of the level of sunlight shining on it, or the effects of shadow. It is the temperature of the light which creates these different colours of white: a warm white being orangey, and a cool white having blue tones. A digital camera records the white balance when a shot is taken, and this is retained as part of the metadata for the image.

What does it mean?

Metadata is data about data. In digital imaging, this includes the date and time of the shot, and all settings used: focus length, shutter speed, aperture setting

You can adjust the white balance and the colour balance for an image, either to correct the unwanted effects of light when the shot was take, or to create an effect. Figure 6.47 shows examples of different colour balances applied as adjustment layers within Adobe Photoshop®.

What does it mean?

An adjustment layer is a layer of pixels the same size as the original image but with some effect applied to the RGB values so that when the two layers are viewed together an adjustment can be seen.

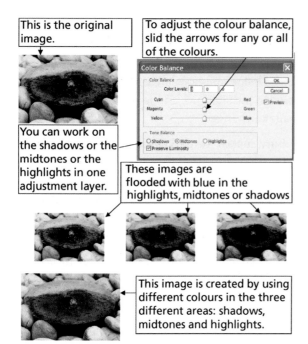

This is the original image.

To adjust the colour balance, slid the arrows for any or all of the colours.

You can work on the shadows or the midtones or the highlights in one adjustment layer.

These images are flooded with blue in the highlights, midtones or shadows

This image is created by using different colours in the three different areas: shadows, midtones and highlights.

FIGURE 6.47 *Adjusting colour balance*

Theory into practice

1 For one image editing software package, follow a tutorial to show you how to adjust colour balance. There may be several ways of doing this. Experiment with them all.

2 Experiment with achieving the same effect in a different image editing software package.

Cropping/layering/filtering

Cropping an image involves cutting away slices from any side of the image until you are left with the part of the image that you want to retain. If the material you want to lose is at the top, bottom, left or right of your image, you could crop to remove it. If the material you want to lose is within the image, then for it to 'disappear' you will need to replace it with something that will not look out of place.

Theory into practice

1 Experiment with cropping in at least two different image editing software packages.

2 Note the similarities in the method, and the things that are different between two packages.

* In Adobe Photoshop®, the Healing Brush tool can be used to touch up spots, scratches and wrinkles on an image.

* In PaintshopPro®, a Scratch Remover tool offers one way to remove scratches, cracks and other defects in an image.

You may need to create a mask, so that only part of the image is affected by the changes you are making. The technique of replacing parts of an image with material copied from elsewhere on an image is called cloning. This can be useful if you want to remove, say a person, from an image, and replace it with what is behind that person. If you have samples of similar background material either side of the person, you can clone that material.

* In Adobe Photoshop®, there is a Clone Stamp tool.

* In PaintShopPro®, a Clone brush is available with different sizes of brush tip and various other options.

Theory into practice

1 Select an image that has some material within it that you would want to remove. Experiment with different software options to replace part of the image with background colouring.

2 In a group, share images that you have worked on to remove material. See if you can spot where the cloning has happened.

A design brief may require a more complex combination of text, scanned imagery and imagery from a digital camera into one final image. A final image is created using one or more layers. Each layer is sourced separately, and can be edited in isolation. The layers can be laid one on top of the other, and depending on the order and the transparency settings, various effects can be achieved.

* A layer mask is a grey-scale image. What you paint in black will obscure the original image; what is left white will allow the original image to show through. Shades between white and black (the grey shades) will show in various levels of transparency.

✳ A vector mask tends to be used when you need to create a sharp image, for example, for some design element. Having created it using a vector mask, you can apply layer styles and, for example, have instantly usable buttons or panels.

Using both techniques, you could create a menu bar that gradually fades away. You might also use a mask to remove an object from a photo, by drawing a selection around the object. There are a number of tools that will help you to do this, depending on the shape of the object, and the complexity of the outline (see Figure 6.22 on page 188).

Setting image transparency/apply mode

Transparency relates to whether you can see through a colour to a background. The term opacity may also be used.

6.6 Producing final printed output

Producing hard copy involves selecting both the printer and the media. Most printers will provide a print out of your images. However, to achieve good quality, for example, for print-ready material or photos, the printer needs to offer high resolution printouts. Having prepared an image, printing out involves selecting the media type. There are many different types available. You might also print direct to a CD.

Effect of print media type

Advances in printer technology (and the paper that is used in these printers) mean that high-quality full colour images can be produced at home.

* Ink jet printers (or bubble jet printers) squirt ink at the page as a series of dots, and there are gaps between these dots which make the image look unrealistic when examined closely.

* Dye-sublimation printers are a recent invention. Within these printers, a transparent film, which looks like sheets of red, blue, yellow and grey cellophane glued together, roll past a heating element. The heat causes the dyes to vaporize and stain the surface of the paper before the dyes cool and return to solid form. Because there is a gentle gradient of colour change, the overall effect is more like a traditional photograph. Also, because the colour is 'soaked' into the paper, it is less likely to fade over time.

Each type of printer works best if you use the appropriate quality of paper.

* Most paper is fibre-based; it is made from trees. The surface of the paper may then be resin-coated. This affects how well the colour sits on the paper. Matching the quality of the paper to your purpose should guarantee the best photos.

* Paper is supplied in different weights, measured in g/m^2. Using an appropriate weight is also important.

What does it mean?

g/m^2 stands for grams per square metre.

In the same way that printer manufacturers stipulate the print cartridges to use, you will be advised as to what paper is best to use to print photo-quality images.

Theory into practice

1 Investigate what paper quality can be used on your printer, and which is best to use for printing full colour images.

2 Research different printers to find the cost of the better printers cost, and the paper costs involved.

6.7 Evaluation

Evaluation is an essential process, necessary to ensure the quality of your work, and to redirect your efforts in future if you fail to hit target in some way. You should evaluate both the end product (the images you create to meet your client brief) and the approach you took in completing the work.

Your client will have some standard that he or she expects you to meet, and, on completion, can tell you whether your work was good enough. You should check, before you start, exactly what standard is expected, so that you can try to meet this performance target and win the approval of your client.

Obtaining feedback from your client is essential; how else can you learn to improve your work? Identifying strengths and weaknesses of your work may seem a painful process, but it is only by facing up to what you need to improve on, rather than just basking in what you are good at, that you will develop your talent and improve your skills over time.

Part of the success of any project lies in careful planning of your time, and having the right resources available. It is easy to blame failure on the lack of resources or 'bad luck'. However, in the real world, you are responsible for your own success and need to take steps to ensure that nothing prevents you from achieving your goals. This includes being aware of how others can impact on your progress, and making allowances for this.

Think it over...

Discuss, with others in your group, things that went wrong in preparing your work, and how you could have prevented the problems in the first place by better planning.

6.8 Quality of written communication

The portfolio that you produce should demonstrate that you are capable of using, and have used, a suitable and appropriate style of writing. All text must be legible, meaningful and organised appropriately. Standard conventions such as applying headers and footers, using page numbers and title pages should also be applied.

Creating a website

Introduction

The use of the Internet has expanded rapidly over the past decade. Nowadays, many organisations make use of the Internet by having their own website. Nearly all large organisations and many smaller ones take advantage of the benefits offered by the Internet, to promote their products and services to a potentially global marketplace.

This unit focuses on the knowledge and skills required for setting up and managing websites. It will help you to understand the technology related to the Internet, and to appreciate the requirements for setting up a website. You will learn about the main techniques for transferring and displaying information over the Internet, and learn to design and construct a website for a client.

This unit will help you to understand better how Internet services can be of use to an organisation, and give you the opportunity to develop skills in using Internet tools. You will learn about what contributes towards good and poor website design, and then use your skills to produce web pages for a client, publishing them on a website for others to access.

> ### What you need to learn

By the time you have completed this unit, you should have achieved these learning outcomes.

✳ An understanding of the technology related to the Internet.

✳ An understanding of the requirements for setting up a website.

* The main techniques for transferring and displaying information over the Internet.

* An understanding of what contributes towards good and poor website design

* Know how to design and construct a website for a client.

Resource toolkit

To complete this unit, you need these essential resources:

* access to computer hardware and software facilities, including browser software

* access to the Internet

* wide range of information sources, such as books, trade journals of the IT industry, newspapers

* contacts working within the IT industry.

How you will be assessed

This unit is internally assessed. There are four assessment objectives:

AO1   Practical capability in applying ICT

AO2   Knowledge and understanding of ICT systems and their roles in organisations and society

AO3   Apply knowledge and understanding to produce solutions to ICT problems

AO4   Evaluate ICT solutions and your own performance.

To demonstrate your coverage of these assessment objectives, you will produce a portfolio of evidence, showing what you have learned and what you can do:

* use information from the client and existing websites to design and produce a website that meets the identified needs of a client, with regard to current legislation

* use software to develop web pages that convey relevant information to visitors

* use the results of testing to evaluate your final website against client needs

* upload your web pages to create a working website

* evaluate your own performance.

Your website will be created for a particular client. You need to ensure that:

* it works using a popular browser

* it includes a number of related, inter-linked pages

* your pages must make use of text, graphics and sound.

Your portfolio must provide documentation to show your how your work on the client's website meets the requirements set out in the assessment criteria for this unit:

* list the websites and URLs that you visited to obtain ideas

* include your initial designs as well as your final website documentation

* include a record of the test procedures carried out and the results obtained

* include your evaluation criteria and an evaluation of your completed work.

You are also expected to adopt standard ways of working to manage your work effectively. Standard ways of working is covered separately in the preliminary pages of this book.

How high can you aim?

The presentation of your portfolio is important. You should aim to present your work in a format that would be acceptable in industry. For this unit, how you produce your website and document it, and how you plan and manage the production of your website, will determine the marks that you earn. Table 7.1 shows the marks available for AO1: Practical capability in applying ICT. Notice that more marks are available according to how well you use technical tools in the production of your website.

Table 7.2 shows the marks available for AO2: Knowledge and understanding of ICT systems and their roles in organisations and society. The focus is on meeting your client's needs.

Table 7.3 shows the marks available for AO3: Apply knowledge and understanding to produce solutions to ICT problems. For full marks you need to upload your website.

Table 7.4 shows the marks available for AO4: Evaluate ICT solutions and own performance. Testing is an essential part of the production process, and you will earn higher marks according to your evaluation methods.

	1–5 MARKS	6–10 MARKS	11–15 MARKS	16–21 MARKS
Use of dedicated software tools	Some used	Yes	Full use	Full and effective use
Use of page formatting structures, text and graphics	Some used	Yes	Good use	Full and effective use
Use of video and sound		Yes	Good use	Full and effective use
Meets client's needs		Yes	Yes	Yes
Use of downloaded code to assist functionality of pages	Yes	Yes		
Annotates downloaded code to show how it assists functionality of pages	Yes	Yes	Yes	
Edits downloaded code to adapt it to the new website's pages			Yes	Yes
Creates a website with links between the site's pages	Limited links	Yes	Yes	Yes
Appropriate links from home page		Yes	Yes	Yes
Links to external sites			Yes	Yes
Justifying the inclusion of links to these external sites and relating them to client needs				Yes
Standard ways of working	Shows some awareness	Yes, attempted	Yes, followed	Close adherence

TABLE 7.1 *How well you use technical tools*

	1–4 MARKS	5–9 MARKS	10–14 MARKS
Background information gained from a briefing with the client	Notes made	Description	Full description
Describes task for which website is produced		Yes	Fully
Hardware and software resources needed to produce the website	Stated	Justified	Justified
How website will be produced	Identified		Agreed with the client
Understanding of client's requirements	Partial	Yes	Full
Research of coding of other websites and downloads required information	Yes		Yes, of several websites, and referenced clearly

TABLE 7.2 *How well you meet the client's needs*

	1–5 MARKS	6–10 MARKS	11–15 MARKS	16–21 MARKS
Sketches of initial designs for the website and its pages	Outline sketches	Outline sketches	Detailed	Detailed
Sketches annotated to show how they meet the needs of the client			Yes	Yes, showing how they fully met the needs
Carries through initial designs to the final website	With limited success	Yes	Yes	Yes
Editing changes to downloaded coding to achieve particular results requested by client	Limited	Attempt to match client's requirement	Extensive editing to match client's requirement	Extensive editing to match client's requirement
Enhances web pages with special effects	Few effects on some pages	Yes, using a range of effects	Described enhancements done using a range of special techniques	Described and justified
Evidence of uploading the website to a host server				Clear evidence

TABLE 7.3 *How well you produce a solution*

	1–4 MARKS	5–9 MARKS	10–14 MARKS
Actions taken to solve problems	Stated for some actions	Commented on	
Own strengths and weaknesses		Attempts to identify	Correctly identified
Areas for improvement in your approach to your work		Attempts to identify	Identifies
Evaluation criteria	Some produced	Yes	Yes
Test plan devised		Yes	Yes
Testing the website and its pages	Some testing done	Yes	Yes
Documents the results of testing		Yes	Yes
Changes that could be made to the website in the light of test outcomes	Suggested	Yes	Yes and justified
Evaluating the completed website against client's needs.	Attempt made	Yes	Yes
Suggestions for further improvements			Yes
Use of written expression to convey meaning	Adequate	Coherent	Suitable in form and style

TABLE 7.4 *How well you evaluate*

7.1 The Internet

In this unit, you will design and create a website to meet the needs of your client. To help you to make the best design, you should research and evaluate existing websites on the Internet.

This section considers how the WWW can be used as a source of information for you and focuses on the organisation of the Internet.

| What does it mean? |

WWW stands for World Wide Web.

The WWW is a massive network of resources that are available on the Internet. The Internet itself is a global network of computers, providing access to the information on the WWW and to a wide variety of other services, such as email. The Internet may seem a new invention, but it was in existence for about 30 years before the WWW, so it is actually the availability of the websites and the option to create your own that is the new development.

There are two categories of computer (and people working on those computers) on the Internet:

* Internet clients (the end users) enjoy access to the Internet to send and receive emails, and to surf the websites of other clients. These users are the people that you want to visit your site: the potential visitors. Internet clients may also set up websites, for others to surf.

* Internet hosts (the ISPs) provide the Internet clients with an access point, from where they can tap into the Internet. They may also house the web pages for their clients.

You need to understand how the Internet is organised, and this involves understanding the terminology.

Domains and the DNS

In the world of networks, your domain is your website. A domain name is used to describe the location of a website; you might call this your Internet address or web address. The address is keyed from left to right but, in some ways it is important to interpret it from right to left.

The final few letters of the domain name are called the domain extension. The domain names are grouped according to these extensions, and may be seen as an indication of the type of website you will be visiting.

* Extensions such as .com or .org or .gov can be used to describe the type of organisation – for example, commercial, charitable, non-profit making or government department.

* The extension may offer even more information about the organisation. For example, .museum is reserved for museums, .name indicates a

private individual's site, and .pro tends to be for professionals. The ones mentioned so far are called generic TLDs.

However, domain name extensions can also indicate the location of an Internet host, using a country-level domain, as in .co.uk. Also, since there is very little control over who is allowed to use particular domain extensions, you need to be careful not to assume too much about the integrity of a website, just based on the domain name.

The front end of the domain name identifies the organisation whose website you want to visit. Organisations need to register a domain name; Heinemann, as a UK company, registered its domain name as heinemann.co.uk. This appears on their letterheads as www.heinemann.co.uk.

If you enter the domain name (i.e. a web or Internet address) as the URL, this points, by default to the home page of the website.

Having decided on the domain name of the site you want to visit, how do you access this website? The WWW is available on the Internet, and the Internet comprises many computers, all linked in a huge network. So, for your computer software to locate the website, it needs to know on which computer the web pages you want to visit are stored. Every computer that is connected to the

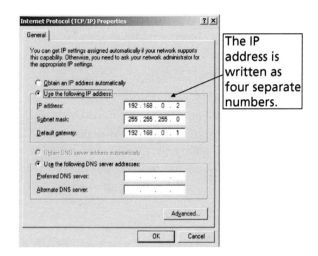

The IP address is written as four separate numbers.

FIGURE 7.1 *Example IP addresses*

Internet, whether a standalone computer or one that is a workstation within a local or wide area network, is a node on the Internet, and needs to be uniquely identifiable. IP addresses (Figure 7.1) are used to identify these nodes and hence the users that may log on at a particular workstation or standalone computer.

A DNS server is used to translate the domain name section of the URL that you key, into the relevant IP address.

The DNS is a database, listing lots of domain names and their respective IP addresses. DNS servers exist all over the world and share information with each other. Your browser will use the DNS Lookup service to convert what you type as the URL into an IP address.

If you get a DNS Lookup Error in a web browser (Figure 7.2), this will be because there is no information available or the DNS server is not working for some reason.

Knowledge check

1 Explain what these terms stand for: ISP, URL, LAN, WAN, DNS.

2 What is the function of a DNS server?

3 What is a browser?

Address field   URL

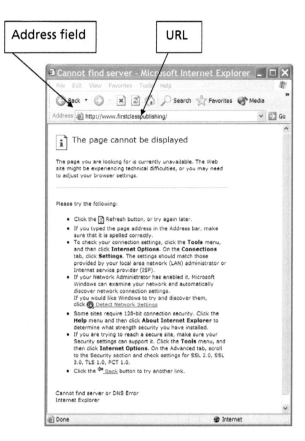

FIGURE 7.2 *Page not found error on Internet*

1 Using your browser, key in the domain name heinemann.co.uk as the URL and press GO. When the web page appears, check the address that appears as the URL.

2 Try entering even less information as the URL. Notice that as you start to type, the software offers URLs that you have accessed previously that start with the same sequence of characters. How successful is the DNS in finding websites when you give incomplete information in the URL?

Modes of access to the Internet, IAPs, ISPs, POPs and Internet services

Modes of access to the Internet fall into two groups: intermittent and continual.

* Dial-up connections, as the name suggests, involve you dialling up to connect to the Internet. Then, when you have completed whatever it was that you wanted to do (send emails and/or surf the net) you hang up, and therefore disconnect from the Internet. You are connected for only a short period of time.

* The second option is to have continual connection, for as long as your computer is switched on. This can be achieved if you subscribe to a Broadband service. There may be an initial dialling up but then the connection is maintained for a long time. You tend to pay for the service, rather than by the minute.

With Broadband Internet connection, a fixed IP address may be assigned to your computer or workstation by your ISP. However, there are only so many IP addresses. Luckily, not every ISP customer is online at the same time. So, in some circumstances, a dynamic IP address is assigned, just for as long as you are connected. The same number can then be released for someone else to use, when you have completed your session. The ISP provides its clients with an a point of presence (POP) and it is from here that they can tap into the information available on the Internet.

An ISP offers its clients a range of services including rich content, web hosting and email. In comparison, an IAP offers access to the Internet but little else.

IAP stands for Internet access point.

POP stands for point of presence. (It also stands for post office protocol, used for sending and receiving emails, see page 220).

A point of presence is a physical connection between an ISP's servers and the rest of the Internet.

1 Describe two modes of access to the Internet.

2 What is a fixed IP address? What is a dynamic IP address?

3 What does ISP stand for? What does IAP stand for?

4 What is a protocol?

5 What does POP stand for?

1 Find out what modes of access are available to you to connect to the Internet. Compare this with others in your group.

2 Sign on to a chat room, and check the IP address that has been assigned to you.

Internet standards and protocols

Not all computers speak the same language, so standards and protocols are used to define how communication may take place. When accessing information on the WWW, your computer will adopt many protocols, each setting the rules for a particular aspect of the Internet communication.

* The DHCP is used to automatically configure a node with its IP address. This IP address then uniquely identifies you, working at your computer and accessing the Internet, so that others can communicate with you, and know that it is you.

* The TCP/IP determines how individual signals are sent over the Internet. It is not a single protocol, but a collection of working practices that allow all Internet users to communicate, regardless of what equipment they are using.

* On the WWW, the HTTP set of rules is needed to transfer HTML files from one computer to another. Effectively, HTTP lets a browser view web pages encoded in HTML, a computer language that is discussed in more detail on pages 228–229.

* FTP allows uploading and downloading of files, and thus for files to be transferred between two computers.

When you first access a web page, it is downloaded to your computer and stored as a temporary file on your hard drive. If you use the Back/Next buttons (Figure 7.3) to surf pages that you have already accessed, you will view the downloaded files, not from the site itself. To see the most up-to-date version of a page, you would need to press the Refresh button, to download the page afresh.

You will use FTP when uploading the website for your client. The software that you use to create the website may also provide an option to publish your website, and this effectively uploads the HTML files for you (see page 233).

There are also protocols for email communication. Some email accounts are entirely web-based and so they follow the HTTP protocol.

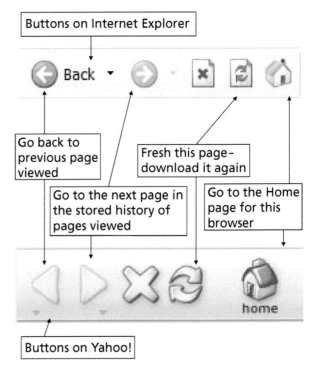

Buttons on Internet Explorer

Go back to previous page viewed

Fresh this page – download it again

Go to the next page in the stored history of pages viewed

Go to the Home page for this browser

Buttons on Yahoo!

FIGURE 7.3 *Forward, Back and Refresh buttons*

For those that are not web-based, other protocols exist. If you use an email program like Outlook or Eudora, then POP3 or IMAP may be used to pick up emails.

What does it mean?

IMAP stands for Internet message access protocol.

POP3, for example, is used to retrieve your messages from a mail server (Figure 7.4). It is a retrieval mechanism only; SMTP is used to send emails across the network. The email is transmitted using SMTP and sits on the mail server until accessed.

What does it mean?

The term server describes a computer on a network dedicated to perform a single task: a print server, a web server and so on. A mail server is a computer dedicated to handling Internet mail. SMTP stands for simple mail transfer protocol.

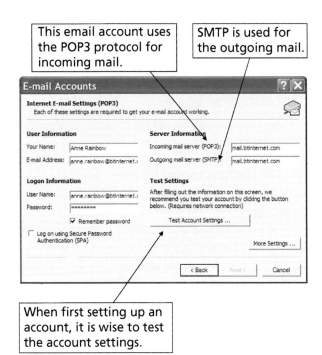

This email account uses the POP3 protocol for incoming mail.

SMTP is used for the outgoing mail.

When first setting up an account, it is wise to test the account settings.

FIGURE 7.4 *Internet e-mail settings*

Knowledge check

1 What do these terms stand for: DHCP, TCT/IP, HTTP, HTML. FTP?

2 Explain these terms: POP3, IMAP, SMTP.

7.2 Internet services

A range of services are available through the Internet. You need to be aware of these services, their purposes, the hardware and software tools you need to use, and the protocols needed to transfer data efficiently.

Think it over...

In a group, brainstorm Internet services. For each one considered, share your experiences of using it.

This section lists and gives brief details of a number of Internet services. The tools needed to make the best use of these sections are discussed in Section 7.4 (page 222).

One of the main purposes of the Internet is to share information. Internet services therefore provide users with options for transferring information to and from the World Wide Web (WWW). The WWW is a hypermedia system, supporting the multimedia variety of data but, using hyperlinks, it includes links to other web pages. In this way, all the pages of the WWW form one huge Internet of data.

❋ Users may communicate with one another by email (pages 220 and 234).

❋ Users may share data files, transferring them between their own computer or workstation and the Internet using file transfer (page 233).

❋ Groups may form to share news and ideas, using newsgroups (page 221).

❋ Users with similar interests may use a bulletin board to advertise information to each other (page 221).

Security issues

However the Internet is used, in every situation, you need to be aware of, and take precautions to minimise, the risks to the security of your equipment and data. Because your computer is connected to other computers via the Internet, you face risks such as virus and Trojan attacks. Hackers may make attempts at illegal access of confidential and sensitive material that is on your computer.

Email

Old-fashioned 'snail mail' has been superseded by email, which reduces postage costs and should arrive sooner. Even internal memos are a thing of the past; employees send a quick email, copying in everyone who might need the message. This is much quicker than typing a memo and can be less time-consuming than picking up the phone to talk to a colleague.

There are two main ways of accessing emails:

* You can go on the Internet and access your emails through the WWW. This is particularly useful when away from your normal place of work, and the only access available to you may be through an Internet café. However, it is relatively slow, and you have to be online while processing your emails.

* You can have your emails downloaded into software, such as Microsoft Outlook, that is resident on your PC. You only need to be online for as long as you are receiving or sending emails and can then work off-line. However, unless you filter your emails in some way, anything that is sent to you will be downloaded, and this can take a long time.

File transfer

The WWW comprises millions of web pages, each one created on a computer somewhere by the web page designer responsible for a particular site. How do these pages reach the WWW?

FTP was established as a protocol on the Internet before the WWW was invented. It has always been the standard for transferring any file across the Internet from one computer to another. When the WWW was developed, it used a limited number of file types: HTML, GIF and JPEG. Since these are precisely the file types you will be creating for your website, FTP is the most natural way to transfer files from your computer to the host computer that you intend to use for your website.

So, once you have created the pages for your website on your computer, you need to upload these pages to your website. This is called publishing your site, and involves transferring files between your computer and the host server, according to how you are connected to the Internet.

You will need to transfer one file per page, together with other supporting files. It is important that these files are organised into folders so that, once on the Internet, the individual pages can be displayed, including all images and other features, like sound and video.

When you transfer files, the size of the file affects the time it takes to upload the data. It also affects how long your page will take to materialise on a visitor's screen. So, it is important to minimise the file sizes. A technique called compression is used to reduce file sizes, so all the data is transferred within a smaller file size, and hence more quickly and efficiently.

With web design, there are two problems that relate to file size: minimising the file size so as to minimise file transfer time when uploading the website, and minimising download time when the visitor is waiting for the display to appear on-screen. Graphic files can take up lots of memory, so it is important to choose a graphic file format that minimises the storage requirements of the image.

Theory into practice

1 For a single image, save it in a number of different formats: GIF, TIF, JPEG, BMP. Which ones generates the smallest file size?

2 For the same image files, enlarge the pictures. In which formats is resolution lost?

Multimedia files can also be large. Software such as Windows Movie Maker will tell you how big your file will be according to the settings you have chosen. You can then try to reduce the file size by changing the settings. However, reduced file size tends to mean a lower quality video, so you have to compromise between size of file and quality of video.

Theory into practice

1 Find out what these terms mean: bit rate, display size, aspect ratio and frames per second.

2 Experiment with software that allows you to make a video to see the effect of reducing file size on the quality of the video.

Newsgroups

A group can comprise any number of like-minded people who decide to form a group so that they can share information and discuss things of interest to them. The group's site may include a bulletin board, and other services for its members.

Theory into practice

1 Visit a newsgroup that relates to a particular interest of yours. Apply to join the group. Explore the newsgroup features to find out what services it offers.

2 Visit the MSN Groups home page to learn how to set up a group.

Bulletin boards

A bulletin board (Figure 7.5) is a place on the Internet where users can 'post' a message so that everyone else can see it, and respond to it if they wish. Bulletin boards are often included as a feature of a newsgroup, today they are often known as forums.

FIGURE 7.5 *Sample bulletin board*

7.3 Internet service providers

There are two main types of Internet service providers:

* some organisations exist solely as Internet service providers

* some organisations happen to be Internet service providers, but this is in addition to their main business. These include telephone companies, computer suppliers and academic institutions.

Connection to the Internet may be on a DUN basis or it may involve Broadband networking. Some ISPs offer one or the other; some ISPs may offer both.

ISPs also vary in the quality and the range of services that they offer. In addition to connection to the Internet, most ISPs also offer other services:

* It is possible to set up multiple email addresses within one email account. This can be useful, for example, if you use the Internet for personal correspondence but also for work-related correspondence. You may also act as the secretary for a club you belong to, and would like any emails addressed to you in that capacity to be kept separate from any personal emails or work emails.

* Many ISPs offer web space for a customer's own website. The ISP may also offer software to help you to create your own website.

* You may also be offered access to a range of newsgroups as described on page 221.

* As with operating systems providers and applications software vendors, your ISP should provide on-screen help pages so that you can make the best use of the communications software that you need to use to access the Internet, send emails, upload your web page and so on.

* A telephone helpline may also be available, depending on the level of subscription. Because it is costly to man such helplines, the cost of calling may be passed to the client.

7.4 Internet tools

In this section, you will learn about the different Internet tools and their protocols so that you are able to transfer data efficiently.

When developing a website, you need to be aware of how the visitor will access it. This can have major implications on the design of your website.

* The visitor will use browser software to view pages on the Internet.

✳ If the visitor does not know the URL of your site, or even which sites to visit to find out whatever he or she wants to know, a search engine (page 226) may be used to generate a hit list of sites to visit.

In producing your website, you will need to know about web programming languages (see pages 228–229). However, to make life somewhat easier for you, you will develop your website using web page development software (see page 229). Entering text onto a web page is relatively straightforward, but to make your website an interesting place to visit you will want to include graphic images. To make the best use of graphics, you need to know how to edit graphics and convert file formats to Internet standards (see page 232). Having developed your website, you need to publish it on the Internet. This involves using file transfer software (see page 233) to upload your site. Finally, if you are to offer the option for visitors to your site to contact you by email you must be able to configure and use an email client program (see page 234).

Browser software

Browsers, such as Internet Explorer, are software applications which let the visitor to a website navigate the website and view the web pages. Browsers interpret the HTML and present the web pages on screen on the visitor's computer. Most popular browsers, such as Internet Explorer, Netscape Navigator and Opera, are self-configuring, but you need to know how to control the settings to suit yourself and your client.

When you open the browser application, the first page displayed is called the start-up home page. It makes sense to set this page as one which you most frequently want to visit (Figure 7.6).

Some settings can adversely affect how the PC works and you need to know about these.

✳ To reduce the time it takes to display a page that has been downloaded from the Internet, the browser stores the page in a disk cache on the hard disk. If you navigate backwards and

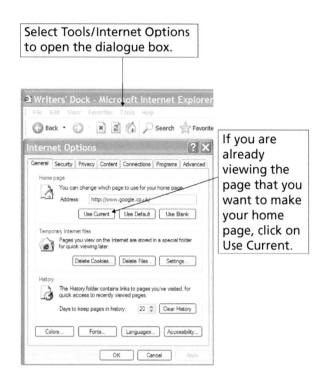

FIGURE 7.6 *How to make a current page your start-up page*

forwards, then instead of downloading again, the pages are displayed straight from the cache. These temporary Internet files can take up a lot of space, so part of the maintenance of your PC should include cleaning the disk of such temporary files (Figure 7.7).

✳ The browser keeps a record of all sites that you have visited in the History folder. If you visit a

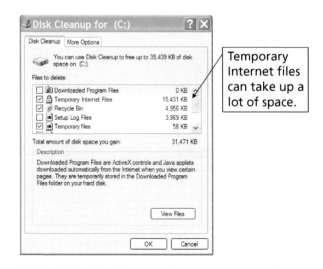

FIGURE 7.7 *Disk Cleanup shows the space to be saved by deleting temporary Internet files*

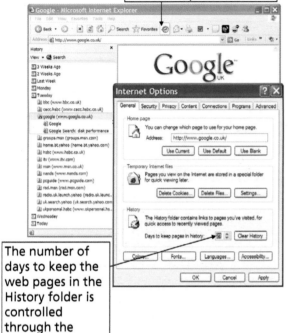

The History folder keeps a record of all sites visited in the recent past.

The number of days to keep the web pages in the History folder is controlled through the Internet Options.

FIGURE 7.8 *Controlling the space used for the History folder*

lot of sites every day, you might consider reducing the number of days records that you want to retain (Figure 7.8). This will reduce the amount of space used by the History folder.

＊ Several players and handlers are included with the most popular browsers (Table 7.5).

These and other add-ons may cause a computer to malfunction, or run more slowly, so you need to know how to disable them (Figure 7.9).

Select Tools / Manage Add-ons to open the dialogue box.

To disable an add-on, click it and then click Disable.

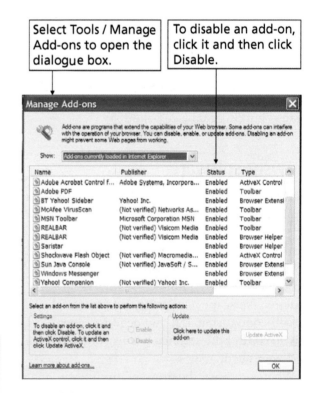

FIGURE 7.9 *Add-on control panel*

PLAYER/HANDLER	FUNCTION
Adobe Acrobat	To read PDF files
Flash	To play Macromedia Flash animations
Windows Media Player, Apple Quick Time, RealPlayer	To play back streaming audio, video and multimedia

TABLE 7.5: *Players and handlers*

Hotlinks appear in blue and are underlined.

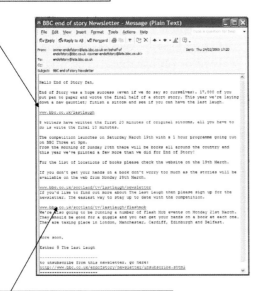

Double-clicking on a link will open the webpage automatically.

FIGURE 7.10 *An email with a hotlink to a website*

To reach a website that you want to visit, you need to know its URL.

✳ If you have visited the site recently, you might access it through your History folder.

✳ If the URL is supplied to you as a hotlink, such as within an email (Figure 7.10), you can just CTRL-click on it.

Otherwise, you will need to key the URL into the address field. Although the browser helps you by offering URLs that match what you have typed so

A hotlink is text or an image which, when clicked on, takes you to another page within a website or to another website altogether.

far, it is even quicker to access a web page if you set up a bookmark (Figure 7.11). Having set up the bookmark, clicking on it takes you straight to the page you want.

If you don't know the URL of the site, you need to search for the website using a search engine.

To bookmark a site, or add it to your Favorites, go to that site and then click on Add….

Tick the 'Make available offline' box if you would want to read the text when you are not online.

Click on Create in to reveal the directory structure of your Favorites folder.

Change the name if you want to, to something that means more to you.

Browse through your Favorite folders to show where you want the bookmark to appear.

FIGURE 7.11 *How to add a web page to your Favourites*

CASE STUDY: REDHOUSE

The Redhouse website presents information about the products that they manufacture and sell.

1 **Visit the Redhouse site through the link at www.heinemann.co.uk/hotlinks. Explore the site and make notes on what you like about it. Note anything that you think you would want to change or avoid.**

2 **Visit two other sites of your own choosing and make further notes on features that you admire, and those that you would avoid in any site that you were to design. Take screen grabs to illustrate your findings.**

3 **Compare notes with others in your group.**

At this stage, you should be visiting websites to obtain ideas on layout that you can then use in the design of your client's website.

> **Think it over...**
>
> Discuss what might happen if you were caught breaking copyright.

There are some copyright-free web images available online. To use these, you only need to acknowledge the source. You can find some examples through the link at www.heinemann.co.uk/hotlinks.

Having found websites that you admire, you might be tempted to download graphics to use in your own design. However, be warned, such images will probably be copyright protected. The Copyright, Designs and Patents Act (1988) protects intellectual property and establishes the rights of an author. It covers many forms of intellectual property, such as books, music and art. The Act is intended to deter others from passing someone else's work off as their own, and making money from using that material.

> **Theory into practice**
>
> 1 Research the Internet for sources of free graphic images. Bookmark any sites that you consider to be particularly useful for you.
>
> 2 Find out what penalty you might incur if you were to infringe copyright by incorporating a copyrighted image in your own website.

Search engines

Using a browser, you can view web pages on the Internet. First, though, you need to go to the web page you want to view.

* If you know the URL of the site, or if you have bookmarked the site, or if you have it listed in your history folder, can go straight to the site.
* If you don't know the URL of a site, a search engine will allow you to find websites that match criteria set by you. You need to enter a word or phrase that can be used as a search key.

> **Think it over...**
>
> With a friend, discuss search engines that have used. Which ones give the best results?

If you enter a search key into a browser, its search engine will present you with a hot list of sites (Figure 7.12), the contents of which match your search key. However, unless you choose your key phrase carefully, the hot list may have too many entries, or too few, to be of any use to you.

* Entering a single word will probably result in too many hits for you to sensibly find what you want.

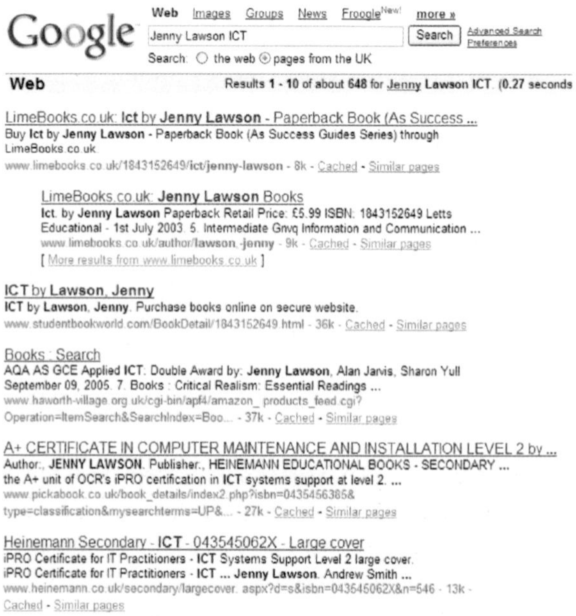

FIGURE 7.12 *Google hit list*

* To narrow a search down, you may use a plus sign (+) or the word AND to link words. Using quotation marks around a phrase will have the same effect, requiring that all the words in the phrase are found.

* When entering more than one word in the search key, put the most important word(s) first. If you have not linked the words (with + or AND or " " as above) then the sites found may have one or more of the key words, not necessarily all of them. This is a good way to widen a search. It has the same effect as using the word 'OR' between them and is particularly useful if you don't know exactly what term might have been used to describe something.

The hot list includes brief details of relevant sites and hotlinks to these sites as URLs. These URLs are shown, either in a different colour or underlined. Double clicking on these hotlinks will open up the web page.

URLs are sometimes provided on sites. So, having found one site that is useful, it may provide an external link to point you to another site. In this way, you can surf the Internet to find whatever information you need.

Theory into practice

1. Open your Internet browser and search using the key: Spurs Tottenham. Use Restore down so that you can see the window and yet have other windows on view too.

2. Open a second window with your Internet browser. This time, search using the key: Tottenham Hotspurs. Use Restore down so you can view both hit lists and compare them.

3. Visit at least two sites (briefly!).

It is important that you understand how the search engine produces its hot list. It will help you to design your client's website so that it too appears on relevant hit lists. Search sites collect information to build a picture of what each site on the WWW offers.

* Some search sites rely on procedures which use robots or spiders to scan web pages automatically, cataloguing the content. From this, a database of key words and matching website addresses is maintained.

* Some search sites add a human dimension. Real people visit sites and manually categorise each site according to its content. This is obviously very time-consuming and, hence, costly.

For a robot or spider to note your website, you should follow a few basic rules in the design of your website:

* The key words that a potential visitor might use must appear somewhere on your site. It would make sense, after you have decided on the content of your website, to think about the terms a potential visitor might use, and then check that you have indeed included them. Don't be tempted to start from this list of keywords though; it may straightjacket your creative thinking processes during the design stage.

* Repeating important key words will make your site more noticeable, but you need to be careful not to overdo it. Excessive use of particular key words may alert the search engine to your ploy, and your site may be excluded.

* Including the key words within headings makes them more noticeable. The search engine pays more attention to headings than it does to the rest of the text. Emboldening a term within normal text also makes it more noticeable.

* There is an option within HTML, called metatagging, which allows you to specify key words. You may think this is the best way to help search engines to know what your site is offering. However, the search engines look at everything on a site, and may be more inclined to notice what you have specified as the TITLE of your site, rather than the key words you have offered.

A search engine will also show sponsored links: sites that pay to be included whenever particular key phrases are used in a search. So, one way to promote a site is to pay. Another option is to arrange with other, maybe better known, sites to include a link to your site. Reciprocal linking involves your putting a link to someone else's site on your site, in return for which they put a link to your site on theirs. Even if the other site is in direct competition with yours, you may both benefit from reciprocal linking.

Another approach is to find out what key words potential visitors are using to search for sites, and then to consider which of these apply to your site. Having identified these, you should make sure the terms appear in your TITLE and/or headings and/or text.

* Lycos provides a weekly report to show the most popular user searches on their site (Figure 7.13). This may help you to identify, not only what is popular now, but since it also offers the previous ranking of any terms, and how long they have been in the top 50, you can see which are passing fads, and which terms really do matter to potential visitors.

* To see which key words are most popular on a number of search sites, you could download a copy of AnalogX Keyword Live. This program analyses the key words that are currently being used, over a period of time determined by you, on a number of search engines. It then presents you will the top 100 keywords

* You may also consider downloading AnalogX Keyword Extractor (KeyEx). This free download extracts all of the key words on a web page, sorts and indexes them based on their usage and position. You can adjust search-engine specific weighting factors and key word criteria for the best possible view of how a search engine sees your site. You can use this software on local files (that is, before you publish your web pages) as well as files on your website, or other websites.

FIGURE 7.13 *The most popular key words for Lycos*

Web programming languages

There are a number of web programming languages you might use for the creation of web pages or components of pages:

* HTML is a computer language that was specially devised to code the data that is to appear on a web page.

* VRML, CFML, ASP, DHTML are all examples of other languages that programmers might use to create web pages. All are beyond the scope of this course.

What does it mean?

VRML stands for virtual reality mark-up language. CFML stands for cold fusion mark-up language. ASP stands for active server pages. DHTML stands for dynamic HTML.

* The original HTML language can now be extended by including scripts – short sections of code written in other computer languages such as Java, Perl, Visual Basic and JavaScript. You need not write these scripts: they are available, some free of charge, and all you have to do is amend them slightly to tailor them for your website.

This unit covers the basic principles of HTML so that you can read HTML code and make amendments to it. You are not expected to know enough about HTML to be able to write web pages in it from scratch! Nor need you incorporate scripts, although your web authoring software may offer easy ways to achieve extra functionality and guide you through the tailoring process using a wizard.

Theory into practice

1 Research the Internet to discover more about script, VRML, CFML, ASP and DHTML.

2 Find out what the downside of using scripts is. Why do some ISPs not allow you to incorporate scripts into your web page code, or insist on vetting the code, at a cost?

HTML consists of elements. An element may be an image or text. Each element then has a tag and attributes and, sometimes, content.

* A tag tells the browser what element is coming next. It appears at the start of the element, and usually at the end (but not always). Tags are easy to spot; they are written within triangular brackets.

* An attribute specifies something special about the element. It may tell the browser the size of an image, the horizontal spacing around an image, or the type face of text to be used. Table 7.6 lists some examples of attributes for images.

Figure 7.14 shows the basic structure of HTML code and illustrates some sample code using the tags and attributes introduced so far.

Knowledge check

1 What do these acronyms stand for? HTML, VRML, CFML, ASP, DHTML.

2 Explain these terms and give examples: element, tag, attribute.

Web page development software

Web pages are written in HTML (or some other web programming language), because that is what the web browser software needs. The early web page designers learned these web programming languages, and it was (and still is) a specialised job to write in this code.

When web page design became desirable for many more people, few of whom were skilled programmers, software vendors began to incorporate the facility to turn documents into HTML coded files. So, to create a web page, you could use any one of a number of the standard software applications:

* Word processing software is one option. Microsoft Word® offers a Save As Web Page option (Figure 7.15). The Microsoft Script Editor® can be used to edit the HTML code that is automatically produced.

* Presentation software such as PowerPoint® may also be used. PowerPoint® was developed to

ATTRIBUTE	NOTES	EXAMPLE
align	Images are aligned relative to text.	align ="left"
alt	The text specified will appear when a mouse over event happens, i.e. when the visitor moves the mouse across the image.	alt ="Photo of Jenny"
border	Your image does not have to have a border but any value greater with 0 results in a border of that thickness (in pixels).	border ="1"
face	Specifies the typeface to be used for following text.	face = "arial"
height	Specifies the height of an image in pixels.	height = "60"
hspace	It improves the look of a page if you have white space, especially around an image; this specifies the space (in pixels) either side of an image.	hspace ="10"
lowscr	An option to provide a low-resolution source image to load quickly before the main high-resolution image, which will take much longer to load.	lowsrc = "Jennylowrespic.jpg"
src	This specifies the filename of the image. Note that the file name must not have any spaces in it. If the file is located in a different folder then the full pathname (i.e. its URL) needs to be given.	src ="JennyPhoto.jpg"
vspace	Like hspace, vspace specifies the space above and below an image.	vspace ="10"
width	Specifies the width of an image in pixels.	width = 40

TABLE 7.6 *Image attributes*

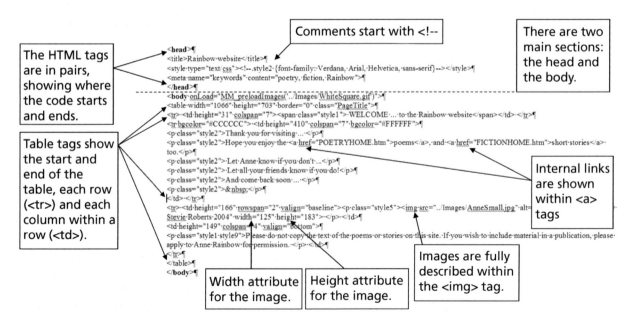

FIGURE 7.14 *Basic structure of HTML code*

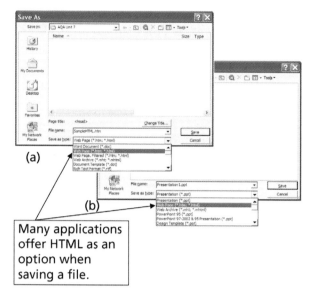

Many applications offer HTML as an option when saving a file.

FIGURE 7.15 *Save As Web Page options in (a) Word® and (b) PowerPoint®*

create slides, and is based on a paged slideshow presentation, so this matches how a visitor may view your website, one page at a time. When you save the files as a web page and choose to edit the HTML code, you will find yourself in Microsoft Script Editor® again (Figure 7.16).

* DTP packages offer a third option. Because these restrict you to creating boxes of text or

Select HTML Source to open the Script Editor.

This map shows one HTML file per slide.

Web Page Title

Notice the text for the title within the code.

FIGURE 7.16 *Microsoft Script Editor®*

images within a paged layout, the document has similarities with how your website will look.

However, the code that these standard applications produce is somewhat clumsy and inefficient, and they do not offer the full range of features you might want to include on your website.

Think it over...

Discuss your experiences of producing web pages using any of the standard software packages. What were the benefits? What were the limitations?

We have now reached the point where software vendors offer web authoring software, so that 'anyone' can design their own website. Having bought and downloaded the web authoring software does not necessarily mean you have the skills to design a good website. However, it does make it easier for people to try to design their own websites and, hopefully, to improve their design skills in the process.

There are many web authoring packages to choose from:

* You might purchase a package such as Microsoft FrontPage® or Macromedia DreamWeaver.

* Some ISPs also offer free or subscription-based web authoring software. Yahoo! SiteBuilder, for example, is available to those who subscribe to Yahoo! for web space. Netscape Composer is available free for those using Netscape.

As with any software, the more sophisticated packages offer the greatest range of clever tools, but carry a price tag to match, and free software may offer only limited functionality.

In theory, the more sophisticated software

Think it over...

Share your experiences of using the more sophisticated web authoring software. What extra features can you incorporate using web authoring software instead of, say, Microsoft PowerPoint®?

packages are also more complicated to use. However, because many provide you with a WYSIWYG design environment, and provide wizards to help you, the process of building the elements of a page and setting attributes is made as easy as possible. The tags are incorporated for you and the HTML code built without your needing to be aware of it.

Also, software designers tend to adopt common

What does it mean?

WYSIWYG stands for 'what you see is what you get'.

techniques like drag and drop, and context-sensitive menus when you right-click, so this makes it easier to transfer skills you have learned using other software, especially software marketed by the same vendor. There are also books available that focus on specific packages, and online help to assist you.

Theory into practice

1 Research the Internet for books on the web authoring software that you will be using.

2 Check what books are available for loan from your library.

3 Check what books others in your group already have. Consider arranging to pool your resources.

Graphic software

Graphic software is used to create and edit images that you may want to include in your website. Creating an image can be done in one of two ways:

＊ You may draw the image, or some component part of an image, using painting software. The tools that you use will include pens or brushes with varying nibs or effects, and a palette of colours. Painting software creates an image

made up from individual pixels, and this is normally stored as a bit-mapped image. If you enlarge a bit-mapped image the gap between the pixels increases and the clarity or resolution of the image is adversely affected.

What does it mean?

Pixel stands for picture element. It is one tiny part of an image. Bit stands for binary digit. A bit-mapped image has one or more bits (depending on the range of colours used) per pixel.

＊ You may construct the image, or a part of it, using drawing software. This can be done using lines and shapes, and colouring these shapes or filling them with colour. These images tend to be stored as vector graphics. You can enlarge a vector graphic without loss of resolution.

What does it mean?

A vector is a maths concept, often used to represent something that has direction and length. In graphic imaging software terms, a vector is used to define shapes, where they are placed and some dimension. For example, a circle can be defined by the location of its centre and the length of the radius.

Graphics software packages tend to offer one or the other (paint or draw) but there can be some overlap of the tools available. You also have the option to save the images in a format of your own choosing.

Think it over...

Within a small group, discuss what graphics software you have used. What tools have you used? What images have you created? What file formats do you normally use to save your images?

You do not have to create your own images; you may not feel you have the artistic skills to do so. Instead, you may source your images from elsewhere. They may have been sent to you as an attachment to an email, or you may have downloaded them from the Internet, scanned them in to your computer, or uploaded them from a digital camera.

Having drawn, constructed or obtained your image in some way, you may need to edit the image:

＊ to alter some of the attributes, such as a change the colouring, for example, to eliminate red eye from a photo

＊ to crop the image so that it shows only the part of interest to you

＊ to create some special effect, such as the page curl effect shown in Figure 7.17

＊ to touch up an image. This may be to disguise a feature, so that it is not legible, or to change the image in some way, for example to add a moustache to the Mona Lisa!

It is important that you compress each image before inserting it within a web page. Compression options are covered in more detail on page 247.

FIGURE 7.17 *Creating a special effect from a scanned photo*

File transfer software

File transfer software allows you to transfer a file (or the many files that form your website) from one computer to another, such as from your computer to the Internet. The process of publishing your client's website involves copying HTML files from your computer onto the Internet, using file transfer software. To achieve this, you need three pieces of information:

＊ you need to know the domain name of your client's website, so that you can specify the destination of the files

＊ you will need to specify your client's user name that has been assigned to him or her by the ISP that is hosting the website

＊ finally, you will need your client's password. Passwords are usually to be kept secret but, in this instance, your client will need to reveal it to you, or do the uploading without your assistance.

You may obtain FTP software in one of three ways:

＊ download free shareware software from the Internet

＊ buy a special application package for file transfer

＊ the option to transfer files may be offered as part of the web-authoring software that you are using, it will be called 'publishing your site' or something similar (see Figure 7.18).

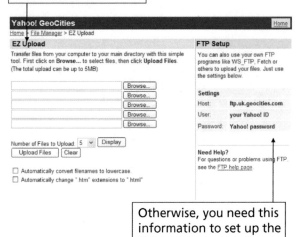

Yahoo offer EZ Upload as one way to upload files to your site.

Otherwise, you need this information to set up the FTP within your web-authoring software

FIGURE 7.18 *File transfer through Yahoo!*

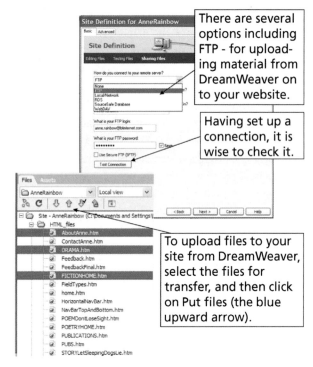

There are several options including FTP - for uploading material from DreamWeaver on to your website.

Having set up a connection, it is wise to check it.

To upload files to your site from DreamWeaver, select the files for transfer, and then click on Put files (the blue upward arrow).

FIGURE 7.19 *Publishing to the web using DreamWeaver*

Knowledge check

1 Explain these terms: domain name, user name, password.

2 Why is it important to keep a password secret? What might happen if someone found out the password you use to access your website?

Email client

Email is the one tool that nearly everyone uses on the Internet. There are two main options for receiving and sending emails:

❊ You may rely on a web-based mail client.

CASE STUDY: TRANSFERRING FILES TO THE INTERNET

Karen Hall is a member of the Photographic Society and her website shows a selection of her photographs. In creating her website, Karen has experimented with using a variety of web authoring software, including Yahoo!'s SiteBuilder.

Anne Rainbow used DreamWeaver to create her site (Figure 7.19).

1 Experiment with free file transfer software. What information do you need to transfer a file to your website? Are there any restrictions on how many files you can transfer?

2 Within a web authoring package, identify how you would upload your web pages to the Internet. Check out any tutorials that are available to explain the process.

3 Compare your findings with others in your group, especially those who have experience of other web authoring software. Identify the common procedures.

CASE STUDY: BT YAHOO

Anne uses BT Yahoo for her email. BT Yahoo! mail is a web-based email. This means that her BT Yahoo! mail account is accessible via a website residing on a BT Yahoo! mail server (Figure 7.20).

Because Anne is using a web-based mail client, her email correspondence is stored in her mailbox on a BT Yahoo! mail server. None of the messages that she sends or receives are stored on her local computer. The browser interface allows her to read, forward, organize and delete email messages that are stored in her mailbox. It also lets her send email messages using her BT Yahoo! mail account. Anne follows this procedure to access her incoming emails:

* She connects her computer to the Internet, using a Broadband link via her telephone line
* She launches the web browser, Internet Explorer
* She goes to Yahoo's mail web page
* She signs on using her user name (anne.rainbow@btinternet.com) and password (flamingo) as shown in Figure 7.21.

1 **Compare Anne's procedure with the one you use. Identify any differences. Compare notes with others in your group.**
2 **Draw a flowchart to explain the general procedure.**

Web browser
Internet
Mail server
Web-based mail client
http://bt.yahoo.com/webmail

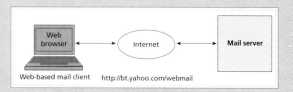

FIGURE 7.20 *How the Internet is used to link a client to the mail server*

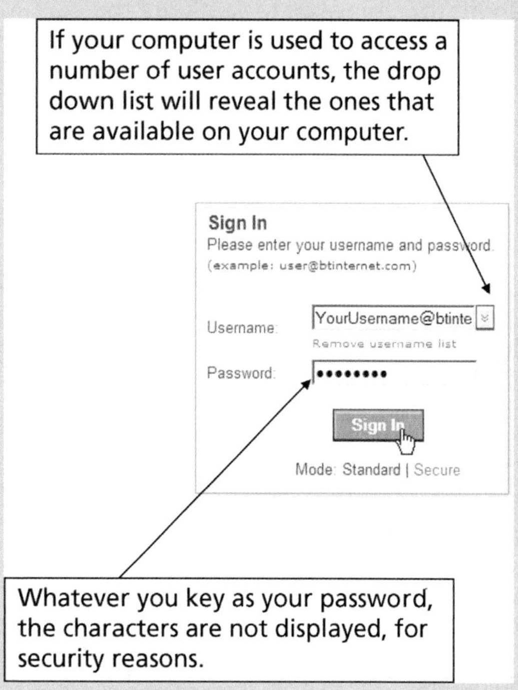

If your computer is used to access a number of user accounts, the drop down list will reveal the ones that are available on your computer.
Sign In
Please enter your username and password.
(example: user@btinternet.com)
Username:
YourUsername@btinte
Remove username list
Password:
Sign In
Mode: Standard | Secure
Whatever you key as your password, the characters are not displayed, for security reasons.

FIGURE 7.21 *Signing on to access mail*

What does it mean?

A web-based mail client is a program (usually a website) that any computer with an Internet connection and a web browser can use to access the mail server.

What does it mean?

A mail server is a software application that receives incoming email and forwards outgoing email for delivery. A computer dedicated to running such applications is also called a mail server.

* You may install communications software, such as Microsoft Outlook®, to collect emails from the Internet, and send emails to the Internet.

For this unit, you must be able to configure and use an email client program.

Anne has Microsoft Outlook® installed on her PC and decides to use this to access her emails. This will mean that her email messages will be stored on her PC, although she can opt for them to be retained on the Yahoo! site for a certain number of days before they are deleted (Figure 7.22).

To set up Outlook® to collect mail from the Yahoo! site, Anne has to configure the software (Figure 7.23).

1 If you do not have a web-based email account, it is easy and free to set one up. Access an email account via a web-based email server. Send an email to someone else in your group. Ask them to send you an email, and reply to it.

2 For the communication software installed on you computer, configure it to accept the emails of a new email account. Check that this works by sending an email and asking someone else to send you an email.

Select Email Accounts, and opt to change an account.
Then click on More Settings ... to open the Internet Email settings dialogue box.

Check this box to leave messages on the server.

You can opt to have them deleted under certain conditions: timeout and/or when you delete them yourself.

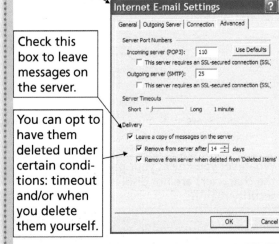

FIGURE 7.22 *Retaining emails on the web server*

Having selected Email Accounts / New, you need to specify the server type.

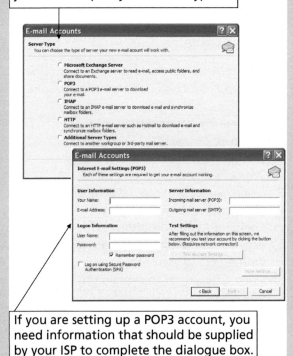

If you are setting up a POP3 account, you need information that should be supplied by your ISP to complete the dialogue box.

FIGURE 7.23 *Configuring Microsoft Outlook for an email account*

7.5 Website creation

You should not underestimate the need for planning and design when creating a website. As with any product, it is important to follow the usual development sequence when designing a website:

* In the analysis stage, you should decide what it is you are trying to achieve. You will establish the scope of your project.

* During the design specification stage, you will think through how you will meet your client's requirements, and write a specification so that

someone else can implement your plan. In practice, you will implement your own plan, but it might help you to design a better website if you try to think of yourself as two different people: the website planner and the website implementer.

✳ The prototyping and implementation stage of website design involves creating a scaled-down version of the website so that your client can see how you have interpreted his or her requirements. Approval of the prototype should be obtained before the more detailed work is done of creating all the web pages and linking them together.

✳ Having obtained the go-ahead from the client, maybe with some adjustments or refinements, work then continues on detailed web page creation. The site will need technical testing prior to publication by uploading the site to the WWW.

✳ The final stage of the design process is to perform an evaluation. Does your web site meet the specification?

In the initial planning stage, you should draw up a task list or action plan so that you can see what needs to be done, by when and then monitor your progress as the development is carried out. Your plan should identify important tasks:

✳ What tasks (broken down into sub-tasks) need to be carried out?

✳ How much time should you allocate to each task and sub-task?

✳ In what order should the tasks be completed?

✳ What are the key milestones for this project?

✳ What factors might cause a delay in the completion of your project?

The purpose of the project plan is two-fold:

✳ Before you start, you need to think about what will be involved, how much time this might take you and how you are going to manage to complete everything before some deadline date.

✳ While you are working on the project, you can use the plan to help you to identify if everything is going well, that is, to manage the progress of the project. If, for example, you are slipping behind schedule, you need to revise your plan. This may involve reducing the scope of the project and/or negotiating an extension of the deadline.

Think it over...

In a small group, discuss what software you might use to help you plan and monitor your progress while developing your website.

This section now looks at the documentation that you might produce as you work through the stages of development of your website, before going into the detail of web authoring software (pages 242) which will allow you to put your ideas into practice.

Analysis

The analysis stage will involve discussions with your client, looking at how things are currently done, and finding out what your client expects of the new website. The analysis stage should establish two important facts:

✳ What is the purpose of the site? Is it to inform visitors? Should it try to sell some product or service?

✳ Who is the intended target audience? What type of visitors does it hope to attract?

During the analysis stage, you should also determine the scope of your site. Where your website stops is almost as important as what it will contain. It is important not to overwhelm visitors. You can provide links to other sites or sources of information if the visitor needs additional information, rather than attempt to include everything in the one site.

In a real-life website creation project, there would also be a limitation due to budget constraints.

✳ How much is your client willing to pay for the development of the site?

* How much of your time does the budget allow you to spend on the development work?

In designing the website, you cannot just dream up whatever suits you or catches your imagination. The website needs to meet the needs of your client and you must identify these needs during the analysis stage.

* You need to have accurate information about the company's contact details. These should be displayed somewhere on the site, maybe running across the bottom of each screen, or on a special screen entitled Contact Us.

* Your client may want to offer products or services through the website. If so, you need to obtain full details of these for every product/service: the product/service name, a short description, size information, pricing, delivery arrangements and maybe an image of the product/service.

* Your client will expect the website to reflect a consistent corporate look, so you need to collect information about the company logo, preferred colours, preferred fonts and so on. Some organisations publish a house style as a guide for suppliers of stationery and web designers.

* Most websites include a facility for a visitor to contact the company direct from the site. Although the site may display a contact telephone number, for some visitors, the option to communicate via email may be preferred. Once the visitor has chosen this route, the communication software (for example, Outlook Express) should automatically load with the To: field in a new email being automatically completed for the visitor. Make sure the hotlink displays the email address within the web page; some visitors may prefer to write it down, and will only be able to do so if the complete address is visible to them.

* Some clients may want the website to offer visitors downloadable material such as an order form. You would need to obtain a copy of any such material in a format that allows the majority of visitors to access it.

* There are a number of ready-made applets and scripts that you might incorporate into your website. For example, your client may be interested in including a hit counter or a banner.

Initial discussions with your client may serve to focus your client's mind on exactly what is required. Your goal throughout is to establish the requirements of your client.

* What is the precise purpose of the client's website?

* Who exactly is the target audience? What characteristics might a typical visitor have in terms of age, gender, occupation, income bracket, interests?

* Once you have developed the website, how will your client access the site, i.e. what hardware, software, and connection method will be used?

* What information is the website to provide to visitors? Who will supply this information to you, or to whoever is responsible for maintaining the site after you have completed the development of the site?

* What features, such as a log counter, are be provided?

* What level of user interaction is required? For example, are downloads to be made available to visitors?

* Is there any information to be collected about visitors to the site? Is a cookie to be placed on the computer of each visitor?

* What plans does your client have for maintaining/updating the site once it is up and running? Who will be responsible for this?

* How are security requirements to be addressed? It will be important to address these issues during the design of the site, so that the website is protected from attack.

* What legal requirements need to be addressed? Your client should be aware of codes of conduct in putting information on to the Internet.

At the end of the analysis stage, you will have collected lots of information and should have a clear idea of what the client needs. You will use this information, plus your own creative ideas on web design, to produce the design specification of the website.

Theory into practice

1 Decide on your client, and carry out the initial analysis stage of your web deign project.

2 Write an analysis report, and discuss this with your client, to clarify any points and to make sure you have fully understood your client's requirements.

3 Prepare a plan that shows how you propose to complete your project: the steps you will take and the time you need to complete the website design and implementation.

4 Identify the resources that you will need, and check that they will be available to you.

Design specification

In completing the design specification stage, it may help you to focus on three separate aspects of your website:

* The content is the data that the visitor will be offered, plus the links that allow him or her to navigate your site. You will rely on your client to supply this information, but will need to decide how best to present it to the visitor.

* The visual design (theme) of your site is important because it creates the atmosphere that will greet each visitor.

* The technical design is also important. It focuses on how user-friendly your site is: Will it be easy to navigate? Does it download quickly or does the visitor lose interest waiting for your images to appear on screen? Do you provide useful aids such as search tools? How many clicks of the mouse are needed for a user to find what they want? (Any more than three mouse clicks may be too many for some users!).

Your design specification documentation should include a site map, showing the structure of your website and how a visitor might navigate the site. It will also outline the content for each page within the site. Links are an essential ingredient of your website:

* internal links allow the visitor to navigate through the site

* links from your site to other sites are called hyperlinks

* links that allow the visitor to send you an email are called email links.

Having determined your links, you should then be able to produce a prototype of your website, as described on this page and page 241. This is a skeleton version of your website, which can be used to confirm with your client that you have interpreted his or her requirements as hoped.

A well-designed website will match these criteria:

* It will establish an identity/brand by the clever use of logos, colour schemes and layout.

* It will be structured to facilitate navigation so that it is easy for visitors to find what they want on the site. Your hyperlinks should be intuitive and there should be no dead ends.

* It will provide the right balance of information on each page.

* It will be responsive and secure.

You will evaluate your website once you have completed the implementation and testing of the site, but you should build in these good design points from the beginning.

Prototyping and implementation

You could produce the first prototype as a storyboard, sketching this by hand. It would include essential features of the proposed site:

* You could draw sketches of the layout of the home page and samples of other pages to give the client a feel for what you intend to produce.

* You could show the links that you plan to include on the main navbar.

* You could propose a colour scheme for the background and for the text.

* You could select some images that you plan to use for information and some others that you might use for decoration.

If the client is happy with your storyboard, you could then go on to develop an electronic prototype, including all the necessary links, but only sufficient text and images to indicate what will go where on the site.

The prototype should show how a visitor will navigate the site, and include enough sample pages to demonstrate the visual design (or theme) that you have chosen: the colour scheme, the fonts, the images, and other aspects of web page design which create the atmosphere of the site. Often, discussions with the client result in slight changes to the specification, or some clarification of what is to be done. It is better this happens at an early stage in the development of a website, rather than after you have completed the development. Therefore, prototyping is a valuable tool in the production process.

You now need to learn a bit about website structure and then think about the software you will use to implement the structure.

Website structure

A website comprises one or more web pages. These pages are linked using navigational tools, such as hotlinks, to form the structure of the website. Although different websites may look very different from one another, there are only really three different basic structures to choose between (Figure 7.24).

＊ The linear website leads the visitor through a series of pages, one at a time. This structure may be useful when you want the visitor to take in small amounts of information, one step at a time. It is unlikely your entire site will use this structure. However, you may have a small portion of the website that is suited to linear presentation, such as the process of placing an order.

＊ The hierarchical website is like a family tree. The top level (the home page) offers a number of options and then these lead onto further options. This is a popular structure. It is simple to visualise and to present as a site map.

＊ The web or mesh structure takes advantage of the linking options and allows the visitor to wander around your site according to their own curiosity. Although it provides the most intuitive navigation for the visitor, this structure can be the most difficult to document, due to the number of links that you offer.

Your visitors need help in finding their way around your site and your design should make this as easy as possible, otherwise the first visit may be the last. Your aim should be to keep it clear and simple; if you have to explain to a visitor how to use your navigation system, then it is not clear enough.

The primary navigation system, the linking mechanism that will take your visitor to the main sections of your website, should be kept together in a compact way, either along the top of the page, or down one side, or across the bottom.

The web browser displays the web page in the browser window. Depending on how long your page is, and what resolution the visitor is using, your web page may not fit into the browser window. Then your visitor will have to scroll up and down to see everything. In this case, you might choose a menu bar to go across the top (and the bottom) of your web page. It is possible to split the browser window into separate frames (Figure 7.25), so that some information, such as the menu bar, remains in place whatever is being viewed in the other areas on the screen. In this situation, even if the visitor has to scroll up and down, the main navigation options are visible at all times.

(a) A linear site

(b) A hierarchical site

(c) A mesh site

FIGURE 7.24　*Website structures*

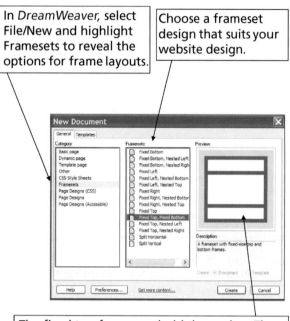

In *DreamWeaver*, select File/New and highlight Framesets to reveal the options for frame layouts.

Choose a frameset design that suits your website design.

The fixed top frame can hold the navbar. The fixed bottom frame can hold the sketch, messages relevant for the page and the logo/email link. The other content can then be scrolled with in the central area.

FIGURE 7.25 *Using frames to split up the browser window*

For your navigational links, you could have images only, or images and text, such as a labelled menu bar. Not all visitors want to see images; the text-only option is a quick way of viewing web pages. The visitor may be using an old browser which does not support all image types. So, you need to make sure your web pages will still make sense if none of your images are on display to the visitor. For visitors who cannot view a graphic, if you complete the alt attribute for the image, at least they will know what they are missing.

If a single word or phrase within a paragraph of text is used as a hotlink, it is advisable to display the linking text in a different colour so that it stands out. You should avoid using underlining for anything but an external link, otherwise this might confuse a visitor.

To help visitors, you might also include an index (Figure 7.26) and/or a site map (Figure 7.27).

Web authoring software

Having determined the needs of your client, decided on a structure, and put together a design using storyboards, it is time to put your ideas into a more practical form: a prototype using web authoring software.

Each page that you create will comprise a number of components:

* According to your design ideas, you will have an underlying theme; a colour scheme and a layout of each page, that you want to use to convey the feel of the website.

* According to the content agreed with your client, there will be text and graphics, and maybe video and sound, to incorporate.

* According to the navigational routes you have decided on, there will be links to implement.

Which particular web authoring package you use will depend on what is available to you. In this section, the discussion focuses on particular aspects of implementation, and these will be possible in whatever software you use. Your task will be to find out exactly how to achieve the effects for yourself.

Themes

Building your website, and changing its appearance, is made easier by the way pages can be parameter driven. Web authoring packages

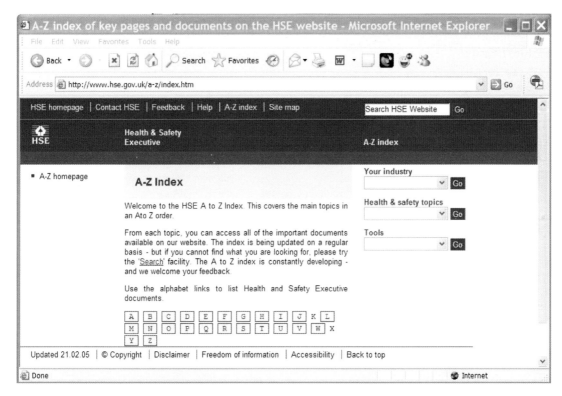

FIGURE 7.26 *An example of an index*

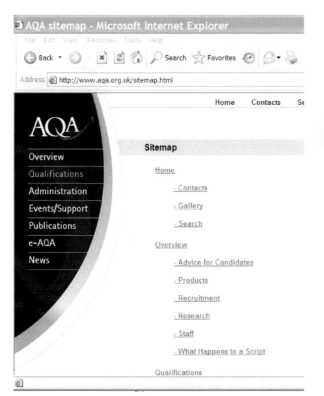

FIGURE 7.27 *A site map*

offer templates (Figure 7.28), and alternative colour schemes (Figure 7.29) so that you can make it a bit more individual. By changing some part of the theme, for example, the background colour, you can change the website quite dramatically.

Theory into practice

1 Find out what web authoring software options you have. Find out also the availability of books and manuals and on-screen support that you can turn to, should you need help.

2 Using at least one web authoring software package, investigate the options for themes that you might use. Choose three or four that you think might suit your client's website. Customise them enough to make them different from the standard ones supplied.

3 Compare your sample themes with others in your group. Amend yours in light of the feedback you are given.

Yahoo! PageWizards

PageWizards are a fun and fast way to make cool web pages. Just by answering a few questions, our PageWizards will collect your information and build a professional-looking web page in minutes.

Photo Page

Baby Announcement

Birthday Invitation

Personal Page

Party Invitation

PageWizard Tips

Tip 1. Making Changes
To make changes to pages you already made, find and launch the PageWizard like you did the first time. This time you will see a pull-down menu that lists the pages you worked on with that PageWizard. Select the page you were working on and make your changes.

Tip 2. Naming your page
To make your page show as your home page, name it **index.html** when you save it. This is the *default* name used for the first page people see when visiting your site. Read more.

Tip 3. Finding help
If you are having trouble or want to find out more, visit the Yahoo! PageWizards Help area.

FIGURE 7.28 *Choosing a page design in Yahoo! SiteBuilder*

Content

Your content will include text, graphics and sound. Images are discussed in some detail on pages 204–207. For sound, you will need to source the audio file (perhaps by recording a *.wav file) and then insert the file as plug-in. You will have to decide what to put where on each page. Most web authoring packages offer a range of templates

---

Yahoo! Personal PageWizard

Launch Yahoo! PageWizard - to begin building your Personal Page.

This Yahoo! PageWizard will walk you through 10 simple steps that should take you about 5 to 10 minutes. What you have on your Personal Page is totally up to you. You can even choose one of the four designs below. With this Yahoo! PageWizard, you can choose to include the following information about yourself:

- your email address
- a picture
- brief descriptions about yourself, your hobbies and interests, and your family and friends
- and, a list of your favourite links and your friends' family members' web sites

Cool Blue

Neon Green

Think Pink

Mellow Yellow

FIGURE 7.29 *Choosing a colour scheme in Yahoo! SiteBuilder*

to help you to set up the layout of each page. It is important to decide on a focal point for each page 196, and to make sure that nothing else stands out so much that it distracts the reader away from this focal point. If there is no focal point, or too many, the overall effect will be poor. Although it is important that the menu bar is clearly visible, it should not be overlarge or more eye-catching than anything else on the page.

To give your website a consistent feel, some elements will be the same on most pages, for example, the same font, the same colour of text, the menu bars in the same position, and so on. These are called repetitive elements. However, to keep interest levels up, and to best present the material, some pages will have a different layout, and use different elements.

You will have seen lots of examples of web pages, but can you recognise the points of good and bad design? Table 7.7 lists some hints about what to avoid, and what to aim for.

Theory into practice

1 Decide which elements will appear on most of your pages and set up a sample page showing these repetitive elements.

2 Set up your home page, with the navigational bar in place. You will need to set up dummy pages (with no content just yet) to test out your navigational system.

3 Include enough content on each page for it to be clear what you intend to place on a page – the heading may be sufficient.

Images

Good choice of images will make your website a place your visitors enjoy spending time on. They can add interest and attraction. Poor choice of images, or using images that take forever to download, could make your website a one-stop only site.

Sourcing your image can be done in one of many ways, as discussed on page 196. The format of your image is also important. There are three formats that have been specially designed for use on web pages:

* GIF files (with the file extension .gif) are suitable for simple images with large blocks of colour. A GIF is made from pixels, the colour of each individual pixel contributing to the overall colour of the image. GIFs only use 8-bit colour values, so are limited to 256 different colours (this is called indexed colour) and would therefore not be suitable for photographs. Regarding transparency, GIFs allow one transparent colour, so instead of it sitting in a white box, it can merge in with the background colour of your web page. Another feature of a GIF is interlacing. This means the image appears a strip at a time; so the visitor can be reading something else while the image gradually appears. A final plus point for GIFs is that a series of GIFs can be combined to create a moving image sequence, a bit like a movie. This is called an animated GIF.

What does it mean?

GIF stands for graphics interchange format.

* JPEG files (with the file extension .jpg) are used mainly for photos, especially those that have subtle colour changes within them. JPEGs are not so good as GIFs for solid blocks or hard lines. Because they offer 16- or 24-bit colour values, they offers 16+ million colours and a photorealistic quality. The JPEG is another high compression format but it has three aspects that are not so good: the compression technique loses some of the data and hence the clarity of the photo, it offers no transparency option, and it is not interlaced.

What does it mean?

JPEG stands for Joint Photographic Experts Group.

	THINGS TO AVOID	THINGS TO AIM FOR
Background	Using default colour (grey) Using a colour that is not a good contrast with the text Having a patterned or too-busy background which distracts the reader	A colour scheme that creates the desired feel for the site
Text	Too long a line length Overuse of capitals, bold, italic Text too close to things next to it; need some space	Accurate, well-written text conveying the message in as few words as possible Contrasting styles to indicate a natural hierarchy, e.g. bigger point size for headings Point size large enough to read, but not overlarge Contrasting colour with background for ease of reading
Images	Overlarge files that take forever to download Images for the sake of it; an image must convey information, not just fill a space Images with special effects around the edges (called **anti-aliasing**) that can result in very large file size and/or distorted view if based on a BMP format	Relevant images, especially for icons Thumbnails to lead the visitor to a full size of same image; but making sure thumb nail is both legible and a lot smaller than actual image, so that enlargement is necessary
Tables	Borders	Clarity of presentation
Navigation	Unclear or scattered hotlinks Overly complex navigation Page titles that don't tell you what will be on the page Icons that don't convey where the button will lead	Easy-to-understand menu system An index and/or site map for large sites
Links	Using default style (blue underlined) Using bold (which will draw attention to them and away from what visitor should be reading) Links that lead nowhere; test your site thoroughly and often	Use underlining, so visitor knows which text is a link Co-ordinate colours with overall theme colours
General	Anything that blinks Animations that never stop – or that will distract the reader Counters (may be important to the client, but shouldn't be relevant for the visitor) Junk advertising Having to scroll, especially sideways Mixture of alignments Voice-overs and other sound tracks that cannot be turned off	A homepage that fits within any standard browser (i.e. 800 × 460 pixels) Pages that download quickly Outside the navigational area and other repetitive elements that give the site a consistent feel, some variety in layout to keep interest of visitor

TABLE 7.7 *Hints for good design of a web page*

PNG (pronounced ping) is the newcomer format and consequently, unlike GIF and JPEG, may not yet be supported by all browsers. PNGs are interlaced (like GIFs); and they include gamma information which allows them to adjust their brightness according to the visitor's monitor settings. However, PNG files can contain embedded information (metatags) which can be detected by search engines, so when they become commonplace, they may become more popular. Also, they claim far greater compression, up to 30 per cent greater than GIF files, which makes these images much quicker to download. They have 256 levels of transparency, as opposed to the GIF one-colour transparency option.

Think it over...

In what other file formats might you save image files? How could you convert them to a compressed file format?

Compression is necessary because the size of a file affects the download time. Too large an image may result in your visitor losing interest and moving on to another site. However, compression should only be done once to an image file. Compressing a file that has already been compressed may reduce the quality of the image.

Photo manipulation packages offer a choice over the level of compression. Remember that a more compressed photo may require less memory, but it will also display less detail.

The size of an image can be measured in one of two ways:

* How big a file is needed to store the image? The size of the file created is measured in bytes, kilobytes or more likely megabytes. The more bytes that have to be downloaded, the longer it takes for your image to appear on the screen.

* How much space (in pixels) does the image take up on screen? Trying to reduce the dimensions of an image on screen does not affect the file size, and hence it does not change the download time. You must minimise your file size by fixing the dimensions of your image prior to compression. If you still find the file size is too large, you will need to rethink the dimensions and start all over again in the preparation of the image.

Theory into practice

1 Convert a file from one format to another. Compare file sizes.

2 Change the dimensions of a file and then compare file sizes. Repeat this for another format.

Having sourced, sized and compressed your images, you should save each image file within a special folder called Images, within the folder in which your web pages are being created. Inserting an image onto your page is then relatively simple in DreamWeaver. Position your cursor where you want the picture to appear and select Insert/Picture/From File. The image stays within its folder, but an <img>tag is put in the HTML code for your web page. This indicates that, when the time comes for your visitor to view this web page, the image will be downloaded and appear just where you want it to.

The <img> tag provides the browser with full information about the image:

* the border width to use

* the source 'src' or where to find the image, that is, its filename

* its dimensions in pixels, (width and height).

In DreamWeaver, changing the image properties is done through the Properties dialogue box (Figure 7.30). Your changes will be reflected in the <img>tag in the HTML code.

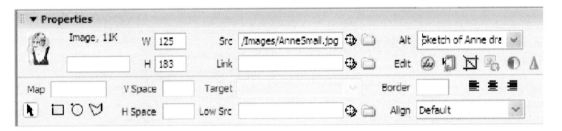

Sketch of Anne drawn by Stevie Roberts 2004

Sketch: Stevie Roberts 2004   © Text: Anne Rainbow 2005

FIGURE 7.30 *Image properties*

The first canvass of the dialogue box is used to enter some descriptive text, known as Alt text. This text appears on-screen when the visitor to your web page hovers the cursor over the image. This may increase the length of time a visitor is prepared to wait for your image to download. More importantly, for blind visitors who rely on text readers, it can be used to tell them what the image portrays.

Background and foreground features

The colour of text can be controlled, but you can also change the background colour of your web page, to create a suitable atmosphere. Within DreamWeaver, the Properties panel lets you control everything and anything that relates to an object on the web page (Figure 7.31)

Notice that the Properties box also shows the colour of text (red in the example) and that you should aim for a good contrast between foreground and background so that it is easy for you visitors to read the text. The tag in the HTML code automatically appears: <tr bgcolor="#CCCCCC">.

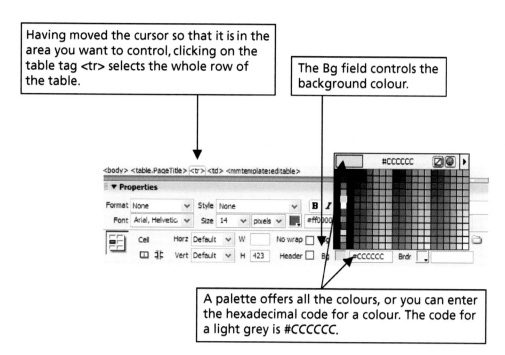

Having moved the cursor so that it is in the area you want to control, clicking on the table tag <tr> selects the whole row of the table.

The Bg field controls the background colour.

A palette offers all the colours, or you can enter the hexadecimal code for a colour. The code for a light grey is #CCCCCC.

FIGURE 7.31 *Changing the background colour for a row of a table*

Tables, forms, interactive features and other appropriate components

Tables can be used on a web page as a way of creating space for text and images on the screen. However, tables are also an important element in web page design; they can be used to create the basic template (Figure 7.32).

Having set up the basic template, you can then add text and images (and more tables) within a page. To insert a table, place the cursor where you want the table to appear and select Insert/Table. The total width of a table includes the widths of all the columns and any borders, plus the cell padding and cell spacing.

What does it mean?

Cell padding is the space within a cell.

Cell spacing is the space between cells.

Accessing various parts of a table can be done through the tags (Table 7.8).

Having created the table, you can then fill the cells with text or images, or another nested table. The <table> tag controls the format of the table but within a table, for each cell, you can also control the cell properties.

* You can fix the width of a cell, so that its column does not stretch when you insert more text. (The width of the cells within one column has to be the same for the whole column.)

* You can set a background colour, and this could be different for each cell.

* You can align the text within each cell both horizontally (left, centre, right or justified) and vertically (top, middle or bottom).

* You may merge cells, for example, to create a heading row.

Your client may need an interactive form as part of the website (Figure 7.33).

The main template of the Anne Rainbow website is based on a table with 6 rows and 7 columns.

The columns are all equal width - and the main navigation bar runs across the first two rows.

The rows are of varied depths to create a layout that will suit all pages.

The cells in this row have been merged into one large area.

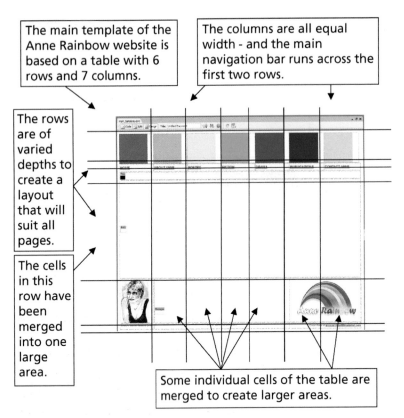

Some individual cells of the table are merged to create larger areas.

FIGURE 7.32 *Using a table structure to set up a template design*

TAG	NOTES
<table>	Sets the table properties: <table width="80%" border ="2" align ="center" cellpadding ="10" cellspacing ="20">
<tr>	Indicates start (and end) of what will appear in each row In the example, there are two rows
<td>	Table data: what will appear in a particular cell of the table, within that row. In the example, there are three cells in each row

TABLE 7.8 *Table tags*

To create this form, a new page was created using the main template, and then a form inserted in the Body editable area (Figure 7.34).

Theory into practice

1 Create a new page based on your template and, within one cell, insert a table with three rows and two columns.

2 Enter text in each cell in the first column, and insert an appropriate image in the second column of each row. Limit your images to 150 pixels wide.

3 Look at the HTML code produced.

4 Experiment with making changes to the table properties, merging cells and creating more nested tables.

5 Review your website design, and incorporate tables where this provides a good way of presenting your content.

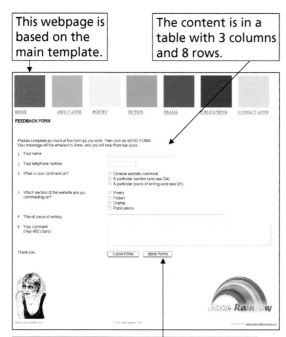

> This webpage is based on the main template.

> The content is in a table with 3 columns and 8 rows.

> The form, when completed, will be sent by email to Anne: the action is to send an email; the method is by POST.

FIGURE 7.33 *A feedback form*

There are a variety of fields that you could include in your form:

* a text field could be used for the visitor's name, and the comment

* buttons can be used to clear the form or to send it to a specified email address

* checkboxes, radio buttons and list/menu fields provide a quick way for the visitor to provide information.

For each type of field, you will need to set the input attributes. Text fields provide freedom for the visitor to put whatever they like. As an alternative, where appropriate, checkboxes, radio buttons and list/menu fields can be used to limit the visitor to a range of responses.

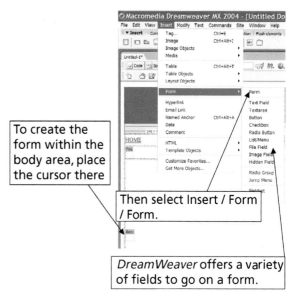

> To create the form within the body area, place the cursor there

> Then select Insert / Form / Form.

> *DreamWeaver* offers a variety of fields to go on a form.

FIGURE 7.34 *Inserting a form using DreamWeaver*

* With checkboxes, the visitor can tick to say 'Yes'.

* Radio buttons can be grouped, and given a common group name, so as to offer the visitor one from many choices. If you wish, you could set one of the buttons on, to start with, so that it becomes the default value.

* The list/menu field offers the options as a drop down menu, which saves space on the screen.

You should test out your form as a prototype form. Simply print out a screen dump, and ask friends to complete the form. Take into account all comments before finalising the form for your website. Then check that it can be completed successfully on-screen, and the responses collected.

Links

Links are an essential ingredient of your website.

✳ You need internal links to allow the visitor to navigate through the site. On the home page, the main navbar (navigation bar) should show the main sections of your site. This same navbar should then be included on each page, so that the visitor can reach the parts of your site that are of interest very easily. The navbar on every page (apart from the home page) should include an internal link back to the home page. If your pages are long, and your visitor needs to scroll, you might include relative links within the same page by setting up named anchors (Figure 7.35) within the page andproviding links to them.

✳ You may provide links from your site to other sites. These external links are called hyperlinks, and can be used to provide a stepping stone from your website to another website. This can be useful for your visitors, but may mean they leave your site sooner than you would wish.

✳ You may provide links which allow the visitor to send you an email. These are called email links. Email links, when clicked, will open up a window in a communications package, such as Microsoft Outlook, so that the visitor can send an email.

An essential part of a link is the address to which the link leads; if this destination changes, either because the name changes or the site is deleted, the link is broken. The visitor will be presented with a warning message saying the site is not available.

Theory into practice

1. Review your website design and check the links that you plan to include.

2. Insert all the links to your own site. Include some hyperlinks to other sites. Check that these work.

Testing

In testing your website, you are challenging yourself to answer each of these questions with a definite 'Yes':

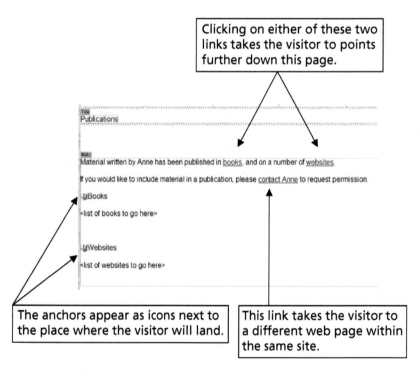

Clicking on either of these two links takes the visitor to points further down this page.

Publications

Material written by Anne has been published in books, and on a number of websites.

If you would like to include material in a publication, please contact Anne to request permission.

Books

<list of books to go here>

Websites

<list of websites to go here>

The anchors appear as icons next to the place where the visitor will land.

This link takes the visitor to a different web page within the same site.

FIGURE 7.35 *Named anchors*

* is the layout and presentation of each page appropriate?

* do the hyperlinks work? Do they lead to where a visitor might expect them to? Are there no dead ends?

* do any interactive actions work as intended?

* does each web page display properly, regardless of which of the common browsers is being used?

* is the web page unaffected by different screen resolutions?

* is the web page accessible to disabled users?

It is important that your testing is systematic. It would help to prepare a test plan and then to carry it out, making notes as to what you find.

Theory into practice

1 Work systematically through each page of your website, making checks on the text, images and general layout.

2 Compare what you have produced with what you agreed with your client. Note any discrepancies.

3 Document the testing that you do, and any changes that you decide to make.

7.6 Evaluation

In evaluating your website, you should focus on two main aspects:

* is the website fit for purpose – has it met your client's requirements?

* does the website meet the needs of the intended end users – the visitors to the website?

You could evaluate the website on your own, but because you have been so involved in its design and implementation, it may be difficult for you to be objective in your evaluation. Instead, you could ask other people to give their honest opinion. You could present them with access to the website and ask them to complete a questionnaire.

7.7 Quality of written communication

The portfolio that you produce should demonstrate, that you are capable of using, and have used, a suitable and appropriate style of writing. All text must be legible, meaningful and organised appropriately. Standard conventions such as applying headers and footers, using page numbers and title pages should also be applied.

Theory into practice

1 Pair up with a friend and test each other's sites. Ask yourself questions like these:

* How useful did you find the site?

* How effective is the design of the site?

* Are you impressed with the content?

* Are you impressed with the presentation?

* Did you find it easy to navigate your way around the site?

* How usable is the site?

* Do you think the level of accessibility meets the needs of all types of visitor?

2 Compare your findings with those of your friend, giving each other constructive feedback.

3 Make amendments to your site, in line with the feedback received and your own evaluation of the site, before presenting it to your client.

GLOSSARY

ActionListener
A section of code that deals with an event such as the program user clicking a button, or making a selection from a check box.

Adjustment layer
A layer of pixels the same size as the original image but with some effect applied to the RGB values so that when the two layers are viewed together an adjustment can be seen.

Algorithms
Formulae or a set of steps for solving a particular problem.

Applet
Short for application, describes a very short program, i.e. a piece of code, written for use on the WWW.

Array
A type of variable that can hold multiple values (all of the same data type). The different values held in the array are accessed by their index number.

ATM (automated teller machine)
An example is the 'hole-in-the-wall' cash dispenser.

BACS (bankers' automated clearing system)
A way of paying employees direct into their bank accounts.

Bit
'Binary digit'. A bit is either on or off and is represented by '1' or '0'.

Bitmapped images
Images comprising many dots (pixels)

Browser
A program which lets you view web pages on the Internet.

Bus
A group of parallel wires, along which data can flow.

Cache
A portion of memory made of high-speed static RAM (SRAM) instead of the slower and cheaper dynamic RAM (DRAM) which is used for main memory.

CAD/CAM
Computer aided design/computer aided manufacture.

CMYK
Cyan, magenta, yellow, key (the key colour is black).

Constructor
A special method of a class which caries out initialisation tasks when an object is created.

Crop
Cut away unwanted parts of an image.

CSV (comma separated variable)
A text file which can be used to store database records. Each field on the file is separated by a comma, and each record is separated by a carriage return. CSV files are easily exported and imported.

Data mining
The analysis of data in a database using tools that look for trends or anomalies without knowledge of the meaning of the data.

Data rate
The number of bytes per second that the drive can deliver to the CPU.

Data type
Determines how many bytes of storage are to be allocated to each attribute, and the kinds of functions that can be carried out on that data.

Data
The raw characters of text, digits and images collected for information.

Database
A collection of data items and links between them, structured in such a way that a number of different application programs can access the information.

DNS (domain naming system)
A database, listing lots of domain names and their respective IP addresses.

E-commerce
Any financial transactions that take place by electronic means, often refers to purchases from online stores, marketplaces and auction sites.

EDI (electronic data interchange)
A method used by businesses to transfer documents electronically over the Internet or other network.

Encryption
A process of scrambling data to ensure that it is kept secure during the transmission process.

Entity
Something (person, thing, concept) in the real world which is represented in a database.

EPOS
Electronic point of sale.

ERD
Entity-relationship diagram.

Ergonomics
The study of the design and arrangement of equipment so that people will interact with the equipment in a healthy, comfortable, and efficient manner.

Field
An area which holds the same category of data for every record in a data file.

Flat-file database
A simple database in which data can be written as a single table.

GIF (graphics interchange format)
A way of storing bitmap image files in a lossless compressed format.

Graphical User Interface (GUI)
A user interface which uses graphical icons, mouse input and program windows.

Hot-desking
A system where employees do not have a personal space within an office, but share any spare desk whenever they come into the office.

HR (human resources)
The department in an organization which deals with employees needs.

Hue
Describes a colour, say, red or yellow. It may be shown on a colour wheel.

IAP
Internet access point.

IDE
Integrated development environment, i.e. an editor, compiler, etc. built into one program.

Induction loop
Technology which allows users to benefit from improved sound and a reduction in background noise for anyone with a suitable hearing aid.

IP
Internet protocol.

ISDN (Integrated Services Digital Network)
An international communications standard for sending voice, video or data over a digital telephone line or normal telephone wires.

ISP
Internet service provider.

Iteration
The name given to each cycle around a loop (q.v.).

Loop
Part of a program that is repeated.

Mathematical precedence
The order in which arithmetic operators are evaluated (i.e. calculations done).

Memory address
A number assigned to each byte in a computer's memory that the CPU uses to track where data and instructions are stored. The computer's CPU uses the address bus to communicate which memory address it wants to access, and the memory controller reads the address and then puts the data stored in that memory address back onto the address bus for the CPU to use.

Metadata
Data about data. In digital imaging, this includes the date and time of the shot, and all settings used: focus length, shutter speed, aperture setting.

MICR (magnetic ink character recognition)
A scanning technique which recognises marks printed in a magnetic ink.

Motherboard
The main circuit board of a computer that provides the base on which a number of other hardware devices are plugged in. The printed circuits on a motherboard provide the electrical connections between all of the devices that are plugged into it.

NI (National Insurance)
Contributions which fund the National Health Service and state pensions.

Object-orientation
A process involving constructing systems from re-useable modules based on real-world things.

OCR (optical character recognition)
A technique for reading forms that have been partly completed by a computer or typewriter.

Opacity
The maximum amount of paint coverage applied by various brush tools.

Opening menu
A menu for a database system providing an interface between the database data and the user.

Organisation
One person, or more usually a number of people who, between them, pool their talents and expertise to provide a service or manufacture a product.

PAYE (Pay As You Earn)
A tax on earnings.

PDA (personal digital assistant)
A handheld device that combines computing, telephone/fax Internet and networking features. A typical PDA can also function as a cellular phone, fax sender, web browser and personal organiser.

Personal data
Information about living, identifiable individuals. It can be as little as name and address.

Pixels
The dots which make up picture elements.

POP
Point of presence (it also stands for post office protocol, used for sending and receiving emails).

Protocol
A set of rules, or standards or code of practice, that are adopted by all parties to a communication.

Prototyping
A method used for evolutionary development of a product. An initial version is presented to the client and then refined in line with their reaction.

QBE
Query by example.

RAM
Random access memory.

RDMS
Relational database management software.

Record
A collection of items all relating to a single individual or object, treated as a single unit for computer processing.

Relational database
Database where the data are collected into two-dimensional tables, each table holding the data for a particular entity.

RGB
Red, green, blue.

ROM
Read only memory.

ROM-BIOS
Read Only Memory Basic Input Output System.

Saturation
The vividness of a colour that results from the amount of grey in the colour, measured on a scale of 0 (all grey) to 255 (saturated colour).

Seek time
The amount of time between the CPU requesting a file and when the first byte of the file is sent to the CPU.

SMS (short message service)
The process of transmitting short messages to and from a mobile, fax or an IP address.

Spamming
The process of sending junk email to another user/users without them authorising or requesting the send. Spam emails usually consist of advertising materials being sent by companies.

SQL
Structured query language.

Syntax
The spelling and grammar of a programming language. All programming languages have strict syntax which defines how instructions are written.

Tint
A global colour with a modified intensity. There are many tints of colour, some brighter, some lighter.

TLD (top-level domain)
The broadest categories of computer host on the Internet.

URL (uniform resource locator)
Identifies where a resource such as a file that holds a web page can be found.

USB (universal serial bus)
A higher speed serial connection standard that supports low speed devices such as mice, keyboards and scanners as well as high speed devices such as cameras.

Utility
A company which provides something useful like water, gas or electricity.

Variables
Areas of the computer's memory reserved for storing data while a program is running.

VAT (Value Added Tax)
An indirect tax applied to most products and collected by the vendor on behalf of the government.

Vector image
An image comprising lines, shapes and text.

Vector
In mathematics, something that has magnitude (size) and direction.

Vendor
The person or organisation selling a product or service to customers.

WAP (Wireless Application Protocol)
A secure specification that allows users to access information instantly via a handheld wireless device such as a mobile phone.

Wizard
A step-by-step aid that can help a designer. Wizards are provided for many activities like setting up a table, setting up a query or setting up a report.

INDEX